European Intellectual History
Since Darwin and Marx

The CONTEMPORARY ESSAYS Series

GENERAL EDITOR: LEONARD W. LEVY

European Intellectual History Since Darwin and Marx

Selected Essays

Edited by

W. Warren Wagar

HARPER TORCHBOOKS   *The Academy Library*
Harper & Row, Publishers
New York, Evanston, and London

*To the memory of
my father*

EUROPEAN INTELLECTUAL HISTORY
SINCE DARWIN AND MARX

Introduction, compilation and notes copyright
© 1966 by W. Warren Wagar.

Printed in the United States of America.

First edition: HARPER TORCHBOOKS, 1967
Harper & Row, Publishers, Incorporated,
49 East 33rd Street,
New York, N.Y. 10016.

Library of Congress Catalog Card Number: 67–10495.

Designed by Darlene Starr Carbone

Contents

40269

1.

Introduction

W. Warren Wagar

THE MOST PROFOUNDLY EMBARRASSING PROBLEM OF THE INTEL-
lectual historian is to define his discipline. Is he an historian
of ideas or thought or opinion, a sociologist of knowledge,
a biographer of the intellectual class, a philosopher of the
Zeitgeist, or, perhaps, something of a charlatan? Each definition so far offered by practitioners in the field has its own
distinctive emphasis. Crane Brinton argues that the "main
job" of the intellectual historian is "to try to find the relations
between the ideas of the philosophers, the intellectuals, the
thinkers, and the actual way of living of the millions who
carry the tasks of civilization." He follows the "often tortuous
path" of ideas from their origins in ivory towers to their
application in the daily lives of ordinary people. H. Stuart
Hughes distinguishes between intellectual history as "retro-
spective cultural anthropology," as "ethico-political history,"
and as the study of "the fund of ideas available at any particular time to men who have received a superior general
education." In the first instance, the historian describes ideas
and sentiments held by the masses, in the second he studies
the values of ruling elites, and in the third he is concerned
primarily with the thinking of the intellectual avant-garde.
This last, Hughes admits, "is the *via regia* of intellectual history." The other approaches lead the scholar more into social
history than into the history of ideas *per se*. In the same essay,

1

Hughes also suggests that "the discovery of the spirit of the
times is . . . the intellectual historian's highest achievement."
F. L. Baumer characterizes the intellectual historian as a
student of "climates of opinion and the way they change from
age to age . . . in relation to the milieu or social context, and
as they become objectified in institutions."[1]

In my own courses, I sometimes define intellectual history
as "the history of mental climates, of the movements, ideas,
and traditions prevalent in these climates, and of the intellectual classes who originate and popularize these movements, ideas, and traditions, set against the background of
society and politics, showing the interrelationship of ideas
across time, space, and disciplinary boundaries, and the
interaction of thought and events." I never intend this definition to be taken seriously, although sometimes (student
respect for father-figures being what it is) I find every word
of it coming back to me at examination time. Clearly, scholars have not yet been born or trained who could perform
the variety of tasks involved in such a definition. Whatever
it should be, intellectual history in practice reduces to something far less comprehensive. And yet a little of the broad,
synthetic spirit always informs even the most recondite
journal articles in the field. Intellectual history differs from
other kinds of studies of human thought in at least one respect. It is not narrowly analytical. It is not concerned primarily with the internal and technical development of ideas.
It makes a deliberate effort to reach out beyond the confines

[1] Crane Brinton, *Ideas and Men* (Englewood Cliffs, N.J., 1950), pp. 7–10;
H. Stuart Hughes, *Consciousness and Society: The Reorientation of European
Social Thought, 1890–1930* (New York, 1958), pp. 8–11; and Franklin L.
Baumer in Baumer, ed., *Main Currents of Western Thought* (Second Edi-
tion, New York, 1964), p. 5. Cf. Baumer, "Intellectual History and Its
Problems," *Journal of Modern History,* XXI (September 1949), 191–203;
Arthur O. Lovejoy, Jr., "The Study of the History of Ideas," the first
lecture in his book, *The Great Chain of Being* (Cambridge, Mass., 1936);
John Higham, "Intellectual History and Its Neighbors," *Journal of the
History of Ideas,* XV (June 1954), 339–47; and John C. Greene, "Objec-
tives and Methods in Intellectual History," *Mississippi Valley Historical
Review,* XLIV (June 1957), 58–74.

of a single discipline and examine ideas in the context of socio-political conditions and the intellectual milieu as a whole. In this way, it earns the right to be called a field of historical study.

But of course there are many different kinds of intellectual history. Much of it is not written by professional historians at all, especially in Britain and France. Specialists in literature, philosophy, history of science, theology, political theory, and sociology have contributed more to intellectual history in our time than historians, although from the historian's point of view these contributions are frequently "marred" by lapses into ahistorical thinking. Nevertheless, we cannot afford to deprive ourselves of the light they can bring to our research. Who would ever seriously contemplate studying or teaching intellectual history without benefit of the books of such "non-historians" as Isaiah Berlin, Ernst Cassirer, F. C. Copleston, Etienne Gilson, Erich Heller, Arthur O. Lovejoy, Jr., Karl Löwith, Karl Mannheim, George Sabine, Ernst Troeltsch, Max Weber, Basil Willey, and Edmund Wilson?

A further and more serious problem is the division of intellectual history into a number of competing camps distinguished by their preference for this or that set of disciplines. Some tend to specialize in ideas in literature and the arts. Others focus on science, religion, and philosophy. Yet another group devotes itself almost exclusively to social, political, and economic thought. These distinctions can be important enough in investigating premodern eras, but they become absolutely decisive in exploring the intellectual history of the nineteenth and twentieth centuries. Such is the fragmentation of the modern spirit that it would be quite possible to write three almost entirely different intellectual histories of the West in the last 150 years, the first running, let us imagine, "from Goethe to Beckett," the second "from Hegel to Bultmann," and the third "from Burke to Morgenthau," not one of which would necessarily contain more than fleeting references to the men and movements dwelt on at great length in the others. Any honest effort to penetrate the major systems of the major thinkers and determine the configuration of the mental climate as a whole is vitiated from the start by the principle of selection employed. A similar problem emerges when the modern intellectual historian limits himself largely to Anglo-American or to Franco-German thought, for example, and tries to represent his work as a history of "Western" thought.

The present anthology surveys some of the main currents of thought in Western Europe alone, and only for the period since 1870. By "1870," I do not mean to invoke memories of the Franco-Prussian War, or the publication of *The Descent of Man,* or the founding of the German Social Democratic Labor party by Marx and Liebknecht, or any other specific historical event. But from our perspective a century later, 1870 has much the same symbolic value as 1789 or 1648. It marks the beginning of a new era in Western civilization, an era of flourishing and dynamic industrialism, of imperialism, of vastly enlarged potentialities for war-making, of new moral and religious freedom, of atheism, and the "transvaluation of all values." In Europe, collectivism triumphed over individualism; conflict between established Great Powers replaced political and national revolution as the principal threat to peace and stability; the middle classes finally achieved the ascendancy for which they had struggled with such limited success in the first half of the century. All the forces which transformed Europe in the years after 1870 were present in embryo fifty or even a hundred years before, but they did not until then appreciably change the tempo and texture of European life.

The epoch from Sedan to Versailles may in turn be divided into two generations of about twenty-five years each. In the history of ideas, the first of these generations is dominated by a robust, systematic, and rather doctrinaire scientism. In and of itself, the scientific orientation of thought was not new. The mathematical physics of the seventeenth-century Scientific Revolution had clearly served as the inspiration of the thought of the Enlightenment. Although the romantic movement of the early nineteenth century could be seen, in part, as a protest against the intellectual ascendancy of the natural sciences, its influence was already on the wane by 1830. Science and romanticism had even joined forces, in at least one sense, in turning their attention to the problem of evolution in nature, and in adopting the vision of reality as process, in place of the static, mechanical world-picture of Newtonian physics. What the philosophers of the romantic era, Fichte, Hegel, Schelling, and Schopenhauer, had attempted to achieve in the sphere of metaphysics, Lamarck, Oken, Chambers, and—ultimately—Darwin achieved in the sphere of biology. But the physical sciences also continued to flourish. The thought of the middle decades of the nineteenth century might well be represented as a second Enlightenment.[2] Utilitarianism in Britain, Postivism in France, Materialism in Germany, were all philosophies of science. Marx put socialism on "scientific" foundations, and Darwin published *The Origin of Species.*

The thinkers of the post-1870 generation were also predominantly positivistic and scientistic in their loyalties. The followers of Comte and Littré preached the Positivist gospel in France and the movement took root in England under the leadership of Frederic Harrison. Marx and Engels carried on their work, establishing Marxism as the orthodox school of socialist thought on the Continent. The physicalist monism of Haeckel in Germany, and in Britain the evolutionism of Spencer and Huxley, reasserted the sovereignty of science and reason. Darwinian concepts pervaded the new science of sociology, as illustrated by the work of Gumplowicz, Ratzenhofer, Novicow, and Kidd. In far greater numbers than in the earlier part of the century, the intellectual avant-garde turned to atheism and agnosticism, professed most typically in terms of a commitment to the scientific world-outlook. Naturalism and realism prevailed over romanticism

[2] See Baumer's concept of the "New Enlightenment" in *Main Currents of Western Thought,* pp. 454–57.

in literature. What distinguishes the post-1870 generation
from its immediate predecessor is not the basic attitude toward science, but the preoccupation with the problem of
struggle as a law of life, the militant character of the "warfare
between science and theology," and the rise of collectivist
ideologies, accompanied by a corresponding deterioration in
the currency of liberal values. Although Western Europe was
at peace from 1871 until 1914, and revolutionaries manned
the barricades of Paris no more, post-Darwinian thought distinguished itself by its tough-mindedness. It was, in Carlton
Hayes' apt phrase, "a generation of materialism." It read the
novels of Zola and admired the blood-and-iron politics of
Bismarck, as an earlier generation in a quite different spirit
had cultivated Byron and doted on Napoleon.

Toward the end of the century, however, the *Zeitgeist*
changed again, and a second post-Darwinian generation
began to assert itself, very dissimilar from the first. Like
Jean Barois, the hero of Martin du Gard's novel, the positivistic avant-garde found itself almost suddenly unfashion-
able. It did not collapse all at once, and it retained much of
its authority among middlebrows, especially in England and
America. But there was quite clearly a change of forces at
the head of the line of march. Three recently published books
by intellectual historians have focussed on the work of this
generation; in each instance, the authors point out that it
anticipated significantly the leading tendencies in thought
since the first World War; and in each instance, they trace it
back to the 1890's.[3]

[3] Hughes, *Consciousness and Society;* Gerhard Masur, *Prophets of Yesterday:
   Studies in European Culture, 1890–1914* (New York, 1961); and John Weiss,
   ed., *The Origins of Modern Consciousness* (Detroit, 1965). The leading
   figures examined by Hughes are Pareto, Croce, Sorel, Bergson, Freud,
   Dilthey, Troeltsch, Meinecke, Durkheim, Weber, Péguy, Gide, Mann,
   and Spengler. Masur's prophets include Wilde, George, von Hofmannsthal, D'Annunzio, Barrès, Gide, Dilthey, Rickert, Weber, Ibsen, Mann,
   Bergson, Croce, Shaw, Freud, van Gogh, Gauguin, Unamuno, and
   Sorel. The papers in the volume edited by John Weiss study American
   pragmatism, Nietzsche, Bradley, Barrès, Bergson, Bourget, Freud,
   Valéry, Meinecke, and Weber.

The thought of this second post-Darwinian generation was heralded by a major shift in taste in literature and the arts, which overlaps in its opening phase with the last phase of the realist movement. Especially at first, the new sensibility resembled in many ways the older "new sensibility" of the romanticists. Its patron saints were Schopenhauer, Baudelaire, Dostoyevsky, and Nietzsche, all largely neglected in their own time, and its leading exponents included Verlaine, Mallarmé, Rimbaud, Huysmans, Barrès, Proust, and the early Gide in France; Swinburne, Wilde, Beardsley, Hardy, Dowson, Shaw, and Conrad in England; Wedekind, Rilke, George, and von Hofmannsthal in Germany and Austria; Strindberg in Sweden; and D'Annunzio in Italy. In the arts, the impressionists, postimpressionists, and symbolists, and the music of Debussy, Delius, Mahler, and the early Schönberg paralleled the movement in literature. These neoromanticists are as difficult to classify as the romanticists before them: what they exhibit in common, if anything, is a distaste for the rational and commonplace. They were nearly all spiritual aristocrats, afflicted with nostalgia, pessimism, and anxiety about crime and death, or (in a spirit of conscious "counter-decadence") full of exuberant lust for life and "higher" values. They rebelled against the "facts" of science and the "bourgeois" gospel of automatic progress. They were interested in inner truths, in psychology and religion. They preferred the vital and organic to the physical and mechanical. Sometimes we can observe the change in spirit in the life of a single artist: witness, for example, the transformation of George Moore from apostle of Flaubert and Zola in his early novel *Esther Waters* to religious mystic in such later works as *The Brook Kerith* and *Héloise and Abélard.*

Turning to the intellectuals, one must rely again more on impressions than on exact definitions; but the second generation of post-Darwinian thinkers was clearly of a different set of mind from the generation of Spencer and Haeckel. In philosophy many of the tendencies of romantic idealism and historicism returned in new forms, as reflected in the idealist revival promoted by Green, Bradley, Bosanquet, Wundt, Eucken, and Croce, and also in the vitalist movement. If one enlarges the familiar textbook definition of vitalism to include all the quasi-romanticist philosophies of "evolution," "life," "organism," "process," and "time" which flourished in the period 1890–1919, the schools of the romantic era seem to recapitulate themselves more faithfully in vitalism than even in the neo-Hegelian movement. Dilthey was the new Herder, Barrès the new Fichte, Nietzsche (or Shaw) the new Goethe, Bergson the new Hegel, Alexander (or Whitehead) the new Schelling, and Spengler the new Schopenhauer. Another theme pervading much of the thought of the age was a new and penetrating interest in human psychology, with an emphasis on the structure and function of the irrational, the unconscious, and the primitive or infantile. The principal schools of psychoanalysis were established. Pareto, Le Bon, and Wallas investigated irrational behavior in politics and society. Max Weber explored the influence of religious and ethical beliefs in the development of culture. Intellectual history itself crystallized as a discipline under the inspiration of the studies of Wilhelm Dilthey. Sorel, Jaurès, and the British Fabians revolutionized socialist thought. In all of this, one senses, in H. Stuart Hughes' phrase, a profound "revolt against positivism." The old world of matter and reason was dissolving. The twentieth century had arrived. At the same time, the prevailing mood remained hopeful, even buoyant, despite the world-weariness of much *fin-de-siècle* literature. On the whole, life seemed good. The majority of the thinking population faced the future with confidence.

To discuss the intellectual history of the twentieth century proper, the century that begins with Sarajevo and Versailles, is a hazardous undertaking. But clearly the period since 1919 has had two distinct phases, marked off from one another by the close of the second World War. The difference between them is perhaps a difference of temperature more than of spirit, the difference between a heroic age and an age that has settled down into the new pattern of thought established by the heroes: between iconoclasm and life without icons.

The generation of 1919-45 was above all else a generation of disenchantment with man, history, and progress. It bitterly rejected the meliorism—positivist or anti-positivist—of the late nineteenth century. It surrendered all hope of finding meaningful correlations between external nature as man could know it and man himself. Philosophers denied the possibility of verifiable objective truth in the traditional fields of ethics, metaphysics, aesthetics, and epistemology. Political theory went into virtual bankruptcy. Following so closely an age of unprecedented confidence in science and civilization, the horrors of the first World War, the disorders of the Twenties, the economic collapse of the Thirties, and the satanic regimes of Stalin and Hitler generated widespread anxiety and nihilism. In literature and the arts, all of this was conveyed with extraordinary force, and at the same time most of the forms, styles, and techniques of the nineteenth century were discarded in a wild rush of experimentalism which greatly widened the already considerable gap between avant-garde and popular culture. But this was clearly a generation of giants: Einstein and Heisenberg, Russell and Wittgenstein, Husserl and Heidegger, Freud and Jung, Barth and Berdyaev, Spengler and Toynbee, Kafka and Mann, Joyce and Eliot, Gide and Sartre, Picasso and Kokoschka, Schönberg and Stravinsky. It remained demonically creative in the face of every temptation to lapse into silence.

For a few years, in the late Thirties and early Forties, the European spirit rallied, in response to the challenge of totalitarianism. A literature of engagement in the political struggle against fascism and Stalinism arrested the drift to despair. But this counter-tendency has not carried into the postwar era to any notable extent. Some of the younger men of the post-1945 generation are disciples or imitators of the iconoclastic heroes of 1919–45. Others are specialists and technicians, teaching in the expanded university systems of the postwar period, deeply infected with the relativism of modern scholarship, and reluctant to commit themselves to any system or program of ideas whatsoever. The ideologies of the Thirties, from communism to fascism, have lost their magic. The Cold War and the perennial menace of nuclear annihilation have prevented a resurgence of old-fashioned meliorism,but the social and economic triumphs of the technocratic Welfare States installed throughout Europe after 1945 have made life too physically comfortable to give much scope for revolutionary activism or even political passion. Anxiety has, at least to some extent, been replaced with indifference; the howl of despair with the ironic shrug. The new mental climate is captured most convincingly in literature: *The Stranger, The Bald Soprano, Endgame, The Tin Drum* are products of a generation which has avoided disillusionment simply because it never allowed itself any illusions at all. We live today, so it seems, in a glacial age of the spirit. There is no reason to imagine that it will go on forever. Past experience would suggest that a thaw is more or less inevitable. But the historian, as historian, should not presume to prophesy.

Although the articles selected for this anthology do not by any means touch on all the main currents of thought since 1870, most of them are synoptic. They present broad views of significant movements and in most instances they provide discussions of the background of ideas and events necessary for an understanding in historical depth of the movements concerned. The reader will also notice that some of the authors are not historians at all. This only reinforces the point made some pages ago that intellectual history is a discipline still too much in its infancy to be able to rely exclusively on specialists in the field; and by its very nature it will perhaps never be able to do so.

I must, of course, apologize for all that has been left out. The last hundred years have produced more books, more thinkers, and more thought than all the rest of Western history taken together. The articles included here have little or nothing to say, for example, about vitalism, surrealism, neo-

Thomism, logical positivism, phenomenology, or contemporary liberal humanism. The reader will look in vain for articles on the varieties of democratic socialism or fascism. Little attention is paid to recent thinking in such disciplines as sociology, anthropology, and economics. But I hope that full measure has been given within the limits set for the anthologies in this series. To those who would like to pursue further the study of modern intellectual history, I especially recommend the files of the *Journal of the History of Ideas,* founded in 1940, and the only journal in the English language devoted exclusively to intellectual history. The best general anthologies of source materials are Franklin L. Baumer, ed., *Main Currents of Western Thought* (Second Edition, New York, 1964), and Eugene C. Black, ed., *Posture of Europe, 1815–1940: Readings in European Intellectual History* (Homewood, Ill., 1964). Textbooks in the field especially useful for the period since 1870 include George L. Mosse, *The Culture of Western Europe: The Nineteenth and Twentieth Centuries* (Chicago, 1961), and Roland N. Stromberg, *An Intellectual History of Modern Europe* (New York, 1966).

2.

Darwin and Religion

John C. Greene

EDITORIAL NOTE: *The flood of scholarly lectures, articles, symposia, and books which marked the hundredth anniversary in 1959 of the publication of* The Origin of Species *testifies to the continuing importance of Charles Darwin as an intellectual force, both inside and outside the scientific community. He was also a prophet with much honor in his own time. He did more than any man of his generation to establish the ascendancy of the organic point of view in philosophy in the second half of the nineteenth century. Such radically dissimilar thinkers as Spencer, Haeckel, James, and Bergson cannot be imagined except in the context of the Darwinian revolution. Darwin's influence on the development of scientific psychology and sociology is immeasurable. Perhaps most significant of all for the intellectual historian is the relationship between his work and the moral and religious ideas of the late nineteenth century. John C. Greene discusses this relationship in a paper originally presented at the annual meeting of the American Philosophical Society in 1959, in a program commemorating* The Origin of Species. *Professor Greene concludes with a typically mid-twentieth-century attack on the idea of progress, which had remained, despite all doubts and reservations, the ruling conception of history down to 1914, in no small measure as a result of the thought of Charles Darwin.*

MY PURPOSE IN THIS ESSAY IS TO VIEW DARWIN AND HIS WRITings in the broad perspective of the historical conflict between science and religion. The modern history of that conflict may be divided into three overlapping stages. In the first stage, the new physics and cosmology of the seventeenth century, combined with scientific, technological, and economic progress in the eighteenth, gave rise to natural religion, or deism, as a competitor of revealed religion. In the second stage, reaching its climax with Darwin, the further progress of science undermined the traditional conception of nature as a stable framework of rationally contrived structures, a view which had underlain both Christian natural theology and deism. In the third stage, beginning in Darwin's day and extending to the present, the methods of natural science were applied to the study of human nature and society, and these methods came to be regarded by many as the *only* methods which could yield knowledge of man and nature.

The first of these stages was already well underway by the time Darwin began to think seriously about religion. The Newtonian conception of nature as a law-bound system of matter in motion, when pushed to its logical conclusion, proved irreconcilable with belief in miracles, special providences, prophecies, and the like. These had provided the "external evidences" of the divine origin of the Bible and hence of Christianity. With respect to the "internal evidences," the spread of humanitarian feeling and of optimism concerning the prospects of human life in this world produced a moral revulsion against the God of the Old Testament and the pessimistic view of human nature expressed in traditional Christian doctrines. Finally, the very notion of revealed truth ran counter to the growing demand that all knowledge be based upon clear and distinct ideas derived from experience by reason and observation. In Germany the beginnings of the "higher criticism" made further inroads on belief in the plenary inspiration of the Bible, that is, the belief that everything in the Bible, properly interpreted, is substantially true. Darwin's account of the considerations which led him in the years 1836–1839 to abandon the Christian faith in which he had been reared will serve as a brief summary of these intellectual trends:

. . . I had gradually come, by this time, to see that the Old Testament from its manifestly false history of the world and from its attributing to God the feelings of a revengeful tyrant, was no more to be trusted than the sacred books of the Hindoos, or the beliefs of any barbarian. The question then continually rose before my mind and would not be banished,—is it credible that if God were now to make a revelation to the Hindoos, would he permit it to be connected with the belief in Vishnu, Siva, &c., as Christianity is connected with the Old Testament. This appeared to me utterly incredible.

By further reflecting that the clearest evidence would be requisite to make any sane man believe in the miracles by which Christianity is supported,—that the more we know of the fixed laws of nature the more incredible do miracles be-come,—that the men at that time were ignorant and credulous to a degree almost incomprehensible by us,—that the Gospels cannot be proved to have been written simultaneously with the events,—that they differ in many important details, far too important as it seemed to me to be admitted as the usual inaccuracies of eyewitnesses;—by such reflections as these, which I give not as having the least novelty or value, but as they influenced me, I gradually came to disbelieve in Chris-tianity as a divine revelation. . . . This disbelief crept over me at a very slow rate, but was at last complete. The rate was so slow that I felt no distress, and have never since doubted even for a single second that my conclusion was correct.[1]

One suspects that the process was painless not only be-cause it was slow but also because Darwin had never felt that deep anguish of the spirit to which Christianity ministers and which caused many of his contemporaries to cling to it despite growing intellectual difficulties. This point will be amplified in connection with Darwin's anthropology.

What role did Darwin's writings play in the further trans-formation of attitudes toward the Bible and the idea of re-

[1] Darwin, Charles, *The autobiography of Charles Darwin 1809–1882 with original omissions restored,* 85–86, New York, Harcourt, Brace and Com-pany, 1959. The points developed in this essay are treated more fully in my *Darwin and the Modern World View* (Louisiana State University Press, 1961).

vealed religion? Most importantly they had the effect of bringing the Biblical narrative of the early history of man into doubt. Not that Darwin was the first to suggest that man's origins had been crude and bestial. Rousseau and Lord Monboddo had sketched the evolution of human nature from brutelike beginnings, and Lamarck had plainly implied man's apelike emergence in a long course of organic evolution. But Darwin converted the scientific community to this view. He thereby raised it from the status of a subversive speculation to that of a scientific theory strenuously defended by scientists in an age when the prestige of science was growing steadily. In this sense, Darwin's writings may be said to have acted as a catalyst, hastening a series of reactions which would have taken place eventually from other causes, such as the progress of Biblical criticism and new discoveries of fossil remains, but which now came rapidly.

Darwin himself avoided attacking the Bible, but for Huxley, his doughty champion against all comers, the battle against the doctrine of inspiration, whether plenary or otherwise, was the crucial engagement in the fight for evolution and for freedom of scientific inquiry.

> I am very glad that you see the importance of doing battle with the clericals, [he wrote to Joseph Dalton Hooker]. I am astounded at the narrowness of the view of many of our colleagues on this point. They shut their eyes to the obstacles which clericalism raises in every direction against scientific ways of thinking, which are even more important than scientific discoveries. I desire that the next generation may be less fettered by the gross and stupid superstitions of orthodoxy than mine has been. And I shall be well satisfied if I can succeed to however small an extent in bringing about that result.[2]

Surveying the polemical situation in 1893, Huxley felt that the battle against Biblical authority had largely been won.

> The doctrine of biblical infallibility [he wrote] ... was widely

---

[2] Huxley, Thomas, *Life and letters of Thomas Huxley* 3:123–124, London, Macmillan, 1913.

held by my countrymen within my recollection: I have reason to think that many persons of unimpeachable piety, a few of learning, and even some of intelligence, yet uphold it. But I venture to entertain a doubt whether it can produce any champion whose competency and authority would be recognised beyond the limits of the sect, or theological coterie, to which he belongs. On the contrary, apologetic effort, at present, appears to devote itself to the end of keeping the name of "Inspiration" to suggest the divine source, and consequently infallibility, of more or less of the biblical literature, while carefully emptying the term of any definite sense. For "plenary inspiration" we are asked to substitute a sort of "inspiration with limited liability," the limit being susceptible of indefinite fluctuation in correspondence with the demands of scientific criticism.

This Parthian policy is carried out with some dexterity; but, like other such manoeuvres in the face of a strong foe, it seems likely to end in disaster.[3]

Actually, the response to evolutionary biology within the Christian camp has been rather more varied than Huxley's words suggest. In some churches, notably the Roman Catholic, a slow but definite accommodation to evolutionary biology has taken place within the context of traditional doctrines concerning the inspiration of Scripture. According to the Reverend E. C. Messenger of Louvain, writing in 1949:

Most [Catholic] theologians down to very recent times repudiated any form of evolutionary theory, even of plants and animals. Wiser counsels now seem to prevail, and a decided modification of the attitude of theologians is now being witnessed on the possibility of applying some restricted form of evolution to man. Theologians still seem to hold fast to the absolutely literal interpretation of the narrative of the formation of Eve. But the day may come when it will be more generally recognized that, in addition to the core of historical truth, the narrative contains figurative elements. Inevitably this presents the appearance of a losing battle, and of a rearguard action, in which successive positions are defended to the

[3] Huxley, Thomas, *Science and Hebrew tradition: essays,* "preface," vii, New York, Appleton, 1910.

last, only to be abandoned under the pressure of necessity. A different attitude is surely desirable, and it would at least have the merit of a more wholehearted recognition that Science as well as Theology reveals to us truth concerning God and the world which He has made.[4]

In Protestant circles the rise of evolutionary biology and of the higher criticism produced the opposing reactions known as modernism (or liberalism) and fundamentalism. Modernism abandoned the doctrine of plenary inspiration in favor of an evolutionary conception of the growth of religious ideas and sentiments; fundamentalism reaffirmed plenary inspiration in its narrowest form and rejected whatever in biology could not be reconciled with the letter of Scripture. This conflict of opinions is too familiar to require description here. Of more recent interest is the development of new conceptions of revelation and inspiration in the Protestant fold.

In recent Protestant theology [Walter M. Horton writes] the old scholastic distinction between natural and revealed theology is generally questioned, and a new conception of revelation has appeared, based upon a less rationalistic theory of religious knowledge. According to this view, religious revelation does not consist of the communication of propositions about God to be believed; it consists of the confrontation of God and man through actual historical events, such as the Flight from Egypt, the Babylonian Captivity, and the Life of Christ. What is disclosed in such events is "not truth concerning God, but the living God Himself". . . . Since God confronts us through the

---

[4] Messenger, E. C., *Theology and evolution,* 211, London and Glasgow, Sands & Company, 1949. This book is a useful compendium of Catholic opinion, including papal pronouncements on the question of evolution. In connection with Messenger's call for a new attitude toward evolution, it is worth noting the favorable interest recently shown by the Vatican in a lecture in Rome by Professor Johannes Hurzeler, curator of vertebrate paleontology at Basle University. Hurzeler described a skeleton four feet in height recently unearthed in a coal mine in Tuscany. He indicated that this creature must have lived more than ten million years ago and that it represented a high degree of "humanization."

meaning of events, any report or comment which powerfully conveys that meaning may be divinely inspired, whether or not it is factually inerrant. The Bible can thus convey a true revelation of God, and its writers can be God's inspired interpreters, while at the same time they are thoroughly human and fallible.[5]

Again Horton writes:

For Niebuhr (as indeed for Barth himself . . .) the Word of God is something contemporaneous, or rather something eternal, which impinges upon our age through a human and fallible historic medium. Literal faith in the *ipsissima verba* of Scripture is a form of idolatry which God will punish as he will punish the idolatrous State-worship of our nationalistic contemporaries. But let the words of Scripture be taken as what Niebuhr calls "myths" and Barth calls "tokens"—symbolic expressions of truths too transcendent for human science to grasp, on which nevertheless our human fate depends—and they will lead us back to a fresh appreciation of Christian orthodoxy.[6]

At the same time, say the advocates of this view of revelation, the historic conflict between science and religion will be greatly mitigated, since religion and revelation are conceived to deal with those aspects of reality, especially the value aspect, which are inaccessible to science.

It would appear, then, that, although evolutionary biology has done much to stimulate a rethinking of the doctrines of revelation and inspiration, it has by no means relegated them to the limbo of exploded ideas.

---

[5] Horton, Walter M., Revelation, in: *A handbook of Christian theology: definition essays on concepts and movements of thought in contemporary Protestantism,* 327–328, New York, Meridian Books, 1958. See also Baillie, John, *The idea of revelation in recent thought,* New York, Columbia University Press, 1956.

[6] Horton, Walter M., The new orthodoxy, *The Amer. Scholar* 7:3–11, 1938, quoted in Gail Kennedy, ed., *Evolution and religion: the conflict between science and theology in modern America,* 88, Boston, D. C. Heath, 1957. This volume contains a useful bibliography on the subject of evolution and religion.

In the second stage of the modern conflict between science and religion further scientific progress undermined the static conception of nature which had informed both Christian natural theology and deism. Here again, traditional views had begun to disintegrate before Darwin published, but his influence was nonetheless decisive. In the static version of the doctrine of creation, set forth in such works as John Ray's *The Wisdom of God Manifested in the Works of the Creation* (1691) and William Paley's *Natural Theology* (Darwin said he knew it almost by heart), nature was conceived as a framework of rationally contrived structures fitted as a stage for the activities of intelligent beings. The basic structures of nature—stars, seas, mountains, species, etc.—were thought to be permanent and wisely contrived to fulfill certain functions in the general economy of nature. Change, though ever present, was superficial; it could not alter the fundamental aspect of things. Structure was perfectly adapted to function; harmony and balance prevailed in all the operations of nature. The lower forms of existence ministered to the needs of the higher.[7]

In the eighteenth and early nineteenth centuries this view of nature was seriously shaken by the development of the nebular hypothesis in astronomy, by uniformitarian geology, by paleontology with its long catalogue of extinct species, and by the evolutionary speculations of Erasmus Darwin and Lamarck. Charles Darwin's contribution to the further disintegration of the traditional view was twofold. On the one hand, by converting the scientific community to belief in organic evolution he multiplied a thousand-fold the impact of evolutionary ideas on the traditional faith in the stability and wise design of the fundamental structures of nature. Secondly, in his emphasis on natural selection as the primary mechanism of evolution he knocked the last remain-

[7] For a fuller analysis of the static view of nature and the factors involved in its decline see my article, Objectives and methods in intellectual history, *Miss. Valley Hist. Rev.* 44:58–74, 1957; also, my book *The death of Adam: evolution and its impact on western thought* (Iowa State University Press, Ames, Iowa, 1959).

ing prop from under the static view. Lamarck had recognized that the perpetual mutability of the inorganic environment implied the perpetual mutability of organic forms, but he believed that living matter was endowed (presumably by the Creator) with a capacity to undergo adaptive transformations in response to changing environmental requirements. Hence he was inclined to doubt the real extinction of species. For him, organic change was progressive precisely because it was adaptive. In Darwin's view, however, the variations which determined the survival or extinction of plants and animals were largely unconnected with their efforts to survive. Those organisms which *happened* to vary in such a way as to gain a competitive advantage in the struggle for existence survived; those which happened to vary in less fortunate directions dwindled in numbers and eventually became extinct. Thus, struggle and chance, the antitheses of pre-established harmony and wise design, became the engines of organic change and the architects of such adaptation as could be discerned in nature. This was the last and harshest blow to the traditional view of nature, a blow from which natural theology has not yet fully recovered.

Most of Darwin's contemporaries evaded the full force of the blow by transferring the element of wise design from the structures of nature themselves to the general system of matter in motion which had produced those structures in the course of time. This maneuver gave rise to precisely the kind of evolutionary theism which Immanuel Kant had foreshadowed a hundred years earlier, when, in propounding his theory of cosmic evolution, he declared:

Matter, which is the primitive constituent of all things, is . . . bound to certain laws, and when it is freely abandoned to these laws it must necessarily bring forth beautiful combinations. It has no freedom to deviate from the perfect plan. Since it is thus subject to a supremely wise purpose, it must necessarily have been put into such harmonious relationships by a First Cause ruling over it; and *there is a God, just because nature even in chaos cannot proceed otherwise than regularly and according to order.*[8]

Applied to geology, biology, and eventually to history, this view of things harmonized with the nineteenth-century faith in progress and appealed to a wide variety of men and women, ranging from Christian liberals like John Fiske and Asa Gray to out-and-out agnostics like Herbert Spencer.

Darwin himself took a much less cheerful view of the theological consequences of his theory of natural selection. To those who achieved peace of mind by minimizing the role of natural selection and assuming some kind of directive agency or progressive tendency in the process of hereditary variation, Darwin replied that natural selection was the only means which could bring about the adaptation of organisms to their changing environments. To those who, like Asa Gray and Charles Lyell, proposed that God providentially supplied streams of variation in the right directions from which the environment could select, Darwin was equally unresponsive. If God provided the variations which were selected, did He also provide those which were eliminated? Did He also provide the variations which pigeon fanciers selected to please their own or other people's fancy? Did He determine the shape of Darwin's nose? If so, it amounted to saying that all variations were predetermined, those which resulted in beautiful adaptations and those which did not.

As Darwin saw all too clearly, the conception of nature as a law-bound system of matter in motion, when pushed to its ultimate conclusion, eventuated in stoicism. "The old argument of design in nature, as given by Paley, which formerly seemed to me so conclusive, fails, now that the law of natural selection has been discovered," he wrote. "There seems to be no more design in the variability of organic beings and in the action of natural selection, than in the course

[8] Kant, Immanuel, *Universal natural history and theory of the heavens . . .* , translated by William Hastie in *Kant's cosmogony . . .* , 26, Glasgow, J. Maclehose & Sons, 1900.

which the wind blows. Everything in nature is the result of fixed laws." [9] But Darwin could not look on the production of order and adaptation through the operation of natural laws with Immanuel Kant's optimistic enthusiasm. Presumably the laws of nature implied a law-giver, but what kind of law-giver would achieve the adaptation of structure to function by proliferating millions of variations at random and leaving it to the environment to eliminate those which did not happen to fit? What kind of law-giver would permit the enormous amount of suffering evident in nature? "What a book a devil's chaplain might write on the clumsy, wasteful, blundering, low, and horribly cruel works of nature!" Darwin exclaimed in a letter to Hooker. To Asa Gray he confessed like bewilderment:

> There seems to me too much misery in the world. I cannot persuade myself that a beneficent and omnipotent God would have designedly created the Ichneumonidae with the express intention of their feeding within the living bodies of caterpillars, or that a cat should play with mice. Not believing this, I see no necessity in the belief that the eye was expressly designed. On the other hand, I cannot anyhow be contented to view this wonderful universe, and especially the nature of man, and to conclude that everything is the result of brute force. I am inclined to look at everything as resulting from designed laws, with the details, whether good or bad, left to the working out of what we may call chance. Not that this notion *at all* satisfies me. I feel most deeply that the whole subject is too profound for the human intellect. A dog might as well speculate on the mind of Newton. Let each man hope and believe what he can. [10]

And so it went, around and around, in Darwin's head— law and chance, chance and law. The difficulty was that,

[9] Darwin, Charles, *Autobiography,* 87.

[10] Darwin to Asa Gray, Down, May 22, 1860, quoted in Francis Darwin, ed., *The life and letters of Charles Darwin including an autobiographical chapter* 2:105, New York, Appleton, 1898. See also Darwin's letter to Joseph Dalton Hooker, July 13, 1856, quoted in Francis Darwin, ed., *More letters of Charles Darwin . . .* 1:94, London, John Murray, 1903.

when nature was conceived as a law-bound system of matter in motion, chance was but the other side of a coin stamped law. In the old view of nature, chance and change had been the antitheses of design and permanence. The forms of the species were regarded as designed by God; varieties were products of time and circumstance, of *chance,* not in the sense of being uncaused or not subject to law, but in the sense of not being a part of the original plan of creation. Now, in the evolutionary view of nature, change was everywhere, and everything was either chance or law depending on how one chose to look at it. Adaptation of structure to function was a *chance* outcome of the operations of nature in the sense of not being specifically arranged in terms of a preconceived plan for the economy of nature, but it was certainly not chance in the sense of being uncaused or spontaneous. Thus, Huxley answered the charge that Darwin had introduced chance into nature by pointing out that "chance variations" must result from the operation of definite laws. Darwin, he declared, had in no way destroyed the teleological view of nature, since the element of design was simply transferred from the present structures of nature to the hidden system of laws, elements, and forces which had produced them. Yet he, like Darwin, asserted repeatedly that he could see no purpose in nature. But what was a teleological view of nature which denied purpose, or *telos,* in nature? The old terms had taken on new meanings. Confusion was rampant.

Oddly enough, it was precisely the element of chance variation (taking *chance* not as the obverse of law but rather as its opposite) which recommended Darwin's theory to the American pragmatists Charles Peirce and William James as a means of deliverance from the mechanical determinism of nineteenth-century physics and chemistry—"the block universe eternal and without a history," as William James described it. Peirce's interpretation of the theory of natural selection was totally at variance with Darwin's conception of nature as a law-bound system of matter in motion. "In biology," wrote Peirce, "that tremendous upheaval caused

in 1860 by Darwin's theory of fortuitous variations was but
the consequence of a theorem in probabilities, namely, the
theorem that if very many similar things are subject to very
many slight fortuitous variations, as much in one direction
as in the opposite direction, which when they aggregate a
sufficient effect upon any one of those things in one direction must eliminate it from nature, while there is no corresponding effect of an aggregate of variations in other directions, the result must, in the long run, be to produce a change
of the average characters of the class of things in the latter
direction." [11] Peirce then went on to substitute a statistical
conception of natural law for the traditional idea of natural
law as a rigid pattern of behavior imposed on matter by the
Creator, and to envisage the world process as a gradual
growth of concrete reasonableness in the universe at large.
In his opinion, a cosmogonic philosophy capable of representing the state of knowledge at which the West had arrived
in his day

> would suppose that in the beginning—infinitely remote—
> there was a chaos of unpersonalized feeling, which being with-
> out connection or regularity would properly be without ex-
> istence. This feeling, sporting here and there in pure arbitrari-
> ness, would have started the germ of a generalizing tendency.
> Its other sportings would be evanescent, but this would have a
> growing virtue. Thus, the tendency to habit would be started;
> and from this, with the other principles of evolution, all the
> regularities of the universe would be evolved. At any time,
> however, an element of pure chance survives and will remain
> until the world becomes an absolutely perfect, rational, and
> symmetrical system, in which mind is at last crystalized in the
> infinitely distant future. [12]

Or, as he put it in another place:

[11] Peirce, Charles, MSS., IB 3a "Folder of Late Fragments" ("Why should
a Doctrine of Chances raise Science to a Higher Plane?") (Jan. 25,
1909), 15, quoted in Wiener, Philip, *Evolution and the founders of Pragmatism*, 81, Cambridge, Mass., Harvard University Press, 1949.
[12] Peirce, Charles, *Collected papers of Charles Sanders Peirce* 6: paragraph 33,
quoted in Wiener, *op. cit.*, 84.

. . . the coalescence, the becoming continuous, the becoming governed by laws, the becoming instinct with general ideas are but phases of one and the same process of growth of reasonableness. This is first shown to be true with mathematical exactitude in the field of logic, and is thence inferred to hold good metaphysically.[13]

Likewise, William James, Henri Bergson, A. N. Whitehead, and others, each in his own way, found in the idea of organic evolution the key to a new cosmology in which spontaneity, novelty, and purpose had a place, a place which had been denied them in the cosmology inherited from the seventeenth century. The influence of these new ideas may be seen in the writings of modern students of evolution, as when Professor Dobzhansky writes, somewhat mystically: "In producing life, cosmic evolution overcame its own bounds; in giving rise to man, biological evolution transcended itself. Human evolution may yet ascend to a superhuman level." [14]

To summarize concerning Darwin's role with respect to the second stage of the conflict between science and religion: On the one hand, he gave the death blow to traditional natural theology by drawing out the ultimate implications for biology of the conception of nature as a law-bound system of matter in motion. On the other hand, he helped to precipitate a cosmological revolution (developing independently within physics itself) which threw into doubt the Newtonian cosmology Darwin and Huxley had taken for granted. Nature was open once more to the elements of value, purpose, and novelty which Newton and his contemporaries had extruded from it except in so far as they thought to find them in the wise design of the structures of nature.

We come now to the third stage of the conflict between science and religion, the stage in which the methods and attitudes of natural science were extended to the study of man, his history and institutions, political, economic, re-

[13] *Ibid.* 5: paragraph 4, quoted in Wiener, *op. cit.,* 91.
[14] Dobzhansky, Theodosius, *The biological basis of human freedom,* 27, New York, Columbia University Press, 1956.

ligious, and moral. The hope for a natural science of man and society had been voiced in the seventeenth and eighteenth centuries, but it was Herbert Spencer, in the mid-nineteenth century, who first proposed that the evolution of human history and human institutions be viewed as a simple extension of cosmic and organic evolution, continuous with them and subject to the same general laws. In his essay entitled "Progress: Its Law and Cause," published in 1857, Spencer discerned in the whole universe a progressive development from homogeneity to heterogeneity. Progress seemed written into the structure of things. It was "not an accident, not a thing within human control, but a beneficent necessity." In human history, said Spencer, progress had come about primarily through a competition of individuals and races. Those who were best adapted to the changing requirements of the environment won out over those less well-adapted, thus setting the stage for still further progress.[15]

The relation between Darwin and Spencer is an interesting one. On the one hand, Darwin was highly suspicious of Spencer's intellectual methods. "My mind," he wrote Spencer's American disciple John Fiske, "is so fixed by the inductive method, that I cannot appreciate deductive reasoning . . . such parts of H. Spencer as I have read with care impress my mind with the idea of his inexhaustible wealth of suggestion, but never convince me." [16] On the other hand, there can be no question that Darwin shared Spencer's belief in necessary, if somewhat sporadic, improvement in both nature and history and regarded natural selection as the chief engine of progress in both. The modern reader is rather surprised to see how frequently Darwin uses the terms "improve" and "improvement" in discussing natural selection. When Lyell protested that natural selection need not imply

[15] For a fuller account of Spencer's ideas as well as those of Auguste Comte, see my article Biology and social theory in the nineteenth century: Auguste Comte and Herbert Spencer, *Critical problems in the history of science* (University of Wisconsin Press, Madison, Wisc., 1959), Paper No. 14.

[16] Darwin to John Fiske, Down, December 8, 1874, *Life and letters* 2:371.

natural improvement unless there were some "principle of improvement" at work in nature independently of natural selection, Darwin replied:

> When you contrast natural selection and "improvement," you seem always to overlook . . . that every step in the natural selection of each species implies improvement in that species in relation to its conditions of life. No modification can be selected without it be an improvement or advantage. Improvement implies, I suppose, each form obtaining many parts or organs, all excellently adapted for their functions. As each species is improved, and as the number of forms will have increased, if we look to the whole course of time, the organic condition of life for other forms will become more complex, and there will be a necessity for other forms to become improved, or they will be exterminated; and I can see no limit to this process of improvement, without the intervention of any other and direct principle of improvement. All this seems to me quite compatible with certain forms fitted for simple conditions, remaining unaltered, or being degraded.[17]

But what was the criterion of "improvement"? Not simply survival, for Darwin was quick to concede that natural selection might bring about developments which constituted "retrogression" when viewed against the trend of development as a whole. Improvement in the latter sense seemed to imply some notion of "higher" forms of life capable of surviving in a wider range of environments. But Darwin and his colleagues Hooker and Huxley could never decide just what they meant by "higher" and "lower" forms. "I do not think zoologists agree in any definite ideas on this subject and my ideas are not clearer than those of my brethren," Darwin wrote Hooker.[18] But, if there was no precise criterion of "higher" and "lower," there could be no precise meaning to general improvement as distinct from competitive advantage in a specific situation. Ironically enough, Wallace and Dar-

[17] Darwin to Charles Lyell, Ilkley, Yorkshire, October 25, 1859, *Life and letters* 1:531.
[18] Darwin to J. D. Hooker, Down, 1854, *More letters* 1:76.

win both thought that much of the ambiguity in this respect might have been avoided if instead of using the term "natural selection," loaded with implications of intelligent choice, Darwin had used instead Spencer's term "survival of the fittest." Nowadays, on the contrary, biologists lament that Spencer's term was ever adopted, even secondarily, because of the difficulty of defining a criterion of fitness and of stripping it of value implications. The moral of the story would seem to be that biologists can neither live with nor live without normative concepts implying standards of excellence. Thus, G. S. Carter, in his recent survey *A Hundred Years of Evolution,* struggles with the "problems raised by the element of progress in evolution." "These," he declares, "are the most fundamental of all, for it is the progressive nature of biological evolution, its progress from the simple to the complex, towards a 'better' organism and more 'efficient' life, that is the most outstanding characteristic of evolution in living nature." [19] Professor Carter's liberal use of quotation marks in this passage betrays his uneasiness at introducing what are essentially normative concepts into a science which he regards as "necessarily mechanistic."

Whatever the difficulties involved in the notion of progressive improvement by natural selection in the realm of nature, they were as nothing compared to those which Darwin and Spencer encountered when they attempted to carry the idea over into human history. That mankind *had* progressed and would continue to progress Darwin seldom doubted. "I cannot explain why," he wrote to Lyell in 1860, "but to me it would be an infinite satisfaction to believe that mankind will progress to such a pitch that we should [look] back at [ourselves] as mere Barbarians." Again he wrote: "I am sorry to say that I have no 'consolatory view' on the dignity of man. I am content that man will probably advance, and care not much whether we are looked at as mere savages in a remotely distant future." "To believe that man was aboriginally civil-

[19] Carter, G. S., *A hundred years of evolution,* 181, New York, Macmillan, 1957.

ised and then suffered utter degradation in so many regions," he declared in *The Descent of Man,* "is to take a pitiably low view of human nature. It is apparently a truer and more cheerful view that progress has been much more general than retrogression; that man has risen, though by slow and interrupted steps, from a lowly condition to the highest standard as yet attained by him in knowledge, morals and religion." [20] This progress, he added, gave hope for "a still higher destiny in the distant future."

A very comforting, even inspiring, view of things this, but there were ambiguities in it, both as to the criterion of improvement and as to the method by which it had taken place and would take place. These difficulties may be illustrated with respect to Darwin's account of the origin and progress of the *moral sense,* which he regarded as the chief attribute distinguishing man from the lower animals. In Darwin's view, the moral sense sprang from the interaction of the social instincts with man's superior intellectual powers, the whole process being guided by natural selection.

It must not be forgotten [he wrote in *The Descent of Man*] that although a high standard of morality gives a slight or no advantage to each individual man and his children over the other men of the same tribe, yet . . . an increase in the number of well-endowed men and an advancement in the standard of morality will certainly give an immense advantage to one tribe over another. A tribe including many members who, from possessing in a high degree the spirit of patriotism, fidelity, obedience, courage, and sympathy, were always ready to aid one another, and to sacrifice themselves for the common good, would be victorious over most other tribes; and this would be natural selection. At all times throughout the world tribes have supplanted other tribes; and as morality is one important element in their success, the standard of morality and the number of well-endowed men will thus everywhere

[20] Darwin, Charles, *The descent of man, and selection in relation to sex,* new edition, revised and augmented, 145, New York, Appleton, 1886. See also Darwin's letter to Lyell, Down, January 4th?, 1860, *Life and letters* 2:56, and another letter to the same, Down, April 27, 1860, *More letters* 2:30.

tend to rise and increase. . . . But as man gradually advanced in intellectual power, and was enabled to trace the more remote consequences of his actions; as he acquired sufficient knowledge to reject baneful customs and superstitions; as he regarded more and more, not only the welfare, but the happiness of his fellow-men; as from habit, following on beneficial experience, instruction, and example, his sympathies became more tender and widely diffused, extending to men of all races, to the imbecile, maimed, and other useless members of society, and finally to the lower animals,—so would the standard of his morality rise higher and higher. . . . Looking to future generations, there is no cause to fear that the social instinct will grow weaker, and we may expect that virtuous habits will grow stronger, becoming perhaps fixed by inheritance. In this case the struggle between our higher and lower impulses will be less severe, and virtue will be triumphant.[21]

But, it may be asked, if human sympathies become extended to all mankind, to all races and nations, to the imbecile and the mained, the so-called useless members of society, what becomes of the competitive struggle and hence of the progress of man? Here, indeed, was a dilemma, and Darwin was caught squarely on the horns of it.

Man, like every other animal, [he wrote] has no doubt advanced to his present high condition through a struggle for existence consequent on his rapid multiplication; and if he is to advance still higher it is to be feared that he must remain subject to a severe struggle. Otherwise he would sink into indolence, and the more gifted men would not be more successful in the battle of life than the less gifted. Hence our natural rate of increase, though leading to many and obvious evils, must not be greatly diminished by any means. There should be open competition for all men; and the most able should not be prevented by laws or customs from succeeding best and rearing the largest number of offspring.[22]

This would seem a frank enough avowal of Spencer's "Every

[21] Darwin, *Descent of man,* 124–125, 132.
[22] *Ibid.,* 618. See also pages 133–134.

man for himself, and the devil take the hindmost," but Darwin immediately adds that the moral qualities, though developed in part by the struggle for existence, are developed even more "through the effects of habit, the reasoning powers, instruction, religion, &c." than through natural selection.

Darwin's reference to the elevating influence of religion on the moral sense is interesting in view of the precarious state of his own religious beliefs. Speaking as an anthropologist, he thought to find the origin of religious ideas in the fears and dreams of primitive peoples. Presumably it was only in the later stages of social advance that religion exercised a beneficial influence on morality. "The idea of a universal and beneficent Creator," he noted, "does not seem to arise in the mind of man, until he has been elevated by long-continued culture." Yet the latest advances in science, to which Darwin himself had contributed mightily, seemed to undermine belief in such a Creator. Science, in discovering the secret of man's lowly origin and the equally humble origin of his highest thoughts and aspirations, seemed to Darwin to have destroyed confidence in man's reason and in his deepest intuitions when confronted with the ultimate questions of human existence. Darwin himself confessed to an "inward conviction" that the universe was not the result of chance. "But then," he added, "with me the horrid doubt always arises whether the convictions of man's mind, which has been developed from the mind of the lower animals, are of any value or at all trustworthy. Would any one trust in the convictions of a monkey's mind, if there are any convictions in such a mind." [23]

Here, indeed, was agnosticism, an agnosticism which trusted in the power of science to trace the origin of stars and planets, mountains and species, morality and religion, but which to all the deepest questions of the human spirit returned an *Ignoro,* followed by an *Ignorabo.* These were gloomy thoughts, and they were but little relieved by Darwin's

[23] Darwin to William Graham, Down, July 3, 1881, *Life and letters* 1:285.

rather ambiguous belief in the progress of man. For over human progress lay a dark shadow—"the idea," he wrote to Hooker, "or rather I presume the certainty of the sun some day cooling and we all freezing. To think of the progress of millions of years, with every continent swarming with good and enlightened men, all ending in this, and with probably no fresh start until this our planetary system has been again converted into red-hot gas. *Sic transit gloria mundi*, with a vengeance. . . ."[24]

There was, however, an even more dreadful thought which never occurred to Darwin because he assumed that the progress of science and civilization necessarily brought moral improvement in its wake. This was the thought, all too familiar to the present generation, that man might perish not through some natural catastrophe but by his own hand, because the progress of science and technology, of man's intellectual powers, had outrun the progress of human sympathy and understanding.

These difficulties and ambiguities in Darwin's reflections on nature, man, and God would not be worth rehearsing at such great length if they had been *his* difficulties alone. After all, he was primarily a biologist and a very great one. It would perhaps be too much to expect any biologist since Aristotle to be simultaneously a great moral philosopher and social thinker. But Darwin's difficulties and inadequacies were those of his age and of the age which succeeded. They entered deeply into biological and social thought and still do. The genetic fallacy which led Darwin to suppose that the religious beliefs of mankind were adequately accounted for in terms of the dreams and fears of primitive peoples was to permeate sociology and cultural anthropology for many years to come. The sociological positivism which indentified Kant's categorical imperative as the voice of society built into the individual by a long course of social training was to reappear in Freud and Durkheim. The anti-metaphysical bias which relegated to the realm of the unknowable every-

[24] Darwin to J. D. Hooker, Down, February 9, 1865, *More letters* 1:260–261.

thing which could not be formulated scientifically was to become even more pronounced. The conception of human progress as an outcome of competitive struggle between individuals, nations, and races was to wreak incalculable havoc in the custody of men less deeply humanitarian than Darwin. Finally, the confident assumption that the progress of intellect, especially of science and the scientific attitude, is necessarily accompanied by moral and cultural progress still lingers on despite the shattering events of our own age and the threat of atomic destruction. "Judged by any reasonable criteria," Professor Dobzhansky writes in his recent book *The Biological Basis of Human Freedom,* "man represents the highest, most progressive, and most successful product of organic evolution. . . . Most remarkable of all, he is now in the process of acquiring knowledge which may permit him, if he so chooses, to control his own evolution. He may yet become 'business manager for the cosmic process of evolution,' a role which Julian Huxley has ascribed to him, perhaps prematurely."[25]

What should a sane man think of this? Should he conclude with Sir Julian that the cosmic process, after billions of years of labor, has finally brought forth a creature, man, who is ready or nearly ready to direct the future course of things? Or should he rather regard the very entertaining of such an idea as a symptom of the madness with which the gods afflict those whom they would destroy?

To summarize: With respect to revealed religion, Darwin's writings helped to precipitate a rethinking of traditional doctrines concerning inspiration and revelation, a rethinking which has proceeded in several directions and is still going on.

With respect to natural religion, Darwin shattered its traditional basis by exhibiting the adaptation of structure to function in the organic world as a necessary outcome of random variation, struggle for existence, and natural selection.

[25] Dobzhansky, *Biological basis of human freedom,* 87–88. See also Huxley, Sir Julian, *Evolution in action,* 116, New York, Mentor Books, 1957.

For many of his contemporaries the blow was softened by the indomitable faith of the nineteenth century in progress, a faith which enabled them to view the world-machine as a divinely contrived mechanism for insuring perpetual improvement in nature and history. But Darwin found little comfort in this view. Progress was too slow, too sporadic and haphazard, too precarious to reflect much credit on the Creator, if there was one. But though Darwin remained a prisoner of the law-bound system of matter in motion which he had extended to biology, others found in his theory of organic evolution a way of escape from the gloomy confines of that system. The revolution in biology was soon followed by a revolution in physics and cosmology.

With respect to the third stage of the conflict, in which the methods of natural science were applied to the study of man and society, Darwin played a pioneer role. His writings in this field are valuable not so much for their scientific content as for the light they throw on the difficulties inherent in the concept of social science. Like Spencer, Darwin attempted to apply the concepts of biology to human history; like Spencer, he wound up in hopeless contradictions. Biology afforded no criterion of progress for a creature like man, and Darwin was forced to bring in other criteria, imported surreptitiously from his Christian background. To the very end, he failed to appreciate the morally ambiguous character of human progress. He failed because, like many social scientists today, he had no adequate conception of man. Whatever his origin, man is a very peculiar creature, whose inmost being eludes the abstractions of science. For science, since it adopts the point of view of the detached observer, has no access to those aspects of reality which can be known only from the point of view of the actor. Yet, ultimately, the scientist himself is an actor in the difficult human situation, and science becomes pointless and even destructive unless it takes on significance and direction from a religious affirmation concerning the meaning and value of human existence.

3.

Fate and Will in the Marxian
Philosophy of History

Robert V. Daniels

EDITORIAL NOTE: *One of the great traditional paradoxes in Marxism is the conflict between its allegedly deterministic theory of history and its seemingly voluntaristic theory of revolution. The queston of whether Marx and Engels were determinists or voluntarists becomes especially significant in the twentieth century, when self-styled Marxist political parties have been involved in the making of "proletarian" revolutions in countries not yet prepared by Marxist standards for anything of the sort. One is reminded of the inconsistency in Darwin's theory of the descent of man, which requires both elimination of the unfit and development of altruistic feeling, as discussed in Professor Greene's article above. Robert V. Daniels here demonstrates that the ambiguity of contemporary Marxist philosophy of history has its origins in the work of the founding fathers themselves. Professor Daniels' article also touches on the important problem of the relationship between ideology and socio-political conditions. The vicissitudes of the debate between determinists and voluntarists in the history of Marxist theory obviously make no sense at all except in the light of the changing political needs and opportunities of those involved in the debate. At the same time, the theory itself, with all its ambiguity, continues to shape minds and influence the course of events*

HISTORICAL MATERIALISM—THE ECONOMIC INTERPRETATION OF
history as a travail of class struggles ascending to the classless

perfection of "communism"—has for some years been in a curious position. Non-Marxist critics are constantly assaulting it with bludgeon or scalpel; it is pilloried, slashed, dissected, refuted, time and again. No other dead dragon of the XIXth century has to endure such blows; could there yet be life in the old monster? As for our contemporary representatives of Marxian orthodoxy, we would expect them to stand in firm defense of the doctrine, yet strictly speaking they do not do so at all. If historical materialism is understood in the extreme sense, of the absolutely determining influence of the mode of production, through the class structure, upon the whole fabric of society and the course of its history—and this is the image which the non-Marxist critics have before them when they sally forth to the attack—Soviet theorists are against it also. To them it is "vulgar economic materialism," a perversion of the Master's teaching perpetrated by bourgeois heretics. Both sides are hostile to economic determinism.

In his essay "Dialectical and Historical Materialism" Stalin wrote in 1938: "As regards the *significance* of social ideas, theories, views, and political institutions . . ., historical materialism, far from denying them, stresses the rôle and importance of these factors in the life of society. . . . Once they have arisen they become a most potent force . . . which facilitates the progress of society."[1] While conceding the influence of material conditions in the origin of such ideas and institutions, Stalin refused to recognize them as serious obstacles to the political program which he represented. He declared in 1934:

> There can be no justification for references to so-called objective conditions. . . . The part played by so-called objective conditions has been reduced to a minimum; whereas the part played by our organizations and their leaders has become decisive, exceptional. What does this mean? It means that from now on nine-tenths of the responsibility for the failures and

[1] *History of the Communist Party of the Soviet Union (Bolsheviks): Short Course* (New York, 1939), 116.

defects in our work rests, not on "objective" conditions, but on ourselves, and on ourselves alone.[2]

All of the material conditions of existence, so central in Marx's philosophy of history, are here dismissed by Stalin—they will neither guarantee nor prevent what he wants to have done.

The attitude which Stalin enjoined upon Soviet historical thought between 1934 and 1938 meant an abrupt break with all of the presumed tenets of Communist historical orthodoxy as previously conceived. The sharpness of the change was dramatically underscored by the savage attacks begun in 1936 on M. N. Pokrovsky, the man who had been the czar of Soviet historical study. Pokrovsky enjoyed the curious distinction of being posthumously purged, for he had died with full honors in 1932. Four years later he was denounced in the most violent terms for the "vulgarized" notion of "economic materialism." Additional charges made the indictment of Pokrovsky's ghost an exotic amalgam—"subjective idealism," "denials of objective science," "deviation to mechanism"—all because Pokrovsky had espoused a Marxian determinism as rigid as that which most non-Marxist critics read into the theory.[3] The party line had discovered the historical significance of political institutions and leaders, and a spate of literature followed to establish the new and officially correct interpretation of Marxism, exalting the nation, the state, the idea, the individual—all those categories which the opponents of Marxism had been trying to defend. The inspiration for the Soviet shift was obvious: theory was brought more explicitly into line with reality, as Lenin and Stalin were hailed as the inspired leaders of the October revolution and the creators of the new socialist society. "Lenin and Stalin," declared one writer,

[2] Stalin, Report to the Seventeenth Congress of the CPSU(B), *Problems of Leninism* (Moscow, 1940), 529.

[3] See, e.g., A. Shcheglov, "Metodologicheskie istoki oshibok M. N. Pokrovskogo" ("The Methodological Sources of the Errors of M. N. Pokrovsky"), *Pod Znamenem Marksizma* (Under the Banner of Marxism), no. 5 (1936), 60–62.

"devoted all their strength and experience, all the power of their genius as theoreticians, all their knowledge of the laws of the class struggle and revolution, in order to prepare the working class and the toilers for the consummation of the socialist revolution."[4] Such was the Soviet frame of mind, of course, that this adjustment could not be accepted as a revision of a Marxist dogma disproved by the success of the revolution in Russia; Marxism must needs be restated, so that the new line would appear to represent what had always been the true doctrine. The old reading of Marxism was denounced as a petty-bourgeois perversion, and an old familiar bourgeois philosophy was dressed up in the language of the proletarian revolution. Frankness about this change was as unacceptable to the Stalinists as resistance to it, and Georg Lukács, the Hungarian Communist philosopher of voluntarism, met with his harshest criticism from the Russians at this very time.[5]

The obviously contrived and compulsory nature of the Stalinist reinterpretation of Marxism does not mean that the previously accepted version was entirely accurate. There is good reason to doubt whether Marx and Engels ever really intended their philosophy of history to be understood in the extreme determinist sense which most of their followers gave it in the first quarter of this century. Serious debate over this question took place in Russia before the official change of line in the 1930's. This was the so-called "philosophical controversy," which was conducted with great vigor in the late 1920's until the heavy hand of the party put an end to the debate in 1929–30.

The controversy centered around a rising challenge to the prevailing interpretation of Marxism, which was a strictly mechanistic and deterministic materialism. Of this view the most prominent exponent was Nikolai Bukharin, the party's

---

[4] F. Gorokhov, "Rol lichnosti v istorii" ("The Role of the Individual in History"), *Pod Znamenem Marksizma*, no. 9 (1938), 76.

[5] See Morris Watnick, "Georg Lukács: An Intellectual Biography," *Soviet Survey*, April–June, 1958, pp. 54–55, and Jan.–March, 1959, pp. 80–81.

leading ideologist after Lenin and one of the top chieftains until he came to grief as the leader of the Right Opposition in 1929. Fortified in his belief by the prevailing behaviorist and physiological mode in psychology, and blissfully ignorant of XXth-century physics, Bukharin rejected individual free will and historical accident altogether. History was the determined outcome of social laws, before, during, and even after the socialist revolution.[6] Individual will was a factor, but not an independent agent: physiology and sociology determined its direction. Thus it was even with the revolutionaries: "Marxism does not *deny the will, but explains it.* When Marxists organize the Communist Party and lead it into battle, this action is also an expression of historical necessity. . . ."[7] Socialism would succeed capitalism independently of any individual's will, for it was in the nature of capitalist society to make people embrace Marxism and strive for socialism: "Marxist social science . . . emphasized that Socialism followed 'with iron necessity' from the capitalist system of society and that our ideals and our aims were deeply rooted in the objective development of capitalist society . . ., that Socialism emerges from the objective process of development of capitalist society."[8]

Bukharin had a long tradition of socialist theory on the side of his interpretation. Determinism was expounded *ad nauseam* by the German Social-Democrats, while Plekhanov, the founder of Russian Marxism, was at pains to account for every apparent accident or individual influence as the ultimate product or agent of the material conditions of society.[9] The Italian Labriola went to the point of an explicit

[6] Bukharin, *Historical Materialism: A System of Sociology* (New York, 1926), Ch. 2.

[7] *Ibid.,* 51.

[8] Bukharin, "Report on the Program," Sixth Congress of the Communist International, *International Press Correspondence,* no. 56 (Aug. 27, 1928), 981.

[9] See, e.g. H. W. C. Cunow, *Die Marxsche Geschichts-Gesellschafts-, und Staatstheorie: Grundzüge der Marxschen Soziologie* (Berlin, 1923); George Plekhanov, *The Rôle of the Individual in History* (New York, 1940).

Marxian explanation of Marx and Engels themselves—"to show how the materialist conception of history arises precisely in given conditions, not as a personal and tentative opinion of two writers, but as the new conquest of thought by the inevitable suggestion of a new world which is in process of birth, that is to say the proletarian revolution."[10] Even Lenin, for all the voluntarist implication which he introduced into Marxism with his doctrine of the party and his revolutionary leadership, firmly professed the determinist point of view: "One cannot 'make' a revolution; revolutions grow out of crises and turning points of history which mature objectively (independent of the will of a party or a class)."[11]

The success of Lenin and his followers in scoring a revolutionary victory in spite of the absence of the supposed economic prerequisites impelled some Marxists to think out a new view of the change from socialism. The earliest man to accept the voluntaristic implications of the Russian Revolution was Georg Lukács, who had come to Marx from Hegel and continued to reflect the latter's influence. Writing in 1919, Lukács attacked the "vulgar Marxists" for denying "the rôle of power in the struggle to achieve and preserve victory in the proletarian revolution"; in this struggle he saw "the beginning of the suspension of economism's pure 'conformity to natural law.'" The revolution, Lukács insisted, required violence to divert the natural course of history: "The demand that socialism be realized without 'extra-economic' power, through the immanent laws of economic development, is actually synonymous with the external survival of capitalist society."[12]

Lukács was condemned by the Russians—his revision of Marxism was much too clear for their taste—but Soviet

[10] Antonio Labriola, "Historical Materialism," in *Essays on the Materialist Conception of History* (Chicago, 1908), 158.

[11] Lenin, *Sochineniia* (Works), 1st ed., XIII, 164. On Lenin's implied voluntarism, see my article, "Lenin and the Russian Revolutionary Tradition," in *Russian Thought and Politics* (Harvard Slavic Studies, IV, 1957).

[12] Georg Lukács, "Der Funktionswechsel des historischen Materialismus," in *Geschichte und Klassenbewusstsein* (Berlin, 1923), 246, 252.

thinking began to follow the same course in the mid-1920's. The rising philosophical school of "dialecticians," aided by the publication of hitherto unknown writings by Engels, *The Dialectics of Nature,* and by Lenin (his *Philosophical Notebooks*), began to challenge the prevailing determinist assumptions in both natural and social science.

While the issue was complicated by factional politics and the ambitions of zealous mediocrities, the substance of the dialecticians' criticism of the mechanist point of view was that basic historical changes could occur neither gradually nor as the simple working-out of "objective" forces. A "dialectical" jump would intervene between the two social systems, capitalism and socialism, while the laws of determinist causation applicable to the former would cease to apply after the revolution. The change itself was indeterminate, the result of conscious intervention in the historical process by revolutionary leaders and the revolutionary party.[13]

The new interpretation was quickly reflected in political pronouncements. In the course of denouncing Trotsky before the Sixth Comintern Congress in July 1928, Dmitri Manuilsky interpreted historical materialism as a two-way street: "To deny the influence of 'social organizational' forms upon the level of the material-productive basis means to abandon Marxism. . . . Social-organizational forms were not only the product of the material-productive structure but . . . influenced the latter."[14] One Ksenofontov, discussing the proposed Comintern program in *Pravda,* explicitly asserted the new activist philosophy against the old mechanism:

There exists a view according to which the overthrow of capitalist society "takes place of itself" in accordance with its laws of development. Marxism teaches us, however, that a form of society is superseded by the new form only when the revolu-

---

[13] A good discussion of these issues is included in the remarkable senior thesis written by David L. Auerbach, "Marx and the Mechanist Image of Man" (Harvard University, 1952), 95–109.

[14] D. Z. Manuilsky, Report to the Sixth Congress of the Communist International, "The Situation and the Problems of the CPSU," *International Press Correspondence,* no. 63 (Sept. 17, 1928).

tionary class actively intervenes. . . . The proletarian revolution is accomplished not of itself, but it must be organized.
Capitalism knows no crisis from which there is no way out.[15]

This looks like a voluntarist heresy, and indeed it is if Marxism means what most non-Communists think it does. In
1929, however, Stalin made it Soviet orthodoxy; the mechanist view was condemned as "a clear departure from the
Marxist-Leninist philosophical position," and used by the
Stalinists as evidence against the "kulak deviation" of the
Bukharin faction and the gradualism which they espoused.[16]

Political considerations were at the root of the new voluntarist line and its enforcement. It was admirably suited as a
rationalization of the dynamic drive of the Soviet state, after
Stalin had become its unchallenged leader, to collectivize
the peasantry and transform Russia into a modern industrial
nation. From 1934 on doctrinal revision flowed freely. The
"withering-away" theory of political power and institutions
was abandoned. Stalin discovered in 1939 that the state had
a positive function in building the new social order, while his
apologists hailed in chorus the emergence of "a state of a new
type" and the inspired genius of its leader.

From the 1930's on Soviet writing on historical theory has
systematically obscured the real issue, which is natural
enough, since the point of this latter-day theorizing has
mainly been to sustain the fog of confusion within which the
new doctrine can be made to look like the old one. The real
question in assessing the Soviet revision of the Marxist theory
of history is this: are the proletarian revolution and the development of socialism considered inevitable as the result of

[15] Ksenofontov in *Pravda*, Second Discussion Supplement on the Draft Program of the Comintern, translated in *International Press Correspondence*,
no. 35 (June 28, 1928), 651–652.

[16] Resolutions of the "Second All-Union Conference of Marxist-Leninist
Scientific-Research Institutions," *Pod Znamenem Marksizma*, no. 5 (1929),
6–7; B. Gessen and I. Podvolotsky, "Filosoficheskie korni pravogo
opportunizma" ("The Philosophical Roots of Right Opportunism"),
Pod Znamenem Marksizma, no. 9 (1929), 25–28.

historical laws, or do they depend on chance and the historical accident of correctly inspired and resolute leadership?
Soviet theorists have never faced this question squarely; they
have only fumbled with formulae about the identification of
great revolutionary leaders with the masses, in order to maintain a chain of rationalization between the manifestly voluntarist aspects of the Soviet political record and the objectivist
tradition of Marxism. After Stalin's death Soviet doctrine de-
emphasized the rôle of the individual, only to impute the
same crucial rôle to the Communist Party as an institution.

While Soviet theorists have hesitated to pursue the Stalinist conception of history to its logical conclusion, certain
foreign sympathizers have frankly asserted that leadership
can be decisive. This position has been mainly developed—
with the common sense traditional to their nationality—by
the British school of Marxists. In an assessment of the limits
of the economic factor, the economist Maurice Dobb writes:
"When the objective situation is of a certain kind, and action
has an appropriate direction, such action can have a large,
even an epoch-making effect."[17] Christopher Hill describes
Marxism as the science of how to make society freer, and
notes that if the Russian Revolution had not been led by
Lenin "its course would have been very different."[18]

Similar notions have cropped up in recent years in connection with East European Communist "revisionism." The
East German historian Jürgen Kuczynski incurred the wrath
of the authorities for his "idealist" deprecation of the rôle of
economics and the masses. "Where the spirit of many millions sleeps," he wrote, "then it is just the few, whose spirit
is not asleep, who make history." While he conceded the
mass rôle at critical moments, he asserted of Lenin's rôle
(particularly in deciding on peace in 1918): "I would say . . .

[17] Maurice Dobb, "Historical Materialism and the Rôle of the Economic
Factor," *History* (Feb. 1951), 5.
[18] Christopher Hill, "Le Marxisme et l'histoire," *Esprit* (May–June 1948),
901.

that the survival of the revolution here, at this moment, depended solely on Lenin's genius."[19] The famous young Polish philosopher Leszek Kolakowski took a particularly bold stand to denounce belief in inevitability as the excuse for the crimes of Stalinism: "It is enough to believe in Providence in order to bless the brick which hits one on the head. . . . One needs a certain skepticism in the face of any prophetic philosophy of history which sees the future with excessive certainty."[20]

The curious conclusion which emerges from this brief survey of various latter-day adherents of Marxism is that they reject strict economic determinism just as vigorously as do the opponents of the doctrine. Everyone, explicitly or implicitly, repudiates the inevitability of impersonal laws of history and the remorseless primacy of the mode of production in determining the future of mankind. The two points of view—Marxist and anti-Marxist—differ only as to whether Marx himself agrees with them. The Communists have tried to make him square with their own interest in the power of the party and the guidance of the leader, while anti-Communists have endeavored to make of him a straw man of mechanistic determinism whom they could disprove with ease and pleasure. What Marx really meant with his philosophy of history is the question which we must now try to resolve.

Marxism—the original version—is shot through with dualism, notwithstanding the assertions of its exponents (and critics) that it is a "monistic" philosophy. A careful reading of Marx and Engels, as we shall see, indicates that the extreme determinist reading of the doctrine is almost as much an exaggeration as the latter-day Soviet voluntarism. The de-

---

[19] Jürgen Kuczynski, "Der Mensch, der Geschichte macht," *Zeitschrift für Geschichtswissenschaft* (East Berlin), no. 1 (1957), 4, 16.
[20] Kolakowski, "Responsibility and History," *East Europe* (Feb. 1958), 18, (Mar. 1958), 27.

terminist distortion is not hard to understand: emphasis on the economic factor was the distinctive feature of the Marxian interpretation of history, so much so that it was easy for both its friends and enemies to conclude that the theory ended simply with that. "Marx and I," conceded Engels, "are ourselves partly to blame for the fact that younger writers sometimes lay more stress on the economic side than is due to it. We had to emphasize this main principle in opposition to our adversaries, who denied it, and we had not always the time, the place or the opportunity to allow the other elements involved in the interaction to come into their rights."[21]

One form of dualism in Marxism is widely recognized—the opposition between theory and practice, scientific (or pseudo-scientific) analysis and revolutionary action. Marxists everywhere until after the Russian Revolution were convinced that they had scientific proof of the objective inevitability of the proletarian revolution, while at the same time they worked with energy and dedication in their Marxist parties to bring about this event. The logical contradiction between a determinist philosophy of history and the vigorous pursuit of political action is obvious, but in psychological terms it makes a great deal of sense. This might be termed the "predestination paradox," which Marxism shares with much Christian theology: the man who is convinced of the inevitability of his cause strives all the more vigorously to make sure it succeeds. This is a puzzle only if the unwarranted assumption is made that the action is motivated by the doctrine. According to the Marxian approach, or from any sociological point of view, the revolutionary is so oriented not by virtue of any theory but because of the effect which his social situation has had upon him. The man thus inclined to revolution embraces Marxian determinism as an appealing rationalization for his own impulses, which continue to impel him to

[21] Engels to J. Bloch, Sept. 21, 1890, *The Selected Correspondence of Karl Marx and Friedrich Engels* (New York, 1942), 475, 477.

action. Philosophy does not create the will to action, but
only reinforces it. A man is Marxist because he is revolutionary, not vice versa.

This situation allows broad opportunity for the reinterpretation of Marxian doctrine, whose complexity permits a
wide range of emphases without breaking from the prophet.
Voluntarist conclusions, if they turn out to be more conge-
nial, can be stressed. They would be, in fact, much more in
accord with revolutionary actuality, especially in Russia.

By stages, precisely such a revision was carried out by the
Bolsheviks, first in action and tactical ideas which bore voluntarist implications, and then in the explicit reinterpretation of the theory. Lenin's doctrine of the party turned, in
the last analysis, on the assumption that without deliberate
organized action by correctly inspired leaders—i.e. Bolsheviks—the proletarian revolution would never come to pass.
The Bolshevik Revolution itself was the triumph of one
man's overriding will. The ensuing stages of the Communist
reinterpretation of Marxism have been discussed already—
the philosophical revisions of 1928–29 and the application
of the new line to history and political theory beginning in
1934. The end product under Stalin was the so-called Marxism in which the wisdom of the leader, the power of political
institutions, and the virtue of the nation governed every
decisive step in history.

Among Marxists elsewhere and by the Mensheviks in
Russia determinism was held to much more strictly, but here
again temperamental considerations are involved. Roughly
with the turn of the century the psychological referents of the
determinist belief changed. Previously it had been an inspiration to revolutionaries; subsequently it was more and more
the resort of people who temperamentally were not really
revolutionary at all. The fatalistic connotations of historical
materialism, as Bolshevik polemics have graphically pointed
out, served to justify the evasion of deliberate revolutionary
action, at a time when the socialist tradition still made it po-
litically difficult for socialist leaders to forswear their radical

terminology. Kautsky in Germany and Plekhanov in Russia were the outstanding examples of this state of mind. Something more than temperament was involved, however; as we shall see, the philosophical question of determinism and voluntarism involves implications about the social process which bear intimately on fundamental political preferences.

These conflicting trends of interpretation suggest a further question which is actually the key issue in the present study. Marxism involves a second duality, contained within the first or theoretical term of the familiar theory-practice dichotomy. This is a duality—or perhaps inconsistency—in the objective interpretation of the historical process, quite apart from the subjective question of taking action to affect that process. Is the course of history shaped or influenced more by the determined action of "material conditions" that operate through material laws independent of the will of any given individual, or by the ideas, decisions, and impulses of certain individuals? Are human events a matter of collective fate or individual will? Does history make man or does man make history?

Marxism—popular notions to the contrary—does not offer a simple and entirely one-sided answer to this question: man makes history *and* history makes man, as Marx put it in so many words. It is therefore possible, depending on personal preferences, political requirements, and the changing intellectual fashions of succeeding generations, for Marxists to find in the scriptures whichever emphasis they wish to make, and they have done so.

It will readily be observed at this point that our two dualities are related. The man who is interested in theoretical understanding more than in revolutionary action can readily stress the deterministic reading of the theory. The man of contrary bent, the revolutionary activist, will naturally seek out and put his emphasis on that aspect of the theory which accords a decisive rôle to willful action. This sums up the doctrinal development of the Bolsheviks. Activist Marxists, they molded their beliefs into an activist Marxism. There is nothing inherently inconsistent about their development, though at certain critical points it was forced along by political command. On the other hand, there was no logical necessity for this particular development, and its far-reaching political implications cannot simply be laid at the doorstep of Marx and Engels.

The task which now confronts us is to demonstrate where the actual position of Marx and Engels lay. Trying to correct the exclusively idealist conception of history which prevailed in their time, they allowed themselves to be identified with the opposite extreme. Some of their oversimplified statements, and particularly Marx's introduction to the *Critique of Political Economy,* do give precisely such an impression of unqualified economic determinism. However, there are a number of important qualifications of this extreme determinist view contained in the other writings of Marx and Engels. The explicit statement of these reservations was primarily the work of Engels after the senior partner died in 1883. They can be subsumed under three major points, which in sum make clear the subtle complexity of the Marxian philosophy.

The first basic qualification in Marxian determinism concerns the relationship between the economic forces of the social "base" and the political and intellectual forces of the social "superstructure." The relationship is one of "reciprocal interaction," in which each sphere affects the other, but with the stronger and in the long run more independent causative influence being attributed to the economic base.[22]

Once an important and occasionally decisive rôle is accorded the political and intellectual superstructure, the question naturally follows as to what importance the Marxists saw in these forces for the success of their own movement. To what extent is the proletarian revolution not blindly inevitable, but subject to acceleration, shaping, retardation,

[22] See, for example, Engels to Bloch, Sept. 21, 1890, and to Conrad Schmidt, Oct. 27, 1890, *Correspondence,* 475, 480–481.

or deflection to another line of development? To what extent is it the undetermined product of willful action?

Marx always stressed that historical necessity operated through the agency of conscious action. He did not deny the efficacy of will and of political power, but claimed to have explained their nature and direction on the basis of economic forces and the class struggle. Freedom of the will is an illusion —the individual is unconsciously made to want what he does by the social and economic circumstances which shape his mentality.

When Lenin undertook to justify revolutionary action, he departed sharply from Marx's identification of necessity and will, though he had Marx's stress on the latter as his sanction. Lenin assumed that consciousness and willful action were not only independent of social circumstances, but decisive in acting upon them. Consciousness, embodied in specially endowed individuals, would be injected into the historical process from the outside, and would dictate the ultimate success of the revolution. Lenin stated this in so many words:

> Class political consciousness can be brought to the workers *only from without,* that is, only from outside of the economic struggle, from outside of the sphere of relations between workers and employers. . . . Give us an organization of revolutionaries, and we shall overturn Russia.[23]

Remarks of this sort were made by Lenin not with any intent of challenging the philosophical presuppositions of Marxism, but only in immediate justification of the organizational and tactical measures which he insisted that the revolutionaries take. Nevertheless, the implications of Lenin's thinking were immediately apparent to orthodox Marxists like Plekhanov, who seized upon them for purposes of rebuttal: "The disputed question consists in this: Does there exist an economic necessity which calls forth in the proletariat a demand for socialism, makes it instinctively socialistic, and

[23] Lenin, "What Is to Be Done," *Selected Works* (Moscow, 1950), I–1, 287, 339.

impels it—even if left to its own resources—on the road to
social revolution, notwithstanding the stubborn and continual effort of the bourgeoisie to subject it to its own ideo-
logical influence? Lenin denies this, in face of the clearly
expressed opinions of all the theorists of scientific socialism.
And in that consists his enormous mistake, his theoretical
fall into sin."[24] Thanks to Lenin, the Bolsheviks' Marxism
was highly inconsistent by the time the party took power.
Most Bolsheviks, like Lenin himself, thought themselves to
be out-and-out determinists, however their political practice
contradicted this belief. But the materials were present for
a thorough reinterpretation when the course of Soviet politics
pressed upon Lenin's successor the need for a correction in
his doctrinal justifications.

The second major qualification of Marxian determinism
is the concept of historical causation as a matter of probabilities. This aspect of the doctrine has been almost completely neglected, which is unfortunate, since its implications
are extremely interesting. The essence of this notion of
probabilities is to concede to individual actions and historical
accidents a broad play, but to insist that the net resultant
of the constellation of events—after the probabilities are
added up and opposite quantities cancel each other out—is
governed by economic forces and the basic social structure.
As Engels expressed it in 1890:

> History makes itself in such a way that the final result always
> arises from conflicts between many individual wills, of which
> each again has been made what it is by a host of particular
> conditions of life. Thus there are innumerable intersecting
> forces, an infinite series of parallelograms of forces which give
> rise to one resultant—the historical event. This again may itself
> be viewed as the product of a power which, taken as a whole,
> works *unconsciously* and without volition. For what each indi-
> vidual wills is obstructed by everyone else, and what emerges

---

[24] Plekhanov, "The Working Class and the Social Democratic Intelli-
gentsia," *Iskra* (Aug. 1, 1904), as quoted in Max Eastman, *Marxism, Is
It Science?* (New York, 1940), 223.

is something that no one willed. Thus past history proceeds in the manner of a natural process. . . .[25]

The clarity of Engels' formulation can easily be improved upon with the use of more modern terminology, though his meaning does not seem to be in doubt. What he is trying to express is the statistical nature of the laws of social causation. Causative forces do not operate with rigor in any individual case, where either accident or free will can indeed operate. The basic economic and social factors have their effect as probabilities, which become decisive as large numbers of individual cases are reached. We might take suicides or traffic deaths as understandable, if morbid, examples: the rate of such mishaps for a whole country over a year's time can be predicted with fair accuracy on the basis of past experience—beyond certain relatively narrow limits of variability, the rate of these fatalities is the inevitable consequence of the sum total of social circumstances. On the other hand, barring exceptional cases of obvious pathology, no one can anticipate the fate of any particular individual. Statistical law, acting only as a probability, leaves undetermined the individual instance, but it may become a practical certainty for the society as a whole. The analogy with the physical concepts of indeterminacy and the merely statistical lawfulness in the behavior of atomic particles is very close.

Further sense can be made of Engels' proposition by calling upon the modern psychological concepts of unconscious motivation. While Engels can hardly be called a forerunner of Freud—his catalogue of the basic human motives reads far differently—the idea that in general people can be governed by forces of which they are not consciously aware answers neatly to Engels' aim of "investigating the driving powers which—consciously or unconsciously, and indeed very often unconsciously—lie behind the motives of men who act in history. . . ."[26] Granting a measure of reconcilable

[25] Engels to Bloch, Sept. 21, 1890, *Correspondence*, 476.
[26] Engels, *Ludwig Feuerbach and the End of Classical German Philosophy* (Moscow, 1950), 74.

truth to the concepts of both depth psychology and Marxism, we can uncover an area where social probabilities may have a strong effect on the individual, even though he feels himself to be a free agent. What people will, according to this approach, is conditioned by their social circumstances and in the preponderance of cases will be governed by these circumstances. Combining the concepts of unconscious motivation and statistical causation, we have a notion of the mechanism whereby historical determinism can operate despite the ubiquity of accident and the appearance of individual will.

This formulation still does not extend to the particular case on which Stalinist voluntarism is based. What becomes of determinism, if it is only a matter of probabilities, in those instances where the course of events is not the resultant of many individual wills but is dictated by a few or even one particular will, as in the case of an authoritative political leader? To be sure, the posssibility of such a concentration of decision-making power may perhaps be attributed back to the social structure, as Plekhanov insisted: "Individuals can influence the fate of society. Sometimes this influence is very considerable; but the possibility of exercising this influence, and its extent, are determined by the form of organization of society, by the relation of forces within it."[27] This only means, however, that a given set of circumstances may determine a condition of indeterminacy for a particular society at a particular time.

The concept of reciprocal interaction of base and superstructure, taken together with the concept of the indeterminacy of individual action, permits any kind of social structure to be described in these terms. The superstructure can influence the base; the action of the superstructure may under certain circumstances be governed by one or a few individuals; and the action of these individuals is indeterminate. Here is the avenue for possibly far-reaching indeterminism in a society's historical development. The key point in this sequence is the position and power of individuals within the

[27] Plekhanov, *The Rôle of the Individual in History,* 41.

superstructure—i.e. the nature of the society's political institutions. We can thus deduce from Marxian premises a theory of the decisiveness of political forms.

The third important qualification of Marxian determinism which Engels underscored is the notion of the revolution as a "leap to freedom." One feature of the classless socialist society which the proletarian revolution will establish is the escape of mankind from the determining influence of economic forces. This meant, according to Engels, that "Man's own social organization, hitherto confronting him as a necessity imposed by nature and history, now becomes the result of his own free action. . . . Only from that time will man himself, with full consciousnes, make his own history—only from that time will the social causes set in movement by him have . . . the results intended by him. It is the ascent of man from the kingdom of necessity to the kingdom of freedom."[28]

Underlying this glowing hope is the conviction that human control over the objective forces of history can be established by nothing more than understanding and will:

> Active social forces work exactly like natural forces: blindly, forcibly, destructively, so long as we do not understand and reckon with them. But when once we understand them, when once we grasp their action, their direction, their effects, it depends only upon ourselves to subject them more and more to our own will, and by means of them to reach our own ends.[29]

The human decision which thus prevails over the objective forces is not predetermined. This makes possible a completely indeterminate future, if the conditions which limit the efficacy of the human will can be corrected. Knowledge and a socialist economic organization are presumably enough. If man understands the laws of historical cause and effect, he can foresee the results of his action and secure results which actually correspond to his intentions (thus escaping from the

---

[28] Engels, *Anti-Dühring: Herr Eugen Dühring's Revolution in Science* (Moscow, 1954), 392–393.
[29] *Ibid.*, 387.

blindness of pre-socialist history-making). If the wills of a multitude of contending individuals are replaced with one enlightened social will, pursuing the interest of the collectivity, the cancelling and averaging effect in the atomistic society will be overcome, and the laws of deterministic probability will lose their effect.

It would seem, on the surface, that the new social order is to be scarcely short of an Elysium of untrammeled free humanity, shackled neither by nature nor by social authority. However, the Marxian vision omits a crucial question which is pointed up by our inference about the decisiveness of political power and institutions. Who understands, who plans, whose will is realized? The Russian Revolution gave birth to political institutions which decided this question in a very definite way—the dictatorship of the planner, who has no effective responsibility to the society at large and who subjects the entire population to his personal will on every matter he desires.

Freedom, in Engels' sense of freedom for the social organism to violate economic necessity or alter its course of development, has been achieved in the USSR to a remarkable degree. Guided by dictatorial planning, Soviet economic development is relatively free from the forces that act with statistical determinacy through the decisions of a multitude of individuals. The preferences of the multitude have no direct effect, or little, on the decisions of the top authority, and when decisions are made by an individual or a very small group, the laws of determinacy give way to free will. Freedom of choice for the leaders means necessity—political compulsion—for its members. To the degree that it will surmount the forces of economic necessity, the society must become totalitarian.

In like measure, the society without totalitarian controls, where decisions are made independently by a multitude of individuals, will remain more or less at the mercy of impersonal historical forces, which determine with statistical regularity the net behavior of the population. Each individual is free, but all individuals are subject to the pressure of social and economic conditions which establish in a high degree the probabilities of their response en mass. Once an opinion poll has carefully sampled a few thousand people, it can predict with reasonable accuracy the national response on any question whatsoever. Freedom for individuals means that the society will be shaped by impersonal forces beyond the control of any individual.

There exists, of course, a middle ground, though the prophets of Marxism have not explored it. A democratic society need not drift in leaderless anarchy. It can—and does, in some measure—have an authority representing the collective will which takes action in definite directions, which assumes responsibility, provides leadership, and shapes events. For such action to be effective without totalitarian power, however, the leadership must have reliable knowledge of the objective forces which are operating in the society, so that it can intervene in the way which will procure the desired results.

The ultimate paradox is that the opposing totalitarian and democratic societies of East and West are each wedded to historical conceptions that only make sense for the other. The dictatorial Soviet Union clings to the formula of a deterministic philosophy while all its political experience has revolved around the most exaggerated voluntarism. American democracy treasures the illusions of free will while the central virtue of its system guarantees that impersonal forces will have a preponderant influence on society's future course. Partisans of individual liberty who rail against historical determinism as a denial of human freedom are as illogical as Soviet spokesmen who denounce "bourgeois idealism" as a menace to the rule of the Communist Party. Neither side has carefully faced history's real challenge—to devise ways for society intelligently to plan the future and still preserve freedom for its individual members.

4.

Wilhelm Dilthey and the Critique
of Historical Reason

Hajo Holborn

EDITORIAL NOTE: *Of the many challenges to the authority of the natural sciences laid down by thinkers of the generation immediately preceding World War One, few had such lasting effect as the life-philosophy of Wilhelm Dilthey. As Hajo Holborn argues below, Dilthey was a forerunner of existentialism; a major influence in the development of modern psychological and psychoanalytical theory; a founder of contemporary philosophy of history; and perhaps the single most important figure in the movement which gave rise, at the turn of the century, to intellectual history as a discipline. Professor Holborn's article reveals Dilthey in all his variety and depth. Since its publication in 1950, Dilthey has come to be much better known and appreciated in the English-speaking world. A useful introduction to his historical thought, together with generous excerpts in translation from Volume VII of his collected works, may be read in H. P. Rickman, ed.,* Pattern and Meaning in History *(New York, Harper Torchbooks, 1962).*

I

IT MAY BE DOUBTFUL WHETHER OR NOT ORTEGA Y GASSET IS right in calling Wilhelm Dilthey "the greatest thinker of the second half of the nineteenth century," but there can be no question that his work has a lasting place in the history of the past seventy-five years and has had an influence on contemporary philosophy that is still growing.

Dilthey was born the son of a Calvinist minister in the Rhineland in 1833, a year after Goethe's death and the year of Johannes Brahms' birth. He intended to study theology when he went to Heidelberg and Berlin, but before long philosophy absorbed all his interest. In 1864 he became lecturer on philosophy in Berlin, in 1867 professor in Basel, where he met Jakob Burckhardt. But before Nietzsche arrived there Dilthey had already gone to Kiel. From 1871 to 1882 he was professor in Breslau, where he formed a close friendship with Count Yorck von Wartenburg, a Prussian landed nobleman who was a philosopher of high rank.[1] In 1882 Dilthey returned to Berlin to occupy Hegel's chair for the next twenty years. He died at the age of 77 in 1911.

Dilthey was highly regarded by his colleagues. His vote carried weight in faculty deliberations, and even more in the Academy of Sciences. His lecture courses, however, did not attract wide attention until the very end of the century, when they had to be given in the largest lecture hall of the university. His sudden success was probably only one more reason for his voluntary retirement at an early age. The last ten quiet years of his life were devoted exclusively to the completion of his work, though he probably knew he would not complete it, and certainly that he could not do so in the manner in which it had been begun. In his early forties he confessed to his mother: "It is strange how completely I have lost every worldly ambition in the wish to accomplish my great studies. The great crisis in the sciences and in European civilization in which we are living occupies my mind so deeply and completely that the desire to be useful in it has destroyed every personal ambition." [2] There was in him a

---

[1] Cf. Fritz Kaufmann, *Die Philosophie des Grafen Paul Yorck von Wartenburg* (Halle, 1928).

[2] *Der junge Dilthey,* ed. by Clara Misch (Leipzig, 1933), p. V.

lofty disregard of outward recognition by the academic world of his own time, which is the more impressive as he climbed the academic ladder so easily and successfully.

At the time of his death Dilthey was known as a man who had produced some of the finest studies in the history of philosophy and literature, in which he had created a new method of writing the history of ideas. He also received recognition for his rôle in the resurrection of German idealism, and in making a clear distinction between the methodologies of the natural and cultural sciences. But in this latter respect he was overshadowed by Heinrich Rickert, who systematized the logos of the age of William II so much more clearly that he imposed his concepts even on its critics like Max Weber. Dilthey's studies in anthropology and psychology were also frequently consulted as noteworthy investigations. But only some of his closest students, who knew the full sweep of his philosophy, dared to call the deceased a philosopher of higher rank than Nietzsche.

Dilthey's students prepared his work for final publication. The first World War interrupted this edition, and his most significant writings, which have made it possible to judge the real intent of his philosophizing, became available only during the twenties. Particularly important was the publication of volume V of the *Collected Writings* in 1924, of volume VII in 1927, and volume VIII in 1931. Today there are in all twelve volumes of *Collected Writings,* with one additional volume still unpublished.[3] Outside this collection we have the first volume of his *Life of Schleiermacher,*[4] a masterly study of the growth of the classic philosophical movement in eighteenth-century Germany. There is also the book *Inner*

---

[3] W. Dilthey, *Gesammelte Schriften* (Leipzig, 1914–36). (Hereafter cited as I, II, etc.)

[4] *Leben Schleiermachers* (Berlin, 1870). A second edition, augmented by parts of the projected, but never finished second volume, was published by H. Mulert (Berlin, 1922).

Experience and Poetry, among all his writings the most widely
known in Germany. It was later supplemented by a posthumous publication *On German Poetry and Music.*[5] We have also
important biographical sources, above all the correspondence
between Dilthey and Count Yorck,[6] together with a volume
of letters and notes of the young Dilthey.[7]

These publications have produced a rich discussion of
Dilthey's philosophy. The most important contributions to
a systematic study of Dilthey were made by Georg Misch, in
his extensive introduction to volume V of the *Collected Writings,* and in his discussion of Dilthey's relations with the
phenomenological and existentialist schools, written after
the publication of Martin Heidegger's *Sein und Zeit,* which
was profoundly influenced by Dilthey.[8] Among other German studies, the most notable is that by Otto Friedrich
Bollnow, which modestly claims to be only an "elementary
introduction" to Dilthey's philosophy, but is a most valuable guide in its interpretation both on account of the well-

[5] *Das Erlebnis und die Dichtung* (Leipzig, 1905; ten more editions have been
published). *Von Deutscher Dichtung und Musik* (Leipzig, 1932).
[6] *Briefwechsel zwischen Wilhelm Dilthey und dem Grafen Paul Yorck von Wartenburg, 1877–1897,* ed. by Sigrid von der Schulenburg (Halle, 1923). (Hereafter cited as *Dilthey-Yorck Briefswechsel.)*
[7] *Der junge Dilthey, 1852–70,* ed. by Clara Misch-Dilthey (Leipzig, 1933).
Also *"Briefe Wilhelm Diltheys an Bernhard und Luise Scholz, 1859–64,"* ed.
by S. von der Schulenburg, *Sitzungsberichte der Preussischen Akademie
der Wissenschaften, Phil.-hist. Klasse* (1933), 416–471. These letters show
Dilthey's lively interest in music. Dilthey was a leading member of the
philosophical faculty of Breslau University that conferred the honorary
degree on Brahms for which the composer expressed his gratitude in the
Academic Festival Overture. Other Dilthey letters were published by
E. Weniger, *"Briefe Wilhelm Diltheys an Rudolf Haym, 1861–73,"* *Abhand-
lungen der Preussischen Akademie der Wissenschaften* (1936), *Philosophisch-
Historische Klasse,* No. 9.
[8] G. Misch, *"Lebensphilosophie und Phänomenologie," Philosophischer Anzeiger ,*
III (1929), 1–102, IV (1930), 175–324, subsequently published as a book
(Leipzig, 1930). Cf. also some smaller articles by the same author, re-
cently brought together in *Vom Lebens-und Gedankenkreis Wilhelm Diltheys*
(Frankfurt, 1947).

chosen excerpts from Dilthey's writings and of the author's comments.[9]

But Dilthey's influence has spread into other countries. The close contact between French and German philosophy created French interest in Dilthey. Some of his major works have been translated into French, and studies of him have appeared.[10] Even more has been done, however, in Latin America, where apparently Ortega y Gasset awakened an early interest.[11] In 1943–45 all of *Dilthey's Collected Writings* appeared in Spanish translation.[12]

Dilthey is still little known in the English-speaking world. He has exercised a very strong influence on R. W. Collingwood, in spite of the rather unsympathetic and partly misleading treatment in his posthumous *Idea of History*.[13] The small book by H. A. Hodges was the first serious English attempt at an analysis of Dilthey's work.[14] American interest

[9] O. F. Bollnow, *Dilthey, Eine Einführung in seine Philosophie* (Leipzig, 1936). The most extensive Dilthey bibliography is contained in H. A. Hodges, *Wilhelm Dilthey, An Introduction* (London, 1944), 161–7. The numerous studies of Dilthey's philosophy in German are rather uneven in value, some of them being partly antiquated by the publication of the *Collected Writings;* other and more recent ones are marred by a Nazi slant. I have found most useful the following: E. Spranger, *Wilhelm Dilthey* (Berlin, 1912). M. Scheler, *"Versuche einer Philosophie des Lebens,"* in *Umsturz der Werte,* II, 135–181 (Leipzig, 1923). J. Wach, *Die Typenlehre Trendelenburgs und ihr Einfluss auf Dilthey* (Tübingen, 1926). A. Stein, *Der Begriff des Verstehens bei Dilthey* (Tübingen, 1926). L. Landgrebe, *"Wilhelm Diltheys Theorie der Geisteswissenschaften,"* *Jahrbuch für philosophische und phänomenologische Forschung* (1928). Fritz Kaufmann, *Geschichtsphilosophie der Gegenwart* (Berlin, 1931). C. Cüppers, *Die erkenntnistheoretischen Grundgedanken Wilhelm Diltheys* (Leipzig, 1933). J. Stenzel, *Dilthey und die deutsche Philosophie der Gegenwart* (Berlin, 1934). D. Bischoff, *Wilhelm Diltheys geschichtliche Lebensphilosophie* (Leipzig, 1935).
[10] R. Aron, *Essai sur la Théorie de l'Histoire dans l'Allemagne Contemporaine, La Philosophie Critique de l'Histoire* (Paris, 1938).
[11] Cf. his article on Dilthey in *Concord and Liberty* (New York, 1946).
[12] Mexico City, ed. by Prof. Imaz, 8 vols.
[13] London, 1946. It should not be forgotten that the author did not complete the manuscript and that it was not designed for publication in its present form.
[14] See note 9 *supra.*

in Dilthey started in an accidental and personal fashion. William James met him at the house of Hermann Grimm, the art historian, when he came to Berlin in 1867. He was greatly attracted by Dilthey and curious to learn more about him. He was quite disappointed that Dilthey parted from him without inviting him to his house.[15] Actually Dilthey himself was a mere visitor in the German capital and was on his way to Basel. If, however, he still remembered the meeting with William James in later years he must have regretted its briefness. He did not praise many of his contemporaries as highly as he did "the psychological genius of William James."[16] *The Varieties of Religious Experience* appeared to him the highest achievement in the psychological understanding of religion, the American contribution to the modern study of religion that began with Pascal, Lavater, Herder, Schleiermacher, and others.

It is impossible to say how deeply Dilthey studied the American pragmatism of his time and to what extent James or Peirce was aware of Dilthey. In retrospect Dilthey's "philosophy of life" and American pragmatism seem to have faced the identical problems of the age, and their answers offer many analogies. Both philosophies also show some anticipation of contemporary existentialism.[17] But American philosophy after James turned in other directions, and it was only twenty years ago that the first extensive critical report on Dilthey appeared.[18] Now, however, some of Dilthey's works are being prepared for publication in America.

---

[15] Henry James, ed., *The Letters of William James* (Boston, 1920), I, 109–111.

[16] VI, 293, 303; cf. also VIII, iii. According to a letter from Dilthey to Count Yorck in 1896 Dilthey and James exchanged letters. *Dilthey–Yorck Briefwechsel,* 210.

[17] K. Jaspers goes so far as to call American pragmatism a "preparatory stage of existentialism," *Die geistige Situation der Zeit* (Leipzig, 1931), 146.

[18] H. L. Friess, "Wilhelm Dilthey," *Journal of Philosophy,* XXVI (1929), 5–25. Also G. A. Morgan, "Wilhelm Dilthey," *Philosophical Review,* XLII (1933), 351–380.

II

The most decisive influence Dilthey received during his student years was exercised by the historians. When he came to Berlin, Ranke was at the height of his career. He appeared, Dilthey said in later years, as "the personified capacity of the historical mind." But there was also the great historical tradition created by Niebuhr, Humboldt, Boeckh, the Grimm brothers, F. C. Baur and others, and in addition the rich production of the next generation represented by Rudolf Haym, J. G. Droysen, Theodor Mommsen, Scherer and the like. In these great achievements of historical research and writing Dilthey saw another expression of the prevailing trend of the modern age, which he called its "unsatiable desire for reality." [19] Its most powerful manifestation has been the growth of the natural sciences, which had been chiefly responsible for the collapse of the great metaphysical systems. This result Dilthey considered final, and he accepted Comte's construction of the three stages of human development, the religious, metaphysical, and scientific ages.[20]

Dilthey praised the Enlightenment for its confidence in the power of human reason and its secular interpretation of the world. He stated that it had been the dominant impulse of his own philosophical thinking "in the spirit of the great Enlightenment to cling to the world of experience as the *one* world of our knowledge." [21] This was said with reference to the theological metaphysics in which he had grown up; in later years he told his friend Count Yorck, who was a devout Lutheran, that "he did not even wish to gain salvation through a faith that could not stand up to thought." [22] In this attitude he did not differ from the positivists, or for that matter from the eighteenth-century philosophers, to whose creative achievements in philosophy, in the sciences, and in

[19] I, 123.
[20] On the connection between Dilthey and positivism see H. A. Hodges, *op. cit.,* 3 ff., 70 ff.
[21] V, 418.
[22] VIII, 231. Cf. also *Dilthey–Yorck Briefwechsel,* 146.

history as well he returned so often in his own great historical studies.

He attacked positivism, however, for its refusal to take all of reality into consideration. Quite apart from the metaphysical abstractions which linger on in it, positivism seemed to Dilthey "to mutilate historical reality in order to adapt it to the ideas of the natural sciences." [23] In particular, "it was based upon a truncated experience, which was from the outset perverted by an atomistic theoretical conception of psychic life." In contrast Dilthey claimed that it was the basic idea of his philosophy "that never before had philosophy been grounded on whole, full, unmutilated experience, and consequently never before on whole and full reality." [24] Positivism and empiricism show their failure most clearly in the cultural sciences (*Geisteswissenschaften*), which include not only history but also the study of language, law, economics, etc.[25] Dilthey does not deny that man is part of nature, and

[23] V, 3.

[24] VIII, 175.

[25] It is difficult to translate the German term *"Geisteswissenschaften"* into English. The German translator of J. S. Mill's *Logic,* I. Schick, in 1849 rendered the title of the sixth book, "On the logic of the moral sciences," as *Von der Logik der Geisteswissenschaften oder moralischen Wissenschaften.* The term *Geisteswissenschaften* spread amazingly quickly in Germany. For its general acceptance it was most important that Germany's leading scientist, H. Helmholtz, propagated the concept in his famous Heidelberg speech of 1862, "On the relation between the natural sciences and the totality of the sciences." As the English term "moral sciences" superseded the older concept of "moral philosophy," so *Geisteswissenschaften* was used in Germany to describe more aptly what Hegel's philosophy of *Geist* or the romantic theory of *Volksgeist* had aimed at.

Dilthey had not yet used the new term *Geisteswissenschaften* in his article of 1875, "On the study of the history of the sciences of man, society, and the state" (V, 31). Though he mentioned Mill's *"Logik der Geisteswissenschaften,"* he still preferred the term "moral-political sciences." In 1883 his *Einleitung in die Geisteswissenschaften* conceives of the *Geisteswissenschaften* as "the totality of the sciences which have historico-societal reality as their subject-matter." The book made the term classic in Germany. (Cf. for a full history of the term E. Rothacker, *Logik und Sytematik der Geisteswissenschaften* [Munich, 1926] 3–16, in *Handbuch der*

that, for example, physiology is one of the natural sciences.
But as he puts it:

> Mankind, if apprehended only by perception and perceptual
> knowledge, would be for us a physical fact, and as such would
> be accessible only to the natural sciences. Man becomes an
> object for the cultural sciences only in so far as human situa-
> tions are consciously lived, in so far as they find expression in
> living utterances, and in so far as these expressions are under-
> stood. . . . A study belongs to the human studies only if its
> object becomes accessible to us through the attitude which is
> founded on the relation between life, expression, and under-
> standing.[26]

Before we trace, more slowly, the philosophical steps taken
by Dilthey in these few statements, let us first inquire into
his relation to Kant. He actually went back beyond Hegel
and Fichte and their revival of metaphysics to the Kant of
the *Critique of Pure Reason,* and in this respect he can be called
one of the fathers of Neo-Kantianism. All knowledge is
knowledge of experience, and the facts of human consciousness are the only secure foundation of philosophy. Dilthey
calls this the "epistemological standpoint." He also follows
Kant in the formulation of his own fundamental question:
how are the sciences of the human mind—or humanities,

Philosophie, ed. A. Bäumler and M. Schröter.) But even in the last years
of his life Dilthey was still saying: "When beginning with the eighteenth
century the need developed to find a common name for this group of
sciences, they were called *sciences morales* or *Geisteswissenschaften* or ultimately *Kulturwissenschaften.* This change of names itself shows that none
of them is quite adequate to what is to be defined." (VII, 86.) To translate *"Geisteswissenschaften"* as "humanities" is misleading, since they
include the social sciences as well. The translation "human studies,"
which Hodges uses (*op. cit.,* 157), seems inadequate for the same reason.
I have chosen the translation "cultural sciences" as the relatively best.
The chief objection against this translation is that Dilthey himself
emphatically rejected H. Rickert's narrower definition of *Kulturwissenschaften.* However, "culture" is used in America in a broader sense than
Kultur in Germany, and Dilthey's criticism of Rickert would not apply
to "cultural sciences."

[26] VII, 86; translated by H. A. Hodges, *op. cit.,* 142.

or moral, or cultural or historical sciences—possible?—
exactly as Kant had asked how scientific knowledge is possible. The task of philosophy is not to create this knowledge,
but to furnish its epistemological basis.

But Dilthey went beyond Kant in insisting that philosophy
could not be exclusively concerned with natural science, but
would have to explore the foundations of historical knowledge as well. In this sense he termed his own philosophy an
attempt at the writing of a "Critique of Historical Reason."
By defining his objectives in such a manner Dilthey wished
to express his heritage from Kant, or rather his return to
Kant. But at the same time there remained a sharp difference
from Kant. Dilthey aimed at more than the mere addition
of a new field to Kantian inquiry. In the preface to the *Introduction to the Cultural Sciences* he said:

> If I found myself often in agreement with the epistemological
> school of Locke, Hume, and Kant, recognizing with them in
> the facts of consciousness the whole foundation of philosophy,
> I was, on the other hand, compelled to conceive the inter-
> connection of these facts in a different way. Neglecting the few,
> scientifically undeveloped attempts like those of Herder and
> Wilhelm von Humboldt, epistemology, whether empiricist or
> Kantian, explains experience and knowledge merely as be-
> longing to the realm of thought. In the veins of the knowing
> subject that Locke, Hume, and Kant constructed runs no real
> blood, only the diluted lymph of reason in the sense of a mere
> intellectual activity. But I was led, by my historical and psy-
> chological study of the whole man, to make this whole man
> in the diversity of his powers, this willing, feeling, thinking
> being, the foundation for explaining knowledge and its con-
> cepts, such as those of the external world, time, substance,
> cause, however much it may seem that knowledge weaves
> these its concepts only from the material of perception, idea-
> tion, and thought.[27]

Two fundamental theses are contained in this and similar

[27] I, XVIII. In different translations in H. A. Hodges, *op. cit.,* 113, and in
Ortega y Gasset, *Concord and Liberty,* 155.

statements. The first concerns the conception of consciousness, the second, epistemology itself. Consciousness is to Dilthey not merely rational consciousness, but the sum total of feeling, volition, and thought. It is unrealistic to suppose that non-intellectual human activities will not interfere with man's thinking. Consciousness is given and can be experienced only as the totality of all the motives of the human mind. Intellectual consciousness cannot be isolated. What is given to us in our consciousness is the totality of our being, which Dilthey calls life, mind, spirit, or soul.

Dilthey rejects Kant's concept of a "pure" or "transcendental consciousness" and Hegel's "objective spirit" as metaphysical abstractions. He maintained that "thinking cannot go back beyond life," to which he added:

> Kant took time and thereby life itself to be merely phenomena. To consider life as mere appearance is a *contradictio in adjecto:* for in the lived life, in the growing out of the past, and in the tending of the self toward a future, lie the realities which constitute the dynamic unity (*Wirkungszusammenhang*) and the value of our life. If there were something timeless behind life, that runs through a past, present, and future, it would be an antecedent of life. Therefore, it would be the condition of the total structure of life. This antecedent would be just what we do not experience and, consequently, a realm of shadows.[28]

Dilthey's philosophy of life takes as its starting point life itself as it comes to consciousness in the individual as the act of living experience (*Erlebnis*). In this original act of living experience a full identity of subject and object exists. "In the act of living experience perception and the contents of my perception are one." [29] Dilthey expressed this once as "existence possessing itself," a formula that has played an important rôle in modern existentalism.[30] Living experience is an act that takes place in the individual and is determined by the totality of human faculties. The dominant chord in it

[28] V, 5; cf. also VII, 332 ff.
[29] VII, 27, 439.
[30] V, LXXIX.

may be intellectual, or religious, or aesthetic, or conative, and Dilthey is inclined to assign the higher significance to the three latter qualities of the human being, since thinking is actually the process by which reality is transformed into an object.

But this living experience is never a solipsistic experience. The self can never be alone, it exists always and inescapably among other human beings, and finds itself embedded in transpersonal relations with objects and other subjects. To be sure, there is a state of inner quietude, mere "dreams, play, diversion, contemplation, and light motility, like a deeper layer of life." But Dilthey adds:

> Living relations run in all directions. I react to men and objects, take a position toward them, fulfill their demands, and expect something from them. Some make me happy, expand my existence, augment my power—others exercise a pressure upon me and delimit me. . . . The friend is to him [man] a power which exalts his own existence, each family member has a definite place in his life, and everything that surrounds him will be understood by him as life and spirit which have objectified themselves in them. The shady tree, house, and garden gain in this objectification reality and significance. Thus, life creates its own world through the individual.[31]

In this description volition and desire are the agents which drive the individual beyond the indefinite state of quietude into a more definite state of individual activity. The individual, in the midst of the "relations of life" (*Lebensbezüge*) in which he finds himself, tries to cognize the world he experiences in a *Weltbild*, a word that has recently been introduced into the King's English as "world picture." [32] The "world picture" is the foundation of the experience of life (*Lebenserfahrung*), in which an evaluation of this experience takes place through feeling. Upon these values rest the ideals of life which determine the actions of man. It is not difficult to discover in these three layers the traditional definition of

[31] VIII, 78 f; cf. also VII, 131 f.
[32] E. M. W. Tillyard, *The Elizabethan World Picture* (London, 1943).

the faculties of the human mind as thinking, feeling, and
willing. But it is important that Dilthey emphasizes the rôle
of feeling in the totality of human consciousness. Indeed, most
people never get beyond the *Lebensgefühl,* a feeling attitude
towards life. This is not a definite but an oscillating position.
"Continuously," Dilthey says, "the conception and evaluation of life and the world change, like shadows of clouds
which pass over a landscape." [33]

It is the work of the religious, artistic, and philosophical
genius to transform the feeling disposition into a conscious
interpretation of reality, or, as Dilthey calls it, a *Weltanschauung,* a world view or outlook. It should be stressed that
philosophy is only one among these three faculties, and the
least fertile of *Weltanschauungen.* In his analysis of the artistic
and philosophical movement of eighteenth-century Germany, Dilthey tends to credit the poets with the initial creation of the new outlook, which the philosophers from Kant
to Hegel and Schelling translated into philosophical systems.[34] On the other hand, he was convinced, in spite of his
emphasis on the historic place of Christian religion, that the
full realization and preservation of monotheism was the result of Greek philosophy rather than Christianity.

It is the function of philosophy, by an analysis of the statements and premises of the *Weltanschauung,* to secure univer-
sally valid knowledge.[35] "Life is prior to knowledge." [36] But
already in life itself there is inherent a propensity for higher
consciousness. "Thinking can only increase the energy for
raising the realities of life into consciousness." [37] But thinking not only has its roots in life, it also has a function with
regard to life. "Life imperiously demands guidance by
thought." [38] And more explicitly: "The progress of humanity

[33] V, 379; cf. also VIII, 168.
[34] Cf. his inaugural lecture in Basel, "The poetic and philosophical movement in Germany, 1770–1800," V, 12 ff.
[35] IV, 200.
[36] VIII, 264.
[37] VII, 7.
[38] VI, 189.

in the modern age depends on its guidance by scientific knowledge. Therefore, the certainty of this knowledge must be defined and justified against the obscure feeling, the arbitrariness of subjectivity, and the sceptical mind, the ally of both." [39] Dilthey can say: "Philosophy is an action which lifts life, i.e., the subject in its vital relations, into consciousness and thinks it to its end." [40] Or finally: "Philosophy is only the highest energy of consciousness, the consciousness of every consciousness and the knowledge of all knowledge." [41]

III

But what constitutes scientific knowledge? With respect to the natural sciences Dilthey follows Kant. The experience that outward reality obeys the same laws we experience as the structural elements of our thinking, convinces us that our thinking is able to deal with this reality and to perceive its order. On this basis scientific research can proceed empirically within the framework of the general rules of reasoning without fear of mistaking speculations for facts. An outward criterion of the general validity of scientific results is to be found in their universal applicability, irrespective of their individual authors.

The cultural sciences are distinguished from the natural sciences both by their object and their subject of study. "One cannot have nature within oneself and by merely watching it learn what the world and life are and what they mean," he once wrote to his friend, Count Yorck, and the latter said: "The whole psychophysical reality *is* not, but lives." [42] The only method by which a knowledge of man can be gained is through "understanding." We have already mentioned Dilthey's statement that living experience, expression, and understanding constitute the fundamental categories of the

[39] IV, 200.
[40] *Dilthey–Yorck Briefwechsel*, 247.
[41] VII, 7.
[42] *Dilthey–Yorck Briefwechsel*, 247 and 71.

humanities. But we shall have to describe this process in greater detail.

"Understanding" of man, according to Dilthey, cannot be achieved by mere introspection or self-observation. Apart from the limitations of the life of any individual, even the greatest, introspection is conditioned by the questions I ask, and if I want to express them in words I find these words charged with a complex usage.[43] Living experience is an everflowing stream, and no lines and figures drawn on it would last.[44]

> Inwendig lernt keim Mensch sein Innerstes
> Erkennen; denn er misst nach eignem Mass
> Sich bald zu klein und leider oft zu gross.
> Der Mensch erkennt sich nur im Menschen, nur
> Das Leben lehret jedem, was er sei.[45]

The key to a more than merely subjective understanding of one's self as well as of other men lies in the "expressions of life." Dilthey distinguishes three major groups of "expressions of life." The first consists of statements of logical relations, which can be considered without reference to an underlying living experience. The second group comprises actions, which we always try to understand as the result of the living experience of an individual or an individual group, though in Dilthey's words what they express is rather "undeliberate and non-intentional." The third group is made up of the expressions of living experience in the full sense. They stem from the urge "somehow to express the inner self, and somehow to place it before oneself or communicate it to others,"[46] This is the ideal field of "understanding" and interpretation.

43 VI, 317 ff.
44 VII, 280.
45 "Inwardly no man learns to know his innermost being; for he measures himself according to his own measure, often too small and, unhappily, often too large. Man knows himself only in man. Only life teaches everyone what he is." Goethe, *Tasso,* II, 3; quoted in O. F. Bollnow, *op. cit.,* 150.
46 VII, 320.

Dilthey does not disregard the second group of objectifications, and in particular he knows that there are actions which are produced by a highly conscious will. For instance, he sees the lasting contribution of the Romans to Western history in the new position they created for the will. Or, to take a different example, in his studies of the eighteenth century he pays attention not only to pietism, the philosophy of Leibniz, and the music of Bach and Handel, but also to the spirit underlying the codification of Prussian law under Frederick the Great. Still, as a rule Dilthey shies away from mere actions. "What springs from the life of the day is under the sign of its interests. Something terrifying lies in the fact that in the struggle of practical interests each expression can deceive, and the interpretation also changes according to our position." In contrast, a great work of art stands before you "truthful in itself, fixed, visible, lasting, and therefore an artistic and reliable understanding of it becomes possible." [47] The truthfulness of such a work is not to be judged in terms of right or wrong, but of its genuineness, which is determined by its capacity for achieving the full identity between expression and living experience. This applies not only to the works of the artistic genius, but likewise to those of the religious and philosophical.

Understanding becomes possible, since each individual knows from his own experience the process by which life tends to objectify itself in expressions. Man is driven farther and farther in the understanding of the human world by the discovery that a first primitive understanding proves an inadequate guide to the mastery of his practical problems. Life is action, and thinking that arises from life aims at a higher energy of action. But on all levels understanding remains a mere re-living of the living experience of oneself or others. The limits of the expansion of our understanding are set by this fact. We can re-live only what is at least potentially given to us, or, as Dilthey would have said, what it contained in that dynamic unity of life (*Wirkungszusammenhang*) of which our individual life is a part.

[47] VII, 206 f.

72   Hajo Holborn

"Life takes possession of life"[48]—in this formula Dilthey
once expressed the difference between the cultural and the
natural sciences in which phenomena are organized by
means of abstract concepts. In order to avoid misunderstanding at this point, we must keep in mind that Dilthey called
"cultural sciences" all the disciplines of knowledge dealing
with man or mankind, or in other words not only the humane
arts but also the social sciences, "history, economics, jurisprudence, political science, the study of religion, literature,
poetry, architecture, and music, of philosophical outlooks
and systems."[49] All these branches of knowledge are nothing
but a systematic knowledge gained by living experience and
understanding.

It also follows from this that the student of the cultural
sciences does not necessarily have an advantage over the
practical man. A statesman, for example, may have a much
greater insight into personalities or into the interconnectedness of the factors in a political situation, though as a rule he
may not care to lift them into clear consciousness, except with
a view to his immediate practical purposes. On the other
hand, no scholar can amount to anything who has not had
some living experience in the field he wishes to advance. A
political historian without a living interest in political action,
a literary critic without poetic sense, a student of religion
without religious feeling, etc., cannot hope to produce significant knowledge in his discipline. The cultural sciences
require "aliveness" (*Lebendigkeit*) by the very nature of their
form of knowledge.

Another misunderstanding must be avoided. Dilthey never
shared the theory of the cultural and natural sciences developed by the so-called "south-western German school" of
Neo-Kantianism.[50] Following a suggestion by Wilhelm

[48] VII, 136.
[49] VIII, 79.
[50] This has been overlooked by R. G. Collingwood, *The Idea of History,* 172;
also by D. Bidney, "The Philosophical Anthropology of Ernst Cassirer
and Its Significance in Relation to the History of Anthropological
thought," in *The Philosophy of Ernst Cassirer,* ed. P. A. Schilpp (Evanston,
1949), 488 ff.

Windelband,[51] Heinrich Rickert built up the theory that the cultural and natural sciences could be distinguished philosophically as idiographic and nomothetic studies.[52] Whereas the sciences of nature aim at the establishment of laws, the *Kulturwissenschaften* by descriptive and comparative methods study man as he acts under the influence of moral, aesthetic, and intellectual values. Heinrich Rickert's definition of the general as the object of natural science and the individual as that of the *Kulturwissenschaften* induced him, in contrast to Dilthey, to place some branches of knowledge like economics or psychology among the natural sciences.[53]

Dilthey refused to adopt Rickert's distinction. To him the cultural sciences are not confined to the individual, but include as their main problem the relation between the individual and the general.[54] Moreover, as he said as early as 1883,[55] the *Geisteswissenschaften* are characterized by the combination of the historical, abstract-theoretical, and practical direction of interpretation. And in his last years he wrote: ". . . the recently much-used term *Kulturwissenschaften* contains an unprovable, nay one-sided definition of the meaning and goal of history. This is much too friendly and generous an interpretation of human nature, in which the dark instincts of mutual suppression and destruction play a very considerable role." [56]

Dilthey uses a much broader conception of "reality" than most of his neo-Kantian colleagues. He defines it as "life," or, as he calls it quite often, "history." His defintion of man as a man among men applies not only to the present but to a continuum in time. Dilthey would even go beyond this state-

---

[51] W. Windelband, *Geschichte und Naturwissenschaft* (1894); reprinted in his *Praeludien,* 6th ed. (Tübingen, 1919), II, 136–160.

[52] H. Rickert, *Die Grenzen der naturwissenschaftlichen Begriffsbildung* (Freiburg, 1896/1902; *Kulturwissenschaft und Naturwissenschaft* (Freiburg, 1899).

[53] Cf. my discussion of the English and German terms "cultural sciences," *Geisteswissenschaften, Kulturwissenschaften,* in note 25 *supra.*

[54] VII, 172 f.

[55] I, 26.

[56] VII, 323.

ment. The individual himself is a historical being, and the
relations of the life in which he finds himself are historical.
Not only do the actual political and social conditions mould
the life of which the individual is part, but its forms of consciousness and expression are also determined by history.
Therefore, introspection can never answer the question of
what is man; only history can.

Dilthey expressed this idea, which distinguished his own
philosophy of life sharply from that of Nietzsche, in words
which, incidentally, do not do justice to Nietzsche's attitude
towards history, [57] but express Dilthey's ideas quite clearly.

> Nietzsche stands as a warning of where the brooding of the
> individual mind leads, which tries to grasp the essence of life
> within its own self. He denounced history, perhaps in disgust
> at its unlimited critical detail, without which it is not truly a
> science. He believed that he had to disregard everything that
> this history and the community had done to him; he peeled it
> off like skins one after the other. The core, the problem of what
> constitutes man, he thought he could then seize in an ever new
> anguish of brooding about himself, as once Rousseau tried to
> find the natural behind the historical man. And this brooding
> about one's inner self, this ever renewed self-observation, what
> did it find? Exactly what characterizes the present historical
> state of our economic life and of our society: the 'living danger-
> ously,' the reckless expansion of one's own power. History from
> Euripides to the Renaissance had engraved upon his soul only
> this superman: the great trends of his age talked of him. With-
> out pity the theory of evolution seemed to prove the supremacy
> of the man who conquers life. Thus, he found him in himself,
> as he could also have found quite different basic traits and
> could have formed them into an ideal. And out of him he made
> his abstract scheme of man, his abstract empty ideal.[58]

This statement places the emphasis upon the insufficiency
of introspection, but it is equally concerned with the significance of history for a critical understanding of man. "Life

[57] On Nietzsche's attitude towards history see Karl Jaspers, *Nietzsche*
(Berlin, 1936), 205 ff.
[58] VI, 528 f; cf. also VIII, 162 ff., 198.

contains as the first categorical definition, fundamental to all others, being in time (*Zeitlichkeit*)." [59] Natural events also occur in time, but time in nature and history are entirely different. Dilthey compares time in nature to "a line consisting of equal parts, a system of relations, like succession, contemporaneity, duration." [60] Time is nothing but the outward form, in which natural occurrences take place. In contrast to the formal one-dimensional time of nature stands the "real" or "concrete time" which is a substantial aspect of life itself.

"Concrete time consists . . . in the unintermittent advance of the present, in which the present becomes continually the past and the future the present." [61] The present is only a cross-section of the continuous stream of life, and as such without extension. The present, therefore, is beyond experience in the strict sense. It cannot be defined in spatial or one-dimensional terms, but only by its contents. "The present is the fulfillment of a moment of time with reality." [62] We have the present always and everywhere, "where we suffer, remember, or hope, in brief, where we live in the plenitude of our reality;" but we always have simultaneously the consciousness of its moving into the past, "a feeling that at times overwhelms us to the point of acutest grief." [63] Dilthey stresses again and again what he calls the "corruptibility" of life. This means to him both the transistory character of life, which is in the hands of death at any moment, and the fragility of the particular contents of life.[64] In these views Dilthey moves closer again to Kant's transcendental metaphysics as the philosophy of the "boundaries" of man. His ideas have found a modern expression in Martin Heidegger's existential "anxiety" (*Sorge*) and "fear," though in this connection Kierkegaard should not be forgotten.

But there is another side to life. In contrast to the finiteness

[59] VII, 192.
[60] VII, 72.
[61] *Ibidem.*
[62] VI, 315.
[63] *Von deutscher Dichtung und Musik*, 78.
[64] VII, 72, 229, 325; VIII, 79, 140.

of life we have the experience of life as a continuous structural unity, in spite of the fact that we can have an experience neither of our own birth nor of our death. In this respect one can say that the life of an individual can be understood more fully by posterity than by himself.[65] In life, however, Dilthey argues, "the present includes the presentation of the past in the memory, and that of the future in the imagination, which explores its possibilities, and in the activity which sets ends among these possibilities. Thus, the present is filled with pasts and pregnant with the future."[66] In the continuity of these experiences the individual becomes conscious of being a self, extending in time.[67] But together with this consciousness of his own individual structure he acquires the awareness of ever more comprehensive structures of the general life, like nation and civilization, or finally universal history. On all levels understanding aims at grasping "significance" or "meaning" (*Bedeutung*). For "meaning" is the peculiar form of relation which the parts have to the whole in life.[68] Meaning is already the peculiar and also the true principle of synthesis in memory, and it is equally the fundamental category of historical thinking.

Yet meaning is established not only by contemplation but by active decisions as well. The past appears to us an inevitable and determined process, but we think of the future as a "possibility" and as a realm of active freedom. We may be wise enough not to consider it a world of absolute freedom, as, indeed, our interpretation of the past co-determines our actions, but we still consider the future as the world which we can hope to mould according to the lesser or greater power of our decision. The decisions we make by action are the choices among the possibilities we see in our imagination, according to the ends we will. But the actual meaning of the past begins to change, if the reality of life or history is aug-

[65] VII, 233.
[66] VII, 232.
[67] V, 200.
[68] VII, 233 f.; cf. 73, 237, 255; VI, 319.

mented, so that a complete definition of the meaning of history would become possible only when history had come to an end.[69] Historical knowledge, therefore, cannot be identical through the ages, not only because the historian, like all other students of man, including the philosopher, suffers from the limitations of his finite historical position, but also because of the changing nature of his subject of study.

Dilthey had originally believed that all the cultural sciences had a common foundation in psychology. All of them needed in their work a knowledge of human nature, and if they wanted to achieve objective results this knowledge could not be based on subjective intuition or amateurish construction. But when, in preparation for the second volume of his *Introduction to the Cultural Sciences,* Dilthey reviewed psychological science he was dissatisfied with the existing schools. They claimed to be able to explain psychological facts, but had not produced valid answers except in the borderland between psychology and physiology. All the higher forms of mental life had proved to them a sealed book.

Dilthey believed that the false methodology of psychology could be blamed for the failure of psychological research. It had modeled itself on natural science by trying to "explain" psychological events in terms of hypothetical principles to be verified by subsequent observation. Formerly psychology had taken its hypotheses from metaphysics, recently mostly from natural science. But Dilthey argued that the psyche or life of the human mind was not like nature an outer world which could be studied by using hypotheses in order to unify the unrelated perceptions of individual facts. The experience of psychological events is immediate, and there is no need to go outside or behind consciousness[70] by the injection of hypothetical explanations. Psychological events carry within themselves a unifying pattern, a "structure" that does not call for an explanation by general laws and hypotheses but only for analysis and description.

[69] VII, 233.
[70] V, 194.

Dilthey presented in 1894 the blueprint of a "descriptive
and analytical psychology." [71] The new psychology rejected
the whole approach of natural science to psychology as
incapable of dealing with the great and significant creative
actions of the human mind and particularly of penetrating
into the world of history. Experimental and explanatory
psychology can deal at best with certain aspects of the psychological attitudes of present-day men, but it has no way
of experimenting with historical man, which means that it
has to exclude most of the sources from which we must hope
to gain a knowledge of man. In addition, if "scientific" psychology were to live up to its presuppositions it would have
to reduce the vast psychological reality to the interaction of
sensation and feeling. Such individual acts were considered
the primary psychological facts out of which the psychological world could be built.

Dilthey realized that this "scientific" psychology was incapable of ever coming to grips with the true psychological
reality. By confining itself to primitive sensations and feelings, like those of pleasure and pain, it excluded the contents
of the human mind and became formalistic. In contrast,
Dilthey demanded a "realistic" psychology or "psychology
of content" (*Realpsychologie* or *Inhaltspsychologie*). A realistic
and empirical analysis of psychological events will show the
indissoluble interconnectedness of cognition, feeling, and
will in all of them. The attempt to isolate a single function
of the human mind is an arbitrary abstraction. Moreover,
even to make the single individual the basic unit of psychological study is unrealistic. The individual is a member of
society; by its civilization he is moulded, while most of his
actions and reactions are determined by social habits and
values.

The main task of a descriptive psychology is the study of
the structures by which the various functions of the human
mind are organized. The great documents of human self-
introspection, like Augustine's, Pascal's, or Goethe's autobiographical works, and in general the insights into human

[71] *"Ideen über eine beschreibende und zergliedernde Psychologie,"* V, 139–240.

affairs amassed in literature, poetry, and historiography, will be important sources for such studies. This material should be critically analyzed and systematized to find the typical structural forms of the human mind, and to investigate the problems of individuation, and of the creative achievements of man.

Dilthey's "psychology of structure" or, as he often called it in later years, "anthropology," was a marked departure from the psychological schools of the two Mills, Spencer, Taine, Fechner, and Herbart, though there had already started a certain movement away from sensationalism. It found expression in Wundt and most strongly in William James. Dilthey praised again the latter's "amazingly realistic power and capacity of inner perception," [72] but he complained about James's relapse into metaphysical hypotheses, in so far as James attempted a correlation between psychological and physiological events. Dilthey refused absolutely to accept a causal explanation for the higher processes of the human mind.

Dilthey's approach has had a great influence on the development of modern psychology. In contrast to the old atomistic psychologists he emphasized the interconnectedness of all the functions of the human mind and of its creative capacity. Dilthey also stressed the inseparable link between the psychology of the individual and social psychology. It was Karl Jaspers, then still a psychiatrist, who developed Dilthey's ideas further in his *Psychologie der Weltanschauungen*.[73] Jaspers called his work a study in "understanding psychology," which he conceived as a cultural science in contra-distinction to "experimental psychology," which belonged to the natural sciences.[74] Eduard Spranger, a per-

---

[72] V, 177, 167, LXXI. Cf. note 16 *supra*.

[73] First published in Halle (1919), since reëdited in a number of editions. His first work was his *Allgemeine Psychopathologie* (1913).

[74] R. G. Collingwood in his chapter on Dilthey failed to see that Dilthey's psychology was not constructed, as he asserts, on "naturalistic principles." Most of his criticism of Dilthey thus becomes pointless. *The Idea of History*, 171–176.

sonal student of Dilthey, in his *Lebensformen*[75] offered a
typology of man, distinguishing six fundamental types: the
theoretical, economic, aesthetic, social, political, and religious man. Modern *Gestalt* psychology also has some roots in
Dilthey's descriptive psychology, and MacDougall, Freud,
and Jung are to a varying degree indebted to Dilthey.

While Dilthey's "psychological" ideas thus bore rich
fruits, they did not in his own opinion fulfill his original hope
that psychology could be established as the foundation of
all the cultural sciences. His descriptive and analytical psychology was only a cautious systematization of the inner
experiences of the present and past as presented by the
cultural sciences themselves. His attempt to find a common
foundation for all the cultural sciences soon shifted from
psychology to logic and epistemology. In the last period of
his life he endeavored to build up a theory of interpretation
or "hermeneutics." The problem had been with him since
his early years, and no one knew its history as well as he;[76]
but now he turned to its full philosophical analysis.

All the cultural sciences aim at "understanding" (*Verstehen*), and they try to understand something internal through
the analysis of its outward manifestations. Of this attempt
Dilthey now said: "It is a common error to consider psychology as our knowledge of this inner side of the spiritual
process of life." [77] He began to draw a sharp distinction between soul and mind. Soul is the inner life of the individual,
whereas mind is an objective entity. The meaning of a work
of art is not to be found in the psychological experinces of the
creative artist, but in forms and relations which belong to a
deeper layer of life. Similarily, a political system or a system
of art is not to be found in the psychological experiences of the
objective mind.

Dilthey presented these ideas at the very time when Ed-

[75] Halle, 1927.
[76] See in the first place his important article, *"Die Entstehung der Hermeneu-
tik,"* V, 317–338. Cf. also E. Spranger, *"Zur Theorie des Verstehens und zur
geisteswissenschaftlichen Psychologie,"* *Festschrift für Joh. Volkelt* (Munich,
1918), 357 ff., and J. Wach, *Das Verstehen,* 3 vols. (Tübingen, 1926–33).
[77] VII, 84.

mund Husserl, the founder of modern phenomenology, was banishing psychology from philosophy.[78] But Dilthey was far from retreating into an unhistorical Platonism. He continued to believe that a knowledge of man could be gained only from history. But he began to consider the objectifications of life, like religion, art, science, politics, economics, law, etc., as philosophical organs for an objective comprehension of man, since they were, as he once said, manifestations of the "immanent transcendence of life."[79] Dilthey put forth these ideas rather tentatively while he was trying to prepare the final statement of his philosophical position which his death made impossible.

Closely connected with these studies of his last years were his efforts to redefine the task of philosophy itself. Like Hegel, Dilthey believed that philosophy could expect a solution of its questions only from history, but Dilthey could not accept Hegel's absolute spirit as the prime mover of the historical process. The historic systems of philosophy constitute the high-points in man's own understanding of himself and of the world. They are not the reflections of the movement of the absolute spirit, but the demonstraton of life's own capacity to rise to higher levels. Philosophy consequently is the highest expression of life, through which it advances to new stages. The unity of philosophy does not rest in its actual statements but in its power to realize the creative nature of life by the ability to raise experiences into consciousness and transform them into systematic ideas.[80]

Dilthey demanded a philosophical study of the historical forms of philosophy with a view to its general function in translating life experiences, as expressed in world pictures and world views, into philosophical systems. By such study we could hope to see the full breadth of human self-expres-

---

[78] E. Husserl, *Logische Untersuchungen* (Halle, 1900). On the relation between Husserl and Dilthey see G. Misch, *Lebensphilosophie und Phaenomenologie*, 1.c.

[79] J. Stenzel, *Dilthey und die deutsche Philosophie der Gegenwart* (Berlin, 1934), 17.

[80] *Dilthey–Yorck Briefwechsel*, 52; also VII, 248.

sion and advance to a greater human self-understanding. The systematic study of world views, *Weltanschauungslehre,* leads to a new speculation on philosophy itself which Dilthey termed "philosophy of philosophy."

The philosophical systems which have appeared in history are relative, and though they have a unity in their common origins in life, their substantive statements cannot be harmonized. There are three major and irreconcilable types of philosophy beyond which the conflicting schools of philosophy cannot be reduced. Dilthey names naturalism, the idealism of freedom, and objective idealism as primary types of philosophy. Democritus, Epicurus, Hume and Comte are representatives of naturalism; Aristotle, Kant, Fichte, Bergson and William James, of the idealism of freedom; the Stoics, Bruno, Spinoza, Leibniz, Shaftesbury, Goethe, Hegel, Schelling, and Schleiermacher, of objective idealism.[81]

These types are not always pure; they are rather the points around which all philosophical interpretations crystalize. But the irreducible character of these types of philosophy proves at the same time that "the conflict of world views remains insoluble."[82] Dilthey tried to overcome the difficulty by assuming that life itself is "many-sided,"[83] and that each philosophy "expresses within the limits of our thinking one side of the universe. Each is true in this respect. Each is, however, onesided. We are denied seeing these sides in unity. The pure light of truth we can see only in broken rays."[84]

The ideas of his last years have come to us only in fragmentary drafts for his projected last work, the second volume of his *Introduction to the Cultural Sciences.* He was not able to present them in systematic manner. But the general trend of his thought is clear and it has had a significant influence upon contemporary philosophy.

[81] For a fuller description see H. A. Hodges, *op. cit.,* 99 ff.
[82] VIII, 8, 147.
[83] VIII, 69.
[84] VIII, 222.

IV

Dilthey was a philosopher, but the significance he attached to history as an organ of philosophy made him a historian as well. He was both a great and original historical thinker and a master of historical presentation. His philosophy did not clash with modern historiography. Dilthey rejected completely philosophies of history of the Voltairean, Comtean, or Hegelian type and accepted the general methods of the nineteenth-century historians as the only possible approach to an understanding of history. His own research had made him fully familiar with all the problems of the historical profession. He struggled with the critical edition of Schleiermacher's letters, with the organization of a final Kant edition, and with the interpretation of the unpublished papers of the young Hegel. In brief, he knew the customary worries, thought processes, and methods of the practicing historian from his own research.

But, on the other hand, in contrast to the professional historians of his age who tended to lose sight of the philosophical implications of their methods and findings by embracing a vulgar empiricism modeled after the natural sciences, Dilthey was aware of the philosophical character of historical studies. This enabled him to criticise constructively the work of the nineteenth-century historians and to add to it by his own historical writings.

Dilthey maintained a profound admiration for Ranke all through his life. Ranke had displayed a unique will and power in achieving historical objectivity and had been the first "to express fully that the foundation of all historical knowledge and *one* of its highest aims is the presentation of its singular form of connectedness." [85] But this major interest led Ranke to an overwhelmingly aesthetic and "ocular" presentation, and political history offered him the greatest opportunity for composing history in a dramatic and panoramic manner. Though Dilthey probably did not quite agree

[85] VII, 101 ff., cf. also I, 94; V, 4, 8 f.; XI, 216 ff.

with his friend's mocking remarks, Count Yorck's statements about the "magic lantern" or "rug-weaving" technique of Ranke[86] may serve as an indication of the direction of Dilthey's criticism of the Rankean history.

In Ranke, Carlyle, and Tocqueville Dilthey saw the three greatest nineteenth-century historians, in whom the rise of modern historical consciousness had found its most forceful expression. A true Fichtean, Carlyle looked for the historical man and hero. He approached history not by "optical" means, but as a problem of inner life or of the relation of faith and action. Alexis de Tocqueville Dilthey calls "the greatest analytical mind in politics since Aristotle and Machiavelli." [87] As most clearly demonstrated in his classic study of American democracy, Tocqueville tried to isolate the individual elements important for the internal structure of nations and to show the interaction of the various functions in a modern body politic.

Still, Dilthey felt that historical interpretation was not exhausted by Ranke's generation nor by the work of his own contemporaries. His personal concern lay originally in the history of philosophy and religion. He studied the works of the so-called Tübingen school, whose father was the church historian F. C. Baur and whose chief historian of philosophy was the latter's disciple E. Zeller. The history of ideas, religious or philosophical, was to them a self-contained process of intellectual progress or, in Hegelian terms, the unfolding of the absolute idea in the world. The views of the Tübingen school continued to affect very profoundly the conceptions of Christian history expounded by the Ritschlian school in the later part of the century, of which Adolf Harnack was the most brilliant representative,[88] and in the neo-Kantian

---

[86] *Dilthey –Yorck Briefwechsel,* 59 f., 113, 167.

[87] VII, 99, 104.

[88] For a fuller treatment of the history of religion in the nineteenth century, in addition to W. Dilthey's own studies on Baur and Zeller in Vol. IV of his *Collected Works,* see E. Troeltsch, *"Adolf von Harnack und Ferdinand Christian Baur," Festgabe für A. von Harnack zum 70. Geburtstage* (Tübingen, 1921), 282 ff. Also my article *"Karl Holl," Deutsche Vierteljahrsschrift für Geistesgeschichte und Literaturwissenschaft,* V (1927), 413–30.

history of philosophy of Wilhelm Windelband, though increasingly the influence of Schleiermacher and his emphasis upon the creative rôle of the individual made its weight felt.

Dilthey did not believe that this type of history of ideas was capable of furnishing an adequate interpretation of intellectual and religious history. Philosophical and religious ideas spring from the totality of man's living experience. They have to be understood in terms of their origins in this living experience. The study of the living experience, world picture (*Weltbild*), and general world view (*Weltanschauung*) of every age is a prerequisite for a true historical understanding of religion and philosophy. The conception of a separate "history of ideas" is a mere abstraction. *Ideengeschichte* has to be replaced by *Geistesgeschichte,* i.e., a study of the efforts of life to achieve consciousness of itself. Religion and philosophy are only "expressions of life," though expressions of the highest potential of life. Dilthey added art to religion and philosophy as an expression of this creative vitality. We have already seen why this seemed so important to him, and it is not surprising that a major part of his own historical studies, which altogether form half of all his writings, was devoted to defining the place of poetry, literature, and music in the process of history.[89] They give, however, only a segment of his view of history.

We find the ripest fruits of Dilthey's historical interest in such studies as "The Conception and Analysis of Man in the 15th and 16th Centuries."[90] The title of this article, which is a classic in modern historiography, is indicative of Dilthey's historical intention to present the totality of life and analyse its expressions in terms of a critical philosophy of life. The term *Geistesgeschichte,* which literally means history of the human mind, may lead to the belief that Dilthey conceived of history as a mere reflection of the spiritual life of man. It should be clear after our discussion of Dilthey's conception of life and mind that such an interpretation would be un-

[89] These studies revolutionized the history of literature and art in Germany and Austria. I mention here as examples only R. Unger, *Literaturgeschichte als Problemgeschichte* (Berlin, 1924), and Max Dvořak, *Kunstgeschichte als Geistesgeschichte* (Munich, 1924).

[90] *"Auffassung und Analyse des Menschen im 15. und 16. Jahrhundert,"* II, 1–89.

tenable. In his analysis of historical life Dilthey always remained aware of economic, social, and political institutions and events.

In this respect Dilthey's theory of history opened up certain possibilities for the study of the social conditions of consciousness, and both the "sociology of culture" (Alfred Weber) and the "sociology of knowledge" (Karl Mannheim) found in Dilthey suggestive ideas.[91] Still, Dilthey was far from identifying the material conditions of life with the "expressions of life." He never found it worth while to discuss Karl Marx. What separated him from Marx was his belief that "the meaning of history can only be looked for in the significant interrelations of all the forces which are united through the ages."[92]

One might suspect that Dilthey was in greater accord with the history of culture (*Kulturgeschichte*), as represented in his own time by many writers. But though Dilthey admitted that history should not only deal, as in Ranke's work, with events but that it should present the conditions and states of civilization as well, he warned against disregarding the interrelations between the causal and chronological moments of history. History is thus dissolved into the atomic elements, which then have to be grouped under general categories.[93] Dilthey speaks only with scorn of those histories which present civilizations under such chapter headings as court-life, home-life, costumes, manners, etc.

But even Jacob Burckhardt's *Civilization of the Renaissance*, whose brilliant qualities Dilthey was quick to recognize in his review of 1862,[94] he praised only with strong reservations. He found that Burckhardt, in spite of sharp differences in

[91] Cf. among others A. Weber's article on *"Kultursoziologie"* and K. Mannheim's article on *"Wissenssoziologie"* in *Handwörterbuch der Soziologie*, ed. by A. Vierkandt (Stuttgart, 1931). Also K. Mannheim *"Ideologische und soziologische Betrachtung der geistigen Gebilde," Jahrbuch für Soziologie*, II (1926), 424–440.

[92] VII, 187.

[93] XI, 72.

[94] XI, 70–76.

historical methods, was still a descendant of Ranke in his largely aesthetic approach to history. Ranke had used individual events bound together by causal relations as the firm framework of historical narrative. Burckhardt aimed at the description of the general state of an historic civilization as revealed in its intellectual and artistic achievements as well as in its social aspirations. Dilthey criticised Burckhardt's concepts as not genuinely historical categories. His description of the qualities of "Renaissance man" whom Burckhardt conceived as the "the first-born modern," could be applied, and perhaps with even better right, to other periods of history, for example, to the early period of the Roman Empire. Dilthey also raised doubts about other central ideas of Burckhardt, like individualism, as adequate descriptions of Renaissance thinking. Burckhardt's terms, in Dilthey's opinion, were lacking in historical as well as philosophical concreteness, and were terms often used for artistic rather than scientific purposes. A valid structural pattern could be found only in the living experience of the historical generations themselves. Thus his own "Conception and Analysis of Man in the 15th and 16th Centuries" became, almost thirty years later, his final answer to Burckhardt.

The cultural sciences—and they include (in addition to history) law, economics, political science, language, literature, art—are to Dilthey the means of experiencing the full potentialities of man, and the only way to expand the subjective self into a consciousness of the objective "expressions of life." History is more than a presentation of a phenomenal world, or a mere visualization of a dead past. It is the living experience of the student of history as well. Therefore history must also be a way of understanding the world.[95]

But history teaches the existence of a large variety of "expressions of life," determined by the passing conditions of historic time. In Dilthey's words, "historical consciousness demonstrates ever more clearly the relativity of every metaphysical or religious doctrine which has appeared in the

[95] *Der junge Dilthey*, 81.

course of time." [96] History appears as "a vast field of ruins of religious traditions, metaphysical positions, demonstrated systems, possibilities of all sorts." [97]

This may lead to despair, and in any event to mental suffering. For life points beyond itself, and though religious and metaphysical systems can only be considered historical expressions of life, the metaphysical and religious disposition is an essential quality of the human spirit. But over against the "anarchy of convictions" which frightens the modern historical mind stands the positive achievement. "Modern historical consciousness breaks the last chains which philosophy and natural science could not tear apart. Now man stands completely free." [98] It is important to look not only backward but forward as well. It is true that the objectivations of life are bound to pass and be followed by new ones, but these will be created by man. In spite of his own finiteness in time, man has creative capacity. New objectivations of life may wither in time, but they add a new meaning to life as a whole. For life itself grows, and it grows through man.

[96] VIII, 198.
[97] VIII, 76 f.
[98] VIII, 223; cf. VII, 290, VIII, 271.

5.

The Origins of Freud's Political Psychology

Philip Rieff

EDITORIAL NOTE: *Dilthey's critique of positivism focussed on the methodology of the natural sciences, which he considered to be wholly inappropriate in the study of history and of the* Geisteswissen-schaften *generally. In the same years that Dilthey was completing his life's work, social and political psychologists were beginning to rebel against the rationalistic conception of man as a calculating machine who understood his best interests and was free to pursue them with relentless logic in all his relations with his fellow man. These "anti-intellectualists," as they have come to be known, were in fact mounting a belated counter-attack on the psychological ideas of the Enlightenment more than on the thinkers of the generation of Darwin and Marx; but in any event, their insights were fresh, and their accomplishments impressive. Philip Rieff examines the origins and character of Sigmund Freud's contribution to anti-intellectualist thinking in the field of political psychology. As he points out, Freud's work in this area is not well known, but it is clearly representative of the anti-intellectualist movement, and in its special understanding of the relationship between sexual drives and the leader-follower nexus in modern mass society, it makes a penetrating contribution to our grasp of the mechanics of dictatorship.*

OF FREUD'S VARIOUS SUBJECTS, POLITICS APPEARS BY LITERAL standards the least attended; the word is little used and *Group Psychology and the Analysis of the Ego* (1921), his most concen-

trated political essay, is brief even for a writer of such gra-
ciously slim books. Yet we would be only rendering the
suspect obvious in Freud's mind to assume it had no political
aspect—if politics has anything to do with the nature of our
common life. Freud was, it is true, indifferent to an examination of this or that regime, but he was far from indifferent to
the nature of authority or to the general character of rulers
and ruled. Judging the data of politics as mere manifest contents, he intended to give us "its psychological basis"—the
nature of all regimes and of all ruling. The history of institutional orders stayed too high on the surface of politics; it did
not expose the underground irrationality that relates the
organization of society to the ways its members feel and
behave.

There had been an earlier and larger book, *Totem and Taboo*
(1912), at once a theory of the origins of religion and a Hob-
besian myth of the origin of the polity out of much fear and
little prudence. Freud may have been irked by recurrent
criticism of *Totem and Taboo* as a fantastic construction upon
an outmoded anthropology, applying, if at all, to simple,
relatively unorganized, transient, natural groups. Society, as
the criticism ran, is precisely different from the family or the
clan, and a theory based on natural associations was therefore irrelevant as a basis for the study of political associations.
It is worth noting that *Group Psychology*, where Freud leaves
the cover of pre-history and turns toward the contemporaneous, contains an implicit rebuttal to such criticisms of *Totem
and Taboo;* this time "we shall not choose a relatively simple
group formation as our point of departure, but shall begin
with highly organized, lasting, and artificial groups."[1] Needless to say, it came to the same thing in the end.

Group Psychology opens by setting a traditional political
problem: if people are, by their nature, "combined into a
unity, there must surely be something to unite them, and
this bond might be precisely the thing that is characteristic

[1] Sigmund Freud, *Group Psychology and the Analysis of the Ego,* transl. by
James Strachey (London, 1949), 41.

of a group." [2] Freud's word is *Massen* and "group" is not necessarily the most accurate rendering; the English title unfortunately misses the immediate political sense of the German, a meaning explicit in the use of the term 'masses' among
Freud's predecessors in the peculiar new science of social
psychology. Freud was not alone in thinking that the psychology of the group was the essential problem of society;
having narrowed their search to the nature of unity, most
social psychologists have thought they needed only to discover what bond held people together to find out the nature
of politics, for, in Freud's words, "a group is clearly held
together by a power of some kind." [3]

It is in his particular solution to the problem of the power
which unites that the originality of Freud's political psychology lies, although in many respects *Group Psychology* conforms
to a very special genre—mainly French and Italian—which
flourished at the turn of the century. Perhaps Taine's *Origins
of Contemporary France* (1868) is the first example of the school,
and reveals its deepest animus: against the French Revolution and all the democratic yet state-centralizing revolutions
that followed it. Now that the controls of government had
been loosened by democracy, a new dimension of politics appeared to many observers: the emotions of the mass, deeper
by far than the institutions or the abstractions with which
history and philosophy had tried to penetrate the mystery of
political society. The intellectual credentials of the Italian
pioneers of the new theory show its other vital connection,
for the psychology of the mass became "scientific" as a
branch of criminology. In 1886, the first congress of "criminal
anthropologists" was held in Rome, under the presidency of
Lombroso; by the third congress, held in Brussels in 1893,
the movement had become quite international. The French
magistrate and criminologist Gabriel Tarde read two important papers, "The Crimes of Crowds" and "Crowds and
Sects from the Criminal Point of View"; and for some time

[2] *Ibid.*, 7.
[3] *Ibid.*

the two themes—the fear of revolution and the image of the criminal—remained completely interwoven.

Of course, the disdain of the masses was no new motif in the study of politics. But there was a different emphasis behind this particular disdain which earlier political speculation, and certainly the legalistic political science of the nineteenth century, had not emphasized: this difference is the feeling that institutions—churches, armies, parties—really count for less in politics than sentiments. It is this feeling that connects Freud with minds of the most special bent, not only with Taine, Lombroso, and the others, but also with such a figure as Walter Bagehot before them in the whole range of contemporary social psychology. However else they differ, all these as social psychologists share with Freud a common concern for what we ought rightly to call the politics of culture. It is in this way, for example, that anti-Semitism becomes for social psychology not a peripheral problem of group sentiments but incorporated as a fundamental consideration for a political science; Arendt's book on the *Origins of Totalitarianism* bears an inverted resemblance to *The Origins of Contemporary France,* and both of these with Freud's *Massenpsychologie,* for all are concerned to portray with their special terms the mental and moral condition of the masses.

There had been just before and during Freud's early years a renewal of suspicion against popular government even among the most liberal minds. The style of suspicion at the time centered on the experience of French democracy, as today it is supported by the outcome of the Russian Revolution. The case of France reads in a most familiar way; thirty years after Louis Napoleon, the Republic seemed to the liberal Lord Bryce still to maintain "a precarious life from year to year." [4] Walter Bagehot, at once the precursor and most intelligent exponent of the new social psychology, mused in his brilliant "Amicus" letters—they contain, by the way, the most profound appraisal I know of the attraction of the

[4] James Bryce, *Studies in History and Jurisprudence* (New York, 1901), II, 491.

Roman church for literary intellectuals—whether the French "national character" was really suited to freedom. Political freedom in France was "an experiment still," Bagehot concluded, because the French character was too experimental to permit a settled order. Yet democratic institutions did serve the English character, and Bagehot suggested that it was because the English were so much less intellectual than the French.[5] In England, therefore, protected from the incitements of political intelligence, the gloom was not so heavy. Even Matthew Arnold, who especially felt the disintegrative *Zeitgeist* blowing over from the continent to threaten the stability of English culture, had not really worried about the entry of the populace into politics. On the battleground of English culture the political armies still drew up in traditional order, not as mobs excited to ignorant and dreadful actions but as rational corporate expressions of the social structure, Whigs and Tories standing more or less firmly for the vested Anglican and non-Conformist interests in national continuity.

Since it was in England that the new social psychology was born, if men like Bagehot are credited insufficiently by later continental exponents it is perhaps due to the fact that the English did not share in the extremity of the continental polemic against democracy.[6] Imitation was not, in Bagehot's original conception, a pejorative term. But that the English precursors from Burke to Bagehot showed a guarded respect for imitation as a principle of stability only accents the increasingly open disdain of it by continental liberals from Tocqueville onward. We can read the stylish vehemence of the continental reaction against the possibilities of mass democracy in the young Freud, long before he turned his mind to any ordered conception of the emotions that underlie political society. The clichés of national character held good: England, for example, which Freud visited in the summer of

---

[5] Walter Bagehot, *Literary Studies* (London, 1884), I, 331–334.

[6] Cf., on this, Scipio Sighele, *Psychologie des sectes*. Traduction française par Louis Brandin (Paris, 1898), 90 n.

his eighteenth year upon graduating from the Gymnasium,
appeared sober and puritanical;[7] and France, in the winter
of 1885–86 he spent in Paris, was still the France of the Revolution and the Commune. The young Freud reported the
familiar fearful image in a letter to his fiancée:

> The town and the people are uncanny; they seem to be of
> another species from us. I believe they are all possessed of a
> thousand demons. Instead of *"Monsieur"* and *"Voilà l'Echo de
> Paris,"* I hear them screaming *"A la lanterne"* or *"A bas dieser
> und jener."* They are the people of psychical epidemics, of his-
> torical mass convulsions.[8]

Almost forty years later Freud's scientific estimate of the
"masses" in the *Group Psychology* still depended upon the
alarms of the French and Italian writers following Taine.

Freud considered his disdain of the masses so indistinguishable from his sources that he did not even bother to rephrase
his main source, a procedure most unusual for him, but
copied out whole passages from the most popular and intract-
ably hostile of critiques presenting itself as a social psychology, Gustave Le Bon's *The Crowd* (1895). We may wonder
how Freud came to borrow so heavily from this notorious
racist, political anti-Semite, and intellectual servitor of the
French military class. It is well to recall that the socialist
Popper-Lynkeus, whose writings Freud admired, spoke of the
mob in the same tone of horror; and, in our own day, Silone's
The School for Dictators, although by a Socialist, is intended to
warn against the collectivity of emotion one always finds as
a democratic principle in modern totalitarianism. Silone
despairs no less over the inveterate condition of the masses
than did his Italian predecessor in political psychology, Sighele. The difference is that even the most disillusioned
Socialist estimates of democracy still hold on tenaciously to
the promise of collective rationality; for the conservative
psychologists, the fallibility of the crowd is incurable. Thus
it is under the influence of a social psychology implacably

[7] Ernest Jones, *The Life and Work of Sigmund Freud* (New York, 1953), I, 178.
[8] Quoted in Jones, *op. cit.,* 184.

hostile to democracy (although Mussolini's credits are suspect, he did say he had been influenced by Le Bon) that
Freud's *Group Psychology* was composed. His work is touched
—not altogether harmlessly—by the animus of his predecessors.

Let me review quickly the portrait of the mass common to
this school, which Freud transcribes in the first chapter of
his book. It is noteworthy, in the first place, how liberally
the "unconscious" was used by Freud's predecessors, and we
are reminded that the idea was a commonplace both in the
academies and the salons throughout the last two decades
of the nineteenth century, and only later, perhaps in part
because of the startling contents Freud exposed, was it discredited.

The masses, as Freud paraphrased Le Bon, are led almost
exclusively by the unconscious.[9] Freud credits Le Bon with
being the first to stress this fact. Actually, the notion that
unconscious qualities of mind supervene when the individual
gets lost in the crowd had been clearly spelled out by earlier
writers, particularly by Sighele—*The Psychology of Sects* was
published in 1894—who suffered the futile envy of the academic who had written the same book earlier and with less
popular effect than Le Bon; he even accuses Le Bon of out-
right plagiarism. But Freud's exposition has a depth of
clinical insight, though the illustrations are few, which transforms the crude polemical interest of Sighele and Le Bon,
even as his use of the "unconscious" surpasses the earlier and
mechanical Herbartian one. Put with the term 'mass' it not
only suggested to Freud (as it had to Le Bon) a genetic connection between the unruly sandheap of individuals and the
unruly desires of the unconscious, but moreover an identity.
Freud's own portrait of the unconscious *is* a metaphor of the
revolutionary mob; it catches the distractions of individual
behavior not, as we might suppose, from inner reality—the
Unconscious is anyway a construction, an inaccessible mad-
house of desire whose chaos one infers dangerously near the

9 Freud, *op. cit.,* 14.

observable and therefore deceptive surface—but from a standard metaphor of political reality.

Again, in Freud, we read the familiar allegations: the mass is a bundle of positive desires, "impulsive, changeable, irritable," [10] without any intimations of the great civilizing 'No' that tries to rule the world, deaf to the cold echoes of impossibility that inhibits consciousness from testing the fantastic variety of behavior. Everywhere in society there appeared to Freud the same discouraging "weakness of intellectual ability, the lack of emotional restraint, the incapacity of moderation and delay, the inclination to exceed every limit in the expression of emotion and work it off completely in the form of action." Still following Le Bon, Freud "dwells especially on the lowering in intellectual activity which an individual experiences when he becomes merged in a group." Mass politics must in this view be a stupid and exciting affair, for the group's "feelings . . . are always very simple and very exaggerated." [11]

While concentrating on the primitive irrationality of the mass, Freud omitted to blame history, which was at least a consolation Le Bon offered. Le Bon and others before him and after have suspected only democratic politics was a degrading process. Freud, ignoring the distinction between modern and pre-modern politics, and such refinements as between the "people" and the "masses," saw the upthrust of barbarism inherent in all political action. Freud's "masses" were not specially created by industrial urban society. "Mass" or "group" describes the psychological tendency of every people. The personality type of Rousseauist political theory, the independent and intelligent *citoyen*, gets no more place from him than does the increasingly rational proletarian of the Marxist dream; the mass man remains for Freud the servile primitive, a perversely grown child. By his method Freud makes irrelevant the established historical conception of development in political behavior towards the participa-

[10] *Ibid.*
[11] *Ib.*, 92.

tion of the masses, since group "participation" retains its suppliant psychological quality in the most various epochs and cultures. Politics is in this view no mere matter of elections and offices; there must be, beneath the manifest varieties of freedom, more permanent modes by which authority is enforced. In this way, Freudianism undercuts a popular discrimination of contemporary political theory: the masses exercise no unique influence over the dynamics of modern politics, for in Freud's psychology the collectivity as such becomes the common denominator of all politics. The spectre that haunted the cultivated European mind—of which the Marxist was a curiously positive, optimistic inversion—this "mass man" who had arisen to plague high culture in the nineteenth century, was for Freud the eternal *homo politicus*. It is important to notice this difference between the psychology of Freud and the historicist position still maintained by Le Bon, because only by universalizing the historical idea of the mass did Freud transform the specifically anti-democratic animus of the earlier writers into the general anti-political animus characteristic of his doctrine.

Freud correctly remarks that the horror of the mob is not new to Le Bon; it is, indeed, the leading cliché of conservative thought and the perennial caveat by which radicalism indicates its essential respectability. However, from the Freudian perspective the task of social psychology lay not in justifying the conservative fear of mass politics nor in condemning radical hope (with which Freud had an ambiguous sympathy) but in a technical appraisal of the transformation of the rational individual so dearly held by extreme democrats into the mass man who had frightened the conservative critics. How is it, Freud asks, that individuals *en masse* feel, think, and act so differently from themselves alone? For these purposes, Le Bon's text was a fortunate one with which to begin, not because it was the most popular study of the mob and certainly not because it had some special intellectual merit or priority of statement, but because Le Bon showed an electic, synthesizing talent for using all the explanations thus far proposed. At least in the vehemence and spread of his attack, Le Bon was a culmination of the new political psychology, and the economical Freud used him in that way.

I have already mentioned how Le Bon supposed that in the mob the "unconscious" dominates, and further that there was a certain regression to primitive states of mind, which amounted in his estimation—and in Freud's—to the same thing. "Isolated," a person "may be a cultivated individual; in a crowd, he is a barbarian." Mass politics exhibits a creature Freud imagined he had seen on the streets of Paris and among the eternal poor, "a creature acting by instinct." [12] Yet although Freud used this standard characterization, it did not solve the problem of the transformation of personality but only restated it. An alternative explanation of Le Bon's, that in a crowd a new and single entity comes into being differing from the minds of the individuals composing it, is, if understood literally, gratuitous from the Freudian point of view; although he believed that certain contents in the unconscious were collective, Freud never resorted to the separate trans-individual psyche that Jung was to propose. The twin metamorphoses of each person in a crowd—"the intensification of the emotions and the inhibition of intellectual life" [13]—could be accounted for in any case by individual psychic processes. Although the worst failure of the Group Mind theory is moreover that it profoundly over-estimates the community of crowds, Freud did not, for reasons we shall see, give this as a reason for his own rejection of the notion.

"Rational" causes such as intimidation or the arousal of the instinct of self-preservation could not of course satisfy Freud's understanding of mass behavior. But among irrational causes there was one proposed by and for all purposes agreed upon among the varieties of the new social psychology, "even though it is given various names, and that is—the magic word 'suggestion.'" [14] The theory of suggestion, be-

[12] *Op. cit.*, 14.
[13] *Ib.*, 33.
[14] *Ib.*, 34.

cause it seemed capable of explaining everything conceivable by a Group Mind, eliminated a gratuitous spirituality and thus achieved its first place in the social psychology of Freud's time. As it appeared to him, the decline of intellect led back inevitably to the device of suggestion, for if the mass "has no critical faculty, and the probable does not exist for it, it is extraordinarily credulous and open to influence." [15] From here the going was easy; no Group Mind need suddenly turn on in individuals submerged in a mob; the solitary and omni-seminal mind was really only the stimulus of the new emotional environment, with its protective anonymity; it was the natural response of the uncritical mind, trained to its incapacity by the essential discipline of sympathy.

By positing a propensity to suggestion, one can also see how discipline may fail, as when a suggestion does not catch an assent from the emotional predisposition of a crowd it may be met with jeers. Bagehot and Tarde independently had called this same propensity "imitation," and even "unconscious imitation," but Freud agreed with the prevailing criticism that the conception of imitation comes under that of suggestion, and is in fact one of its results.[16] The furthest reach of political psychology until Freud's was that "suggestion (or more correctly suggestibility) is actually an irreducible, primitive phenomenon, a fundamental fact in the mental life of man." [17]

The range of the argument from suggestion was clearly worked through by Bernheim, with whom Freud had studied in 1889. In Bernheim's second book which Freud translated as the *Neuen Studien* (1894), he found Bernheim claiming for his psychology the answer to the major questions of political inquiry and indeed to "the entire history of humanity."

Among all people, therapeutic suggestion was practiced consciously or unconsciously by priests, charlatans, and magicians. Seen from the most general point of view, suggestion has

[15] *Ib.*, 15.
[16] *Op. cit.*, 34.
[17] *Ib.*, 35.

dominated the entire history of humanity. Since the original sin was suggested to Eve by the serpent and to Adam by Eve, until the great wars engendered by religious and political fanaticism, until the bloody horrors of the Revolution and of the Commune, suggestion has played a rôle.

Bernheim's theory of suggestion took care of bad politics and good, although significantly, it could not by itself discriminate between them but depended upon obviously conservative values. "Sometimes a noble and generous idea circulates in the masses and puts all their hearts beating in unison; nobles, priests, workers, bourgeoisie, all fraternize on the altar of *la Patrie.*" Sometimes "ideas of hate, of distrust, of treason, are disseminated by the popular tribunes" and it is for this reason that the masses are sometimes committed to "ferocious evils." Suggestion was the beginning of the best and the worst; "the people are angels or demons, because they are suggestible."[18]

Why, when they both mean the same thing, did the term "suggestion" displace that of "imitation"? Because "suggestion" is a term drawn from the realm of the pathological, from the vocabulary of that then new and sinister addition to the practical sciences, hypnosis. Indeed, hypnosis appeared to Freud not only a therapeutic device but a new way toward a fundamental science of the nature of man and society.

When Bernheim spoke of the suggestibility of crowds, he meant it in the clinical—Sighele and Le Bon would have said "pathological"—sense. Something was "suggested" to the minds in the crowd and the crowd, as if hypnotized, became of one mind; the horrors that crowds committed were explainable by the general fact that "the condition of the individual in a group [is] actually hypnotic."[19] Following the romantic doctors of the nineteenth century with their *universale Medizin,* Freud saw no essential difference between

[18] Hippolyte Bernheim, *De la Suggestion et de ses Applications à la Thérapeutique* (Paris, 1888), 331–337. My translation.

[19] Freud, *Group Psychology,* 13.

the hypnotic relation in the clinic and the emotional organization of society. "The hypnotic relation is (if the suggestion is permissible) a group formation with two members." [20] There are, of course, literal differences which Freud conveniently did not bring to notice; for one thing, the somnambulist usually forgets what he did during his lapse, while members of a crowd remember. But however marked the differences, Freud found similarities more profound: "there is the same humble subjection, the same compliance, the same absence of criticism . . . the same absorption of one's own initiative." [21] In a hypnosis one submitted more or less absolutely to a superior will, and this, not imitation, seemed to describe the essential character of political society. Hypnosis was not simply analogous to authority. Freud stressed that neither he nor his predecessors needed to be satisfied with a safe comparison of the hypnotic relation with the basic emotional structure of political society "because it is truer to say that it is identical with it." [22]

Once, through the contrasting efforts of Charcot and Bernheim, hypnotism had been admitted to a respectable place among the human sciences in the early 1880's, its daemon imagery became a stock item of conservative polemics. Professional ties were fairly close: the social psychologists thought of themselves as pathologists, dealing scientifically but firmly first with race and crime and then finally with the degeneration of modern politics. Sighele taught sociology at the University of Pisa, but Le Bon was a physician by training and had written a manual for the French cavalry on the domination of horses from which higher lessons might be drawn; and Bernheim was a practising hypno-therapist, the great student of hypnotic technique of the day who understood it as the science of domination. Finally, Freud himself had been a hypnotist, the most powerful of rulers, bending submissive

[20] *Ib.*, 78.
[21] *Ib.*, 77.
[22] *Ib.*, 78.

subjects to his will; and he had been repelled by his experience of this power. Training in the arts of Bernheim in the year 1889, Freud could remember feeling

> a muffled hostility to this tyranny of suggestion. When a patient who showed himself unamenable was met with the shout: 'What are you doing. Vous vous contresuggestionnez!', I said to myself that this was an evident injustice and an act of violence. For the man certainly had a right to counter-suggestions if they were trying to subdue him with suggestions. Later on, my resistance took the direction of protesting against the view that suggestion, which explained everything, was itself to be preserved from explanation.[23]

In his own clinical practice Freud quickly dispensed with hypnotism. Breuer's cathartic cure had relied extensively upon it, but this seemed to Freud superficial, since the patient thus remained ignorant of the nature of the illness and there was little chance of control over it. The cooperation of the patient had to be secured in a less drastic way, Freud discovered, and thus the "transference" ultimately replaced "suggestion" in the technique of psychoanalytic therapy.

Thirty years elapsed between the time Freud solved "the riddle of suggestion" as a therapeutic conception and the time he turned to it as a political conception. McDougall's book, *The Group Mind* (1920), seems to have been a stimulus to Freud's decision to reopen the problem in his own writing. While McDougall attempted to explain away politics by an instinct of submission, the satisfaction of which alone can make man happy, Freud considered this a shallow and misleading doctrine, for if we live cursed with an instinct of submission there was no hope for a rational social order, of which Freud did not completely despair. The inclination to make of obedience an instinct was evident in the most diverse minds, not only in psychologists like Le Bon and McDougall but in even more political scientists such as Lord Bryce who put a special instinct at bottom in his famous essay on "Obe-

[23] *Op. cit.*, 35–36.

dience" (1901). But rightly convinced of the sterility of the special instinct hypothesis, Freud moved in quite another direction, towards a deeper identity of our social and natural affections.

If unity expresses the essential mystery of political society, and "a group is clearly held togeher by a power of some kind," to what power could this mysterious unity "be better ascribed than to Eros, who holds together everything in the world?" [24] Language, the refuge of common understanding, had "carried out an entirely justified piece of unification in creating the word 'love' with its numerous uses." And besides Plato's, the finest intuitions had amplified love to connote the essential social purpose: "When the apostle Paul . . . prizes love above all else, he certainly understands it in the same 'wider' sense." But in Freud's mind social science was evidently not so perspicacious as theology for "the authorities make no mention of any such relations";[25] yet, he insisted, the character of political society no less than of the spiritual life was incomprehensible except as the organization and disorganization of erotic sensibility.

Of course Freud was aware that other very powerful answers had been given to the question of why human beings live together, the most persistent of which was the one proposed in so dramatic a way by Thrasymachus: perhaps "community of interest in itself" is the basis of social unity. But the deeper motives, as Freud once said, are never practical. The "leading authorities" of science treat social cohesion in "far too rational a manner," [26] as if unity did not "persist longer than the immediate advantages gained . . . from other people's collaborations" [27] and ceased when advantage ceased. Yet people remain united under the extremest disadvantages, and fall out just in the nicest time. Freud rightly concluded that the established sentiment for expedi-

[24] *Ib.*, 40.
[25] *Ibid.*
[26] *Op. cit.*, 55.
[27] *Ib.*, 57.

ency does not sufficiently explain human unity. And whether his solution—"libidinal ties are what characterize a group" [28] —is correct or not, there is no doubt that he grasped the inadequacy, unadmitted by most, of all solutions of social unity as founded on interest and expediency; his alternative has been singularly influential, in particular upon contemporary American social science.

If social science has discovered bonds stronger than expediency, they chafe all the more, for the erotic gives to society the mode of its unity but no further purpose by which its togetherness can be judged. Having established the primacy of love, Freud made of unity an end in itself. All the associations to which people could possibly belong, from the first family to the world state, were united by a tissue of love. The love relation was Freud's vice of the universal, and he proceeded to bestow it upon individuals not only in their private right but "in the firm expectation of finding in them conditions which can be transferred to the ties that exist in groups." [29] In this transferred sense, the condition of obedience is an erotic one; as all lovers are alike so long as love informs their actions, in the mass "individuals behave as though they were uniform." It is to love we usually find ourselves responding; even the largest, grossest sense of unity gives us pleasure, as anyone knows who has marched along in a squadron of men to whom individually he felt indifferent and even hostile.

But when the "I" becomes a "We" its sense of power is not enlarged; surprisingly, it shrinks. The sources of love, as Freud discovered them, do not strengthen our capacities for discretion but draw us out further into obedience. His entire psychology of obedience depends upon this single theme— the power of love—remarkable for its sinister references even in a mind overcomplicated precisely by a system of sinister references, for Freud has the audacity to tell us "it would be more to the point to explain being in love by means of hyp-

[28] *Ib.*, 54.
[29] *Op. cit.*, 58.

nosis then the other way around." [30] By this connection, Freud reintroduced the category of hypnosis into political analysis, but in a manner the reverse of previous writers; politics became not an elaboration of love but love itself became political, an elaboration of the psychology of obedience. Equally the easy transformation of the individual into the mass-man did not come under the category of an "ineradicable, primitive" suggestibility,[31] as Bernheim conventionally proposed, but under a far more controllable and concrete relation of "absolute" obedience. In Freud's version of the psychology of politics, fanaticism is not some terrible caprice, touched off by a suggestion, but—far more terrible —an intense wistfulness to do the bidding of the loved one or his personification in an idea.

Surely, no one can say Freud treats love sweetly; it is either greedy and triumphant (the "sadistic" component) or it is abjectly submissive (the "masochistic"). It is the second possibility (which incidentally rules out the counter-transference in Freud's therapy, for then the analyst would be submitting to the patient, a superior knowledge to an inferior) that is implied by the Freudian portrait of the mass. Freud made of the love by which a human being becomes a political animal, a personal weakness: the "I" is troubled by a sense of incompleteness that finally defeats it. Thus by virtue of his individuality, the individual gives himself to membership in a group "because he feels the need of being in harmony with them rather than in opposition to them." If everywhere we are born free it is because we are, according to the Freudian psychology, born perfect egotists; if everywhere man puts himself in chains "perhaps after all he does it *'ihnen zu liebe.'*" [32] This is the way Freud reinterpreted Trotter's remark that social gregariousness is only a continuation of multicellularity. Gregariousness "is a further manifestation, which proceeds from the libido, and which is felt by all

[30] *Ib.*, 77.
[31] *Ib.*, 35.
[32] *Op. cit.*, 40.

human beings of the same kind, to combine in more and more comprehensive units." [33] The power of love would thus seem not so sinister a foundation of politics were it not that hypnosis occupied "a middle position," the pivotal one in Freud's description, between politics and love. [34] It is the middle one not only because the clinic is not quite life but because private love has a saving, directly sexual tendency missing as love grows more social.

The clinic was not quite life because in the clinic power was still limited. "The moral conscience of the person hypnotized may show resistance" for he knows "that what is happening is only a game," a deceptive renewal of certain "old impressions." [35] However adequate the hypnosis, it remained "an untrue reproduction of another situation of far more importance to life." But what if political reality itself adopted the techniques of the hypnotist's amphitheatre to fascinate citizenries and put them in the dark? Freud saw a sinister corridor leading from private rooms to the most public places, towards powers of which his understanding in the year 1921 was perhaps only a little premature. Power can create something more dangerous to personality than that pathetic "lack of independence and initiative" loving creates; put together, love and politics induce "an additional element," a "paralysis derived from the relation between someone with a superior power and someone who is without power and helpless." Here Freud sounded an eerie depth in the psychology of modern politics, one never reached even thus momentarily by the psychologies of his predecessors. At the deepest level to which Freud descended into the sense of love as power he referred to "the hypnosis of terror which occurs in animals." [36] By this reference to the animal world Freud anticipates the Kafkaesque reality of the modern political scene: the human animal frozen into immobility by the con-

[33] *Ib.*, 83.
[34] *Ib.*, 78.
[35] *Op. cit.*, 99.
[36] *Op. cit.*, 79.

frontation of Behemoth. It puzzles science to note how many people can be prepared and fixed in just the right position for their own destruction by a direct vision of power. What science has decided to call "apathy" Freud called, perhaps more profoundly, "fascination." The manner in which this "hypnosis of terror" is produced and its relation to sleep is unclear; "and the puzzling way in which some people are subject to it, while others resist it completely, points to some factor still unknown." [37] Nevertheless, Freud was certain that the "parental complex" was one of the factors involved.

Most of us, it appears, have not developed to that stage of emotional maturity at which we will want to resist power. Freud suggests a new stricture on the idea that man is a political animal, for like animals he remains liable to the sudden hypnosis of terror: when power is love, the victim cannot tear himself away. The deepest political sentiment would thus be the capacity for utter devotion without cause; that power may perfect obedience suggests, more abstractly, how a political movement may advance without any conviction save the sense of power and without any confirmation save success. The wave of the future, like a god, is an awesome sight especially as it bears down upon one. In the Freudian political psychology, a special party, a special teaching, even a special leadership would not be necessary to further political success of success is already there. Politics is transformed into a psychological function, a pure holding together, an aspiration to absolute unity as an end in itself with no end superior to it. The Freudian psychology suggests the exquisite connections between love, power, and terror now offered all too insistently by reality; and in this it at least improves on our present dim understanding of the rigid acquiescence with which whole populations endure the disasters of modern politics. Love has become again, but in a way Paul would not admire, comprehensible as power, and fanaticism appears again as the extremest humility.

By putting power under the comparative aspect of a cer-

[37] *Ibid.*

tain relation of love, Freud rephrased the question of domination, but with an expected cast, through "one of the chief elements of the comparison, namely the person who is to replace the hypnotist in the case of the group." [38] Thus the attractive figure of the leader appears, to dominate his followers and Freud's political psychology. Freud found a certain advantage in the hackneyed theory of mass politics and hypnosis, so far as "out of the complicated fabric of the group it isolates one element for us—the behavior of the individual to the leader." [39] Note the direction of the relation: not the behavior of the leader to the individual but of the individual to the leader. Freud rarely examines the leader as such, but only the attitude towards him: through leaders human nature satisfies its original "thirst for obedience." Freud concentrates almost exclusively on the art of being ruled; he has comparatively little to say about the psychology of rulers except as objects of the emotions of the ruled. The psychology of being ruled—the group psychology—is generally more important in Freud's mind than the psychology of ruling—the individual psychology. In this way Freud could ignore the historical reference altogether, for the experience of being ruled is everywhere the same, the ruled being always the one truly conservative class; they have, so to speak, no history but only a psychology. Freud's political theory depends not upon a history of regimes but upon a psychology of obedience, and the implication here is that at the height of the social process the State can be analyzed in the same way as the most natural of groups, the family. The State and the family, the army and the crowd, in fact the natural and the social situation, show the same tendencies and the same emotional structure, even where leadership is not as exotic as in the case of the crowd.

Yet, with the figure of the leader, we move into a new set of Freud's perceptions, one which modern taste shows a certain inclination to believe, not by the ascendancy of

[38] Freud, *op. cit.,* 13.
[39] *Ibid.*

Freud's word—in this respect at least he has gone relatively unnoticed—as by the general air of destroyed will and inevitable accession of leaders that pervades our culture. Modern taste expects Freud's leader to be fully realized in life by 1984; "I love Big Brother" is the perfected cry of erotic submission. It can be matched, on the other side, by the final terrible command—"Kiss me"—Cipolla gives to Mario, the mass-man who lives for love, in Mann's somewhat ornate Freudian allegory of modern politics, *Mario and the Magician*. The idea of the demon lover, suddenly vaulted into politics, was in Freud's version "the idea of a paramount and dangerous personality, towards whom only a passive-masochistic attitude is possible, to whom one's will has been surrendered." [40] In this way the Freudian political psychology achieved a certain pertinence for analyzing the totalitarian state, with its erotic manipulation of the masses. If indeed the Freudian erotic of politics seemed to give all politics a certain quality of madness, it is appropriate to recall that to Freud's mind the state of being in love is "the normal prototype of the psychoses," [41] and the *Führer* is just as easily understood in his sort of romantic psychology as the *Verführer*. Kierkegaard's image of the seducer as the purest sort of lover is in the same spirit as Freud's insight into love as the basis of the state. It is "the credulity of love" that becomes, in Freud's extreme and hostile view, "the most fundamental source of *authority*." [42]

---

[40] Freud, *op. cit.*, 21, 100; Le Bon's phrase. Freud also suggests "passion for authority." *Op. cit.*, 99.

[41] Freud, *Totem and Taboo*, in "Basic Writings" (Modern Library ed.), n.d., 876.

[42] Freud, *Three Essays on Sexuality*, in "The Complete Psychological Works" (London: Hogarth Press, 1953), VII, 150. Freud's italics.

6.

Twentieth-Century Version of
the Apocalypse

Franklin L. Baumer

EDITORIAL NOTE: *If, in fact, modern civilization does collapse and the historical world, as we know it, does come to an end, at least the survivors will be able to congratulate themselves on having had full foreknowledge of their fate. Never before, except perhaps in the writings of the Fathers of the Early Church, has a civilization dwelt so obsessively on the possibility of its own demise. It may almost be argued that this is the controlling vision in twentieth-century European thought, at least during the generation of the two world wars. No other theme expresses so completely and so effectively the spirit of the times. Franklin L. Baumer's "Twentieth-Century Version of the Apocalypse" was prepared for UNESCO's International Commission for a History of the Scientific and Cultural Development of Humanity, and published in its* Journal of World History *in 1954. See also Professor Baumer's discussion of the twentieth century as "the Age of Longing" in his* Religion and the Rise of Scepticism *(New York, 1960), ch. 4.*

I

"FOR THE FIRST TIME FOR MANY CENTURIES MANKIND IS haunted by the idea that *the end of the world* is possible." This statement was made by a Frenchman at the opening session of UNESCO in Paris in 1946. Speaking at the same session, the well-known novelist and art critic André Malraux observed that the war, and events subsequent to the war, had set people to thinking seriously about "the death of Europe." [1]

M. Mounier calls this state of mind the "apocalyptic consciousness." As is well known, the Jews, in the period following the Babylonian Captivity, and the early Christians, exhibited it to a high degree. It is almost as well known that it recurred periodically during the Middle Ages, notably in the tenth century and again in the fifteenth. What is not so well known, at least in the U. S. A., is that twentieth-century Europeans have produced their own version of the apocalypse: a phenomenon surely unexpected in modern culture.

Mounier and Malraux do not alone witness to it; if they did, this paper would never have been written. The fact is, however, that the apocalyptic consciousness has been mounting in intensity since the second half of the nineteenth century when individuals like Burckhardt, Nietzsche, and Dostoievski were predicting the collapse of western civilization. It has become widespread since the first World War, and particularly during the last decade. It impregnates contemporary theology and philosophy, poetry and the novel, the philosophy of history and, one sometimes suspects, even astrophysical thought.[2] The general vocabulary reflects it, and so, not infrequently, do the titles of books, including general books which do not fit snugly into any of the above categories.

Open almost any of these books, and the chances are that your eye will strike sentences denoting apocalyptic time: "The hand on the clock of the worlds moves ceaselessly forward towards the stroke of twelve" (Karl Heim); "It was a bright cold day in April, and the clocks were striking thirteen" (George Orwell); "*The Twenty-fifth Hour* . . . It is not

[1] *Reflections on Our Age:* Lectures delivered at the opening session of UNESCO at the Sorbonne University, Paris (New York, 1949), p. 19, 96. Italics mine.
[2] I refer to that theory, based on the second law of thermodynamics, which holds that energy is being dissipated and the universe inexorably progressing toward heat-death.

the last hour; it is one hour past the last hour. It is Western civilization at this very moment. It is now." (C. Virgil Gheorghiu).[3] Between the first World War and now statements like the following hit the reader like a succession of hammer blows: ". . . there can be no doubt that we are on the threshold of the Apocalypse" (Léon Bloy, 1915); "We are living to-day under the sign of the collapse of civilization" (Albert Schweitzer, 1923); "There is a growing awareness of imminent ruin tantamount to a dread of the approaching end of all that makes life worth living" (Karl Jaspers, 1932); "Realities of our time . . . The Decline of Europe . . . Massacres and atrocities, poverties, famine" (Cyril Connolly, 1946); "Now I happen to believe that Europe is doomed, a chapter in history which is drawing to its finish" ("Julien Delattre" in a novel by Arthur Koestler, 1951); ". . . We are entering upon a time comparable with the darkest periods of human history" (Germain Bazin, 1952).[4] It would be tedious to go on. These statements are, as I believe, symptomatic of an apocalyptic state of mind only too prevalent in twentieth-century European literature.

Note the words that occur with the greatest frequency in these and similar passages. They derive to an amazing degree from the apocalyptic tradition. "Apocalypse", "*dies irae*, the day of the Last Judgment," "Antichrist"—"Satan"—"Belial," "eschatology," "the end:" the apocalyptic imagery is obvious. Did one not know that they implied something rather different, one might be tempted to add to the list the words coined by the existentialists—"nausea," "anguish,"

---

[3] Karl Heim, *The New Divine Order* (London, 1930), p. 87; George Orwell, *1984* (New York, 1949), p. 3; C. Virgil Gheorghiu, *The Twenty-Fifth Hour* (New York, 1950), p. 49.

[4] Léon Bloy: letter to Jean Boussac, Dec. 27, 1915, quoted in Albert Béguin *Léon Bloy* (New York, 1947), p. 231; Albert Schweitzer, *The Decay and Restoration of Civilization* (London, 1947), p. 1; Karl Jaspers, *Man in the Modern Age* (New York, 1933), p. 63; Palinurus (Cyril Connolly), *The Unquiet Grave* (London, 1946), p. 75; Arthur Koestler, *The Age of Longing* (New York, 1951), p. 139; Germain Bazin, "The Devil in Art," in *Satan,* edited by Bruno de Jesus-Marie (New York, 1952), p. 366.

"forlorness," "despair." Nicolas Berdyaev and Arthur Koestler may serve as examples of the several ways in which contemporary writers employ this apocalyptic terminology. To the "religious philosopher" Berdyaev, who ever since his expulsion from Russia in 1922 has been flooding Europe with books about the crisis of western civilization, everything—religion, history, ethics, all sides of modern culture—appears under the sign of the apocalypse. The sentence from his autobiography, "There is an individual eschatology and apocalypse, and there is an historical eschatology and apocalypse,"[5] might well stand as the key to his entire work. Berdyaev preaches "eschatological" as opposed to "historic" Christianity which adapts itself to, and fattens itself on the world—a preachment which, in this one respect if in no other, links him to the whole "neo-orthodox" movement in Protestant theology. History, he tells us, reveals an "internal apocalyptic," "judgment," and history will end in "the Coming of Christ together with those negative anti-Christian forces which must culminate in the coming of the Antichrist."[6]— "Of the Last Things. Eschatological Ethics" is the title of a whole section in his big book on ethics, *The Destiny of Man*. Even Einstein's Relativity is said to be "like an apocalypse of modern physics."[7] In *The Age of Longing* the non-religious but also ex-communist Koestler deliberately uses apocalyptic imagery to heighten the feeling of tension. In the chapter entitled "Interlude," for instance, the Parisians of the year 195– experience the worst heat and drought in human memory. These climatic disturbances, which delight the "Apocalyptists" among the weather statisticians, are followed by "the strangest epidemic ever known" and by "all kinds of curious disturbances in radio-reception, and jagged stars or lightning bolts appeared across the television screens." Who could be certain that at such a time even the seasons would continue in their wonted course? Doubtless, there is con-

[5] *Dream and Reality* (London, 1950), p. 294.
[6] *The Meaning of History* (London, 1936), p. 204.
[7] *The End of Our Time* (New York, 1933), p. 50.

siderable irony in this passage; Koestler is only too obviously
satirizing the ups-and-downs of European political hopes
and fears. But the irony is lacking at the end when M. Ana-
tole's funeral cortege winds its way through the streets of
Paris to the accompaniment of air-raid sirens. "The siren
wailed, but nobody was sure: it could have meant the Last
Judgment, or just another air-raid exercise." As Hydie observed the fearful expression in the eyes of some onlooking
workmen, she thought: "Thus must mediaeval crowds have
stared at the sky Anno Domini 999, waiting for the Comet
to appear."[8]

What does this apocalyptic consciousness signify? The
word "apocalypse" means literally an unveiling or disclosure
of the future. But among the Jews and early Christians it also
denoted a profound pessimism about the world and man. In
the *Revelation of John*, that classic of Jewish and Christian
Apocalyptic, the "new Jerusalem" is established only at the
end of time, and by God's intervention, not human works.
It is preceded, moreover, by the most frightful and hair-
raising events, by the ride of the four horsemen, by plagues
and wars and all manner of natural calamities. It is in this
sense—in the sense of the prophecies of *Revelation*—that I
use the word apocalypse in this paper. "Apocalyptic" signifies a mood utterly at variance with what Karl Mannheim
calls the "Utopian mentality"; a state of mind which takes
a dim view of "time," or rather of what man can accomplish
in "time"; which accepts suffering, conflict, death as permanent data of temporal life; which perceives that demonic
forces are gaining in strength and threatening to overwhelm
human civilization—in a word, "crisis thinking."

To be sure, the twentieth-century version of the apocalypse—the version that I have discovered in such abundance
and in such variegated sources—rarely reproduces exactly
the scheme of the ancient Christian Apocalyptic. In the case

[8] *The Age of Longing*, pp. 360, 362. In Koestler's book the terms "Last
Judgment" and "Comet" symbolize" the shadow of Neanderthal," the
victory of Russian Communism over western liberal civilization.

of some few theologians there has been, indeed, a literal renaissance of John's prophecies: a prediction of the literal end of the world, preceded by heightened conflict between God and the Antichrist, and followed by the establishment of "a new heaven and a new earth." More commonly, however, the "day of the Lord" either signifies "judgment," what Karl Barth calls *Krisis,* God's judgment upon an anthropocentric and self-reliant humanity; or else, more secularly, the end of *a* civilization, the setting in of another "middle age"; or else—and this is the sense in which it is most often used—simply a *warning* of what will surely happen to Europe and Europeans if they do not take stock and do something before it is too late.

The apocalyptic consciousness so defined is undoubtedly the product of catastrophic historical events. We read in Professor Huizinga's *Waning of the Middle Ages* that in the late fourteenth and early fifteenth centuries "the feeling of general insecurity which was caused by the chronic form wars were apt to take, by the constant menace of the dangerous classes, by the mistrust of justice, was further aggravated by the obsession of the coming end of the world, and by the fear of hell, of sorcerers and of devils. The background of all life in the world seems black." [9] The two go together: the catastrophic events and the apocalyptic mood. The ancient Jewish and early Christian Apocalyptic is unthinkable except against the background of Israel's loss of independence, and the persecutions of Antiochus Epiphanes and the Roman emperors in the first century after Christ. By a like token the "crisis thinking" so prevalent in Europe today feeds upon the wars and rumors of war, the concentration camps, the tyranny, the economic and social dislocation and, as I have said in another place, "the Big Machine— the big state, party, business, labor union, the ultimate military weapon, which reduces the individual to insignificance." [10] It is a symptom of the very real decline, economic

[9] London, 1948, p. 21.
[10] F. L. Baumer, *Main Currents of Western Thought* (New York, 1952), p. 578.

and military decline, of Europe relative to Russia and the U. S. A. (for what European or Englishman could now boast, as Hegel once boasted, that "the History of the World travels from East to West, for Europe is absolutely the end of History, Asia the beginning?" [11]). Berdyaev rightly observes that "many people fall victim to eschatological panic because they cannot endure the experience of the decline of an age to which they are bound by all kinds of vested interest, fear and private commitments." [12] But this is by no means the whole story, nor even the most important part of it. Some of the apocalyptists are ex-Communists or ex-Marxists. Some are exiles who, either from personal choice or force of circumstance, have wandered far from home and country. Ultimately, however, twentieth-century apocalyptic reflects the pain and suffering and blighted hopes of the peoples of an entire continent and is confined to no single age-group or nation or class.

I am not inclined to exaggerate the extent of this apocalyptic thinking. It would clearly be a mistake to identify it with *all* contemporary European thinking about history. The Marxists, for instance, though they talk a kind of apocalyptic language—does not the communist "hero" in Koestler's novel profess a mystic belief in "the coming of the Great Change?"—envisage a future that is not apocalyptic at all in the Christian prophet's sense. And no doubt many people, particularly those of a scientific cast of mind, share Bertrand Russell's and Julian Huxley's belief in the possibility of continued progress. Apocalyptic thinking would appear to be, on the whole, less characteristic of the English than of the continental Europeans, and of the apocalyptists considered in this paper, some are obviously less apocalyptic-minded than others. Yet apocalyptic thinking *is* wide-spread in Europe today, and is certainly one of the signs that Europeans live in a "time of troubles."

Since apocalyptic centers in the philosophy of history, let

[11] *Lectures on the Philosophy of History* (London, 1857), p. 109.
[12] *Dream and Reality,* pp. 296–97.

us now see in detail how the twentieth-century apocalyptists size up contemporary civilization, how they account for the present in terms of past events, and what they prophesy for the future.

II

The *Revelation of John* begins with what is in effect an analysis of the present state of the world. To the church in Ephesus John wrote: "Remember therefore whence thou art fallen, and repent." As they survey their world, the twentieth-century apocalyptists likewise see nothing much to delight the eye; they too see a "fallen" world. They have different words for it—"decadence," for example, and "civilization" which Spengler opposed to "culture"—but they all agree that, for a variety of reasons, the West has "fallen." ". . . We feel keenly," Berdyaev wrote in 1934, "that we are living in a fallen world, torn asunder by incurable contradictions."[13]

Evidently, the curve of European self-congratulation has fallen precipitously since the heyday of the apostles of progress. Condorcet and Comte were pretty self-complacent about the present state of western civilization; there was still much work to be done, but the West, having laid the ghost of superstition and having discovered the scientific method was now well on its way towards perfection. But far from taking pride in living in Comte's scientific or "positive" age, contemporary apocalyptists often compare their age with ancient Rome's decline and fall, and employ medical metaphors to diagnose its "diseases" and "disorders." "No doubt our time is full of fever," Huizinga wrote in 1936. "Our whole civilization," says the jaded aristocrat in *The Age of Longing*, "is affected by sclerosis of the arteries and high blood pressure and hardening of the collective glands."[14]

What are the symptoms of the West's disease? Signifi-

[13] *The Fate of Man in the Modern World* (London, 1935), pp. 21–22.
[14] J. Huizinga, *In the Shadow of To-morrow. A Diagnosis of the Spiritual Distemper of our Time* (London, 1936), p. 37; Arthur Koestler, *The Age of Longing*, p. 10.

cantly, the symptoms are said to be mental as well as cultural, to show more in the human mind and character than in the institutional environment.[15] Indeed, some writers speak as though the disease was wholly mental; to quote a famous statement by Jacques Maritain, "the disease afflicting the modern world is in the first place a disease of the mind." [16] The more common description, however, represents the disease as a mixture of the two.

As one might expect, the mental diagnosis is conspicuous among religious writers. Both Catholics and Protestants tend to locate the modern disease in man's sinful nature. "Evil," says the English philosopher C.E.M. Joad, "is endemic in the heart of man." And he adds: "It may perhaps be plausibly argued that there is no more evil abroad in Western civilization than there was at the end of the last century, but it cannot be denied that what there is of it is more obtrusive."[17] In a recent essay Graham Greene tells us how, while still a boy, he read *King Solomon's Mines* and Marjorie Bowen's *The Viper of Milan*. Of the two books he preferred Miss Bowen's because her evil characters seemed truer to life than the virtuous Allan Quartermain. Evil, says Greene, can always find a home in a human body. "Human nature is not black and white but black and grey. I read all that in *The Viper of Milan* and I looked round and I saw that it was so." [18] Greene has tried to show that this is so in his novels, and so do the Catholic novels of François Mauriac, and so does contemporary Protestant theology. Where the older "liberal" theology tended to explain away sin and evil, the newer "orthodoxy"

[15] The anthropologists, I believe, would admit no such distinction between "mental" and "cultural." I make the distinction in this paper because most of the apocalyptists make it. "Mental," as distinguished from "cultural," here connotes the ideas that man has about the universe and human nature, ideas which it is presumed cannot be wholly explained in terms of his culture.

[16] *The Angelic Doctor* (New York, 1931), p. 109.

[17] *God and Evil* (London, 1942), p. 18. In this book Joad describes his "spiritual Odyssey" which he takes to be "not untypical" of the time.

[18] *The Lost Childhood and other Essays* (London, 1951), p. 16.

revives the doctrine of original sin. Karl Barth rejects the Thomistic analogy between Being and beings, and affirms an infinite qualitative difference between "the righteousness of God" and the "unrighteousness of man" which he says is all too evident in the modern world.

This evil "endemic in man" is often associated with, and even objectified in Satan in a way reminiscent of the ancient apocalypse. Modern literature is full of references to Satan or the "demonic"—Berdyaev's "Antichrist," W. H. Auden's "Prince of Lies," H. G. Wells' "the Antagonist," "Belial" in Aldous Huxley's *Ape and Essence,* to mention only a few. Sometimes this is only a manner of speaking, as when Wells, in his last book, evokes an "Antagonist" to account for that force in the universe which appears to oppose life and constructive effort.[19] Occasionally, however, and most spectacularly in a recent collection of essays by continental Roman Catholics, the Devil takes on an objective existence, not sensible to human eyes, of course, but nonetheless real and there to exploit points of entry into man's nature. Some of these essays narrowly avoid Manicheism. "Never before has Satan had such powerful means at his disposal," says Germain Bazin. "Dispossessed of nature, his former kingdom, Lucifer now seems to have installed himself at the very centre of human intelligence . . ."[20] More commonly, Satan simply symbolizes the evil "endemic in man." Paul Tillich appears to use the term "demonic" in this sense. The "demonic," always at work in history and especially so now, is that force in individual and social existence which aims at negation, arbitrariness and meaninglessness.[21] Says the poet Auden, speaking of the Devil:

[19] See *Mind at the End of its Tether* (London, 1945), pp. 12–13.
[20] *Satan,* pp. 366–67. Also see the statement by Heinz-Dietrich Wendland, Professor of Theology at the University of Kiel, at the Oxford Conference of 1937, printed in *The Kingdom of God and History* (London, 1938) pp. 158–159; and Joad, *God and Evil,* pp. 18–19.
[21] See Tillich's essay, "The Demonic," in *The Interpretation of History* (New York and London, 1936).

> You have no positive existence,
> Are only a recurrent state
> Of fear and faithlessness and hate,
> That takes on from becoming me
> A legal personality. [22]

Other signs of mental unbalance, called to our attention *ad nauseam* by the non-religious as well as religious apocalyptists, are loneliness and anxiety; a morbid longing for faith without any discrimination as to what constitutes a valid faith; dehumanization and, paradoxically, extreme extroversion. All these signs culminate in fear—"fear, my good friends," preaches the Narrator in Huxley's *Ape and Essence,* "fear is the very basis and foundation of modern life;" [23]—also in the decline of creative energy—"We are bled out, physically and spiritually. . . . We (French) are in the position of a blood donor dying of anaemia." [24] It would require a whole book to expound the nuances of these words as the apocalyptists use them. Joad tells us in *Decadence* that the disease of the modern mind finds philosophical expression in scepticism and subjectivism—meaning by subjectivism our conviction that "objects" other than our own mental states either do not exist or cannot be known. Albert Schweitzer would say that it consists in a dangerous combination of "world-affirmation" and lack of ethical absolutes, Emil Brunner in our erroneous conception of "time."

In many of these books the mental diagnosis is, as I have said, juxtaposed to a more purely cultural analysis. Indeed, the majority conceive the two to be two sides of the same coin. Thus, Tillich does not fail to point out that "demonism" takes institutional form in capitalism, nationalism, and bolshevism. A list of cultural symptoms would also include fascism (a particularly deadly variety of nationalism), collectivism in general, cultural standardization and specialization, and

[22] *New Year Letter* (London, 1941), p. 31.
[23] New York, 1948, p. 51.
[24] Commanche, a French official, to Hydie in Koestler *The Age of Longing,*
    p. 318.

the "Machine." What particularly strikes an American about this list is that communism appears as only one among many signs of cultural disease. No doubt the Rumanian intellectual Gheorghiu expresses an extreme view when he pictures Russia as simply a more advanced form of robot-civilization than that of the U. S. A. and her western allies. But none of the apocalyptists, not even the ex-communists, reduce the European crisis to a simple struggle between East and West. The symptoms of disease, cultural as well as mental, are too widespread for that.

Of all the cultural symptoms the "Machine" and what Ortega y Gasset calls "the revolt of the masses" attract the greatest attention. Almost all the books contain chapters on the "Machine." In some of them, for example Karl Jaspers's *Man in the Modern Age* and Gheorghiu's *The Twenty-fifth Hour,* it is the major theme. The "Machine" is a symbol of the hypertrophy and dominion of "apparatus" in modern civilization. It connotes "dehumanization," the reduction of the individual to a "category," "function," "grammatical fiction." The soulless city, top-heavy bureaucracy, the "insect state" are its institutional fruits. It manifests itself psychologically in the individual's lack of a sense of beauty and wonder, and especially his conviction that human activities are unavailing. A few examples will illustrate the spleen so often vented by the apocalyptists on the "Machine." Modern technics, says the Swiss theologian Emil Brunner, means "uncounted millions of men massed together in soulless giant cities; a proletariat without connection with nature, without a native hearth or neighbourhood; it means asphalt-culture, uniformity and standardization. It means men whom the machine has relieved from thinking and willing, who in their turn have to 'serve the machine' at a prescribed tempo and in a stereotyped manner. It means unbearable noise and rush, unemployment and insecurity of life, the concentration of productive power, wealth and prestige in a few hands or their monopolisation by state bureaucracy. . . It means also the speedy standardization of all national cultures and the ex-

tinction of their historical origin." [25] The great revolution of
our time, Gheorghiu tells us, is the revolt of the mechanical
slaves against their masters. These slaves are making human
beings over in their image and, with human complicity, "can
become the very beasts of the Apocalypse." [26]

"The revolt of the masses" has attracted scarcely less attention than the revolt of the mechanical slaves. The classic
statement is, of course, by Ortega, but hardly any of the
apocalyptists fail to mark down what Joad calls the "Culture
of the Many" and Arnold Toynbee the "proletarianization"
of culture. The "revolt of the masses" means the accession to
power in our times of a new type of *"Naturmensch"* who
through his contempt for tradition and "principles" crushes
"everything that is different, everything that is excellent, individual, qualified and select." [27] The Fascists and Bolsheviks
are such "mass-men," but so to a scarcely less extent are the
scientists and professional men who adopt "primitive" attitudes toward everything outside their special fields and thus
contribute to the general unbalance of culture.

These are said to be the principal diseases from which the
West now suffers. Why was the West arrested in its march
toward health, and when did the symptoms of disease first
manifest themselves? To answer these questions the apocalyptists must perform an autopsy on the past as well as present, and to their interpretation of the past we turn next.

III

No two evaluations of modern European history could be
more opposed than the "idea of progress" and twentieth-century apocalyptic. Both "schools" of thought regard the
Renaissance and the Enlightenment as turning points in
western history. But the apocalyptists reverse the judgment
of Condorcet and Comte and deprecate these movements as
the harbingers of universal decline rather than progress.

[25] *Christianity and Civilisation,* II (New York, 1949), 10.
[26] *The Twenty-fifth Hour,* p. 51 and *passim.*
[27] Ortega y Gasset, *The Revolt of the Masses* (London, 1932), pp. 18–19.

Schweitzer, it is true, glorifies the Enlightenment, and Arnold Toynbee believes that western civilization, started on its "time of troubles" at the Reformation, rallied briefly in the eighteenth century. But these are but minor variants of a general opinion that the crimes and follies of history have greatly multiplied during "that past three hundred years" (some say "since Descartes"). "As I read history," says the Arch-Vicar to Dr. Poole in *Ape and Essence,* "it's like this: for thousands of years God and Belial fought an indecisive battle; then, three centuries ago, almost overnight the tide starts to run uninterruptedly in one direction." [28] Berdyaev thought that history took an adverse direction at the Renaissance, which culminated in Nietzsche and Marx. The Catholic mystic Léon Bloy heaped his wrath on the eighteenth century, that "marvellously superficial age" which marked the "unparalleled night of the French mind." [29] All, Schweitzer included, agree that by about the middle of the nineteenth century Europe had come to exhibit most of those symptoms of illness which were to threaten its very life in the century to follow.

In diagnosing the causes of Europe's increasing illness over the past three hundred years the apocalyptists reach conclusions that one would logically expect from their analysis of the present. Spengler, as is well known, did not discuss causes. His "morphology of history" simply recorded the "fact" that every culture passes through identical phases analogous to the seasons of the year or the life of the individual man. The majority of the apocalyptists, however, are deeply concerned about causes. They want to know not only how, but why the present calamity was precipitated. In general, they postulate man's freedom, the very freedom of choice that Spenglerian determinism denies. The decline of the West, they tell us, was not inevitable; on the contrary, it was the dialectical consequence of human choice, specifically of man's preference for a false world-view and value-

[28] p. 120.
[29] See Albert Béguin, *Léon Bloy,* p. 206.

system. "As I worked (on my philosophy of civilization)," Schweitzer writes in his autobiography, "I became clear about the connection between civilization and world-view, and I recognized that the catastrophe of civilization started from a catastrophe of world-view." [30] This is not to ignore cultural, including economic, causes, but it does subordinate such phenomena to what man chooses to think about himself and the universe. "All the happenings which come about within nations and within mankind as a whole," Schweitzer continues, "arise out of spiritual causes which are contained in the prevailing world-view." The causes, that is to say, transcend culture; they are primarily mental and only secondarily cultural.

The Arch-Vicar's lecture on history in *Ape and Essence* summarizes the common argument. The lecture starts out on a very dubious neo-Malthusian note. "It began with machines and the first grain ships from the New World." "Feeding means breeding" and "copulation resulted in population," and the overcrowding of the planet led to "the New Hunger" which made inevitable the nationalistic wars of modern times. So far no mention of mental or spiritual causes. But the Arch-Vicar goes on to say that from the very beginning of the Industrial Revolution men became "so overweeningly bumptious by the miracles of their own technology" that they soon lost all sense of reality. It is a fact of history, he lectures Dr. Poole, that "at a certain epoch, the overwhelming majority of human beings accepted beliefs and adopted courses of action that could not possibly result in anything but universal suffering, general degradation and wholesale destruction." The nub of Huxley's argument is contained in the statement made a little farther along by the Narrator: in the morning when the sun rises, "our ape wakes up once more to his own self and the freedom of his personal will—to yet another day of trick playing or, *if he chooses,* to the beginning of self-knowledge." [31] Thus, neither

[30] *My Life and Thought* (London, 1933), p. 176.
[31] *Ape and Essence,* pp. 121–28, 154–55. Italics mine.

machines nor over-population, nor yet Belial, are the real villains of the piece, but rather man himself who *chose,* by ignoring his "essence," to go the way of destruction.

None of the apocalyptists deny that cultural factors operate as secondary causes. One calls to mind the long discourse on "Oligarchical Collectivism" in Orwell's *1984* in which "Emmanuel Goldstein" explains the world's dilemma in terms of the technological revolution and a sort of class struggle in reverse; Ortega's harangue on population and education; Schweitzer's and Jaspers's observations on the Industrial Revolution which they think has developed too far, entailing the "over-organization" of public life and the emasculation of spiritual life; Brunner's chapter on "Technics" in his *Christianity and Civilization.* The machine, we are told, has taken on a "demonic autonomy" in our times. Technology greatly exaggerates the power of evil, exposes western man to almost insuperable temptations, or, as Toynbee would say, confronts him with a challenge such as his predecessors never had to face. In other words, the dragon's teeth, once sown, inevitably produce their crop of armed warriors and bloodshed.

But it should never be forgotten that it was Cadmus who took it into his head to sow the dragon's teeth.[32] This is precisely the point that most of the apocalyptists make. The issue, they say, was decided in man's mind before it ever reached the level of institutional reality. The menace to civilization comes from within rather than from without, comes, as Schweitzer says, from the realm of philosophical ideas under whose influence every age stands or falls.

Neo-orthodox theology says so in no uncertain terms. Brunner, for instance, contemptuously dismisses the theory that would lay society's ills to its failure (as yet) to adapt itself to technological progress. "It is not technics which has created the modern man," says Brunner, "but it is the modern man who has created technics." "The hypertrophy of tech-

---

[32] The metaphor is not exact, for in the legend Cadmus did so on the instructions of the goddess Athena.

nical interest, resulting in a hyper-dynamism of technical
evolution, is the necessary consequence of man's abandon-
ment to the world of things, which follows his emancipation
from God." [33] One is almost tempted to say that for Brunner
the fall of man began not in Eden, but in the seventeenth
century or at the Renaissance.

Berdyaev and Tillich interpret recent history dialectically,
but their dialectic also presupposes human freedom and
decision. Berdyaev, especially, goes into raptures over the
creative powers of man. He will have nothing to do with the
traditional theodicy which would subject man to divine
providence; he appears to have even less use for any crude
theory of cultural or economic determinism. Man is free, as
Tillich would say, to contradict as well as to realize "meaning" in history. Now that is precisely what happened at the
Renaissance. Man chose to tear himself from his religious
center to which all life had been directed during the Middle
Ages, and this "humanism" ended up in the nineteenth century, as one could have predicted it would end up, in its
dialectical opposite, *i.e.,* in "dehumanization" and soulless
collectivism.[34]

Jaspers and Schweitzer, Koestler and Joad say the same
thing in only slightly different terms. Jaspers attributes the
present crisis, at least in part, to the despiritualization of the
world by the philosophers who for centuries whittled away
at the idea of a transcendental Creator existing in as well as
apart from the world he created. As a result of this operation
"we feel the unprecedented vacancy of existence." [35]
Schweitzer has literally no mercy on the philosophers. He
praises the "Illuminati" of the eighteenth century for combining an attitude of "world-affirmation" with ethical absolutes. But he thinks that in the next century philosophy
renounced its duty, ceased to think "elementally," became
engrossed in purely technical problems to such an extent that

[33] *Christianity and Civilisation,* II, 4–5.
[34] See Berdyaev, "The End of the Renaissance," in *The End of our Time.*
[35] *Man in the Modern Age,* p. 21.

it could no longer supply the people with a meaningful philosophy of life. Joad, who might be called an objective idealist, declares that "decadence" became inevitable once the philosophers, and modern people in general, had agreed to "drop the object," *i.e.,* ceased to believe in an objective world of values independent of man. Whenever this occurs in history men become puffed up with pride and invite the disaster that befell the Titans in their war with the gods. Though lacking Joad's religious conviction, Koestler comes to much the same conclusion when he makes his mouthpiece observe that "the reason why Europe is going to the dogs is of course that it has accepted the finality of personal death." "This loss of cosmic consciousness . . . had led to the adoration of the new Baal: Society," [36] which demands the sacrifice of individualism and totalitarian war.

Thus, the apocalyptists repudiate the eighteenth-century "liberal" and Marxist interpretations of history. Europe's plight is said to be fundamentally due, neither to a failure of institutions nor to a temporary cultural lag, but to what men have chosen to think about themselves and the universe. ". . . It is in the spirit, and more especially on the confines of metaphysics and religion, that everything is really decided." [37] What does this portend for the future? Prognosis logically follows diagnosis, and to the apocalyptic prognosis we now turn in the next and final section.

IV

The apocalyptists are not so united on prognosis as on diagnosis. On the contrary, they display a wide variety of attitudes toward the future, attitudes ranging all the way from tempered optimism at one pole to extreme pessimism at the other. But the majority are pessimistic, at least by comparison with the "Utopian mentality" of the eighteenth

---

[36] *The Age of Longing,* p. 136. In the metaphor of the canal lock in *Darkness at Noon,* Koestler, to be sure, offers a more purely cultural analysis of the West's crisis.

[37] Paulus Lenz-Médoc, "The Death of God," in *Satan,* p. 470.

and nineteenth centuries. One cannot imagine any of them sharing the vision of Walter Mehring's father who, according to the son, "had a blind religious faith in the enlightenment of the human species," who thought that "world fraternity and the individual's right of self-determination would be won by the machine—*deus ex machina*," who "was convinced that at the stroke of midnight on the New Year's Eve that marked the transition from the nineteenth to the twentieth century, the hour of intellectual liberation for the world had also struck." "Loyal disciple of the Enlightenment," the father could never have guessed that some day the son would be reading books from his library "while all around culture came crashing down and the West rolled headlong toward the finale of « Götterdämmerung » ." [38]

Let us consider first the attitudes at the two polar extremes. At one end stand the men who come closest to the elder Mehring's vision, men like Bertrand Russell and Julian Huxley who, to quote the title of Russell's most recent book, have "new hopes for a changing world." These thinkers are apocalyptic-minded only in the sense that they recognize the gravity of the present crisis. But the crisis can be surmounted, as so many crises in the past have been surmounted, by human intelligence and faith in the *possibility* of progress, by international institutions, by compensating (Huxley) for Western civilization's over-emphasis on the material side of things. Even if a third world war does break out, Russell expostulates, "it will not be the end of the world; it will be a long illness, but not death, and it will be our duty, through whatever darkness and sorrow, to keep hope alive and to bend our thoughts, in spite of present misery, upon the future of which that misery is perhaps only the labor pangs." [39]

The other extreme contrasts sharply with this not unhopeful attitude. It is the "death-wish": a completely hopeless vision of the future, the desire therefore to destroy or to let

[38] Walter Mehring, *The Last Library. The Autobiography of a Culture* (Indianapolis and New York, 1951), p. 14, 21, 30–31.

[39] *New Hopes for a Changing World* (New York, 1951), p. 144. See also Julian Huxley, "A Re-definition of 'Progress,'" in *Reflections on our Age*, pp. 327–47.

civilization be destroyed without raising a finger to defend it. "The trouble is," observes the American colonel in *The Age of Longing*, "you can't save anybody who has no wish to be saved." "Do you think a whole continent can somehow lose the will to live? . . . You know, I think I am going to read Freud, to find out about this death-bug." [40] Jaspers had already detected the arrival of the death-bug (he called it the "dread of life") in the 'thirties, and Russell himself professes to see it at work in the 'fifties. There is a part of our nature, he says, that actually enjoys the prevailing mood of "impotent perplexity" — "and so we have no firm will to avert misfortune, and there is a deep division in our souls between the sane and insane parts." [41] It would require a whole book to document the death-wish in recent apocalyptic literature. I would not know how better to characterize Spengler's thesis that each culture has "its own death" as well as life, and that recent events are "the prelude of a future . . . with which the history of West-European mankind will be definitely *closed*." [42] How else but in terms of the death-wish can one interpret Bloy's joy at the coming of "the Cossacks and the Holy Ghost," or Cyril Connolly's (also the existentialists') endless prattle about "Angst," from which he cannot rouse himself, and which has its historical counterpart in world neurosis and decadence. [43] Writers like Auden and Koestler fill their books with people who live in fear and trembling and who, like the "Fearless Sufferers" in *The Age of Longing*, expect only the worst. Even the great H. G. Wells was bitten by the death-bug toward the end of his life. [44] These are but a few examples of an essentially nihilistic vision of the future

[40] P. 130.
[41] *New Hopes for a Changing World*, p. 3.
[42] *The Decline of the West* (London, 1934), I, 38.
[43] Léon Bloy, *Au Seuil de l'Apocalypse* (Paris, 1916), p. 351; Palinurus (Cyril Connolly), *The Unquiet Grave*, pp. 23, 33, 92–3, and *passim*.
[44] "The writer sees the world as a jaded world devoid of recuperative powers. In the past he has liked to think that Man could pull out of his entanglements and start a new creative phase of human living. In the face of our universal inadequacy, that optimism has given place to a stoical cynicism" (*Mind at the End of its Tether*, p. 30).

which has been steadily gaining ground ever since the events of 1914–18.

The majority of the apocalyptists take ground somewhere between these two extremes. On the whole, their prognosis is more pessimistic than optimistic. They set limits to what men can accomplish in historical "time." They are not very sanguine about the immediate future. While refusing to make forecasts, they describe, often in lurid detail, what *might* happen to the West at almost any moment, in 195–, 1984, or by 2108. The West *might* commit harakiri— Gheorghiu's novel, for instance ends up with the world once more at war and the barbarians knocking at the gates. In *Ape and Essence* the war has been fought, Europe and America are in ruins, and for a long time to come there is hope only for a few resolute individuals to escape the clutches of Belial. War or no war, the West *might* "advance to insecthood" (Joad) after the manner of the state of Oceania in Orwell's fantastic tale. It *might* plunge into a "new middle ages" (Berdyaev) in which the powers of not-being will vie with Being for the mastery. All this could happen, yet it need not happen—so runs the majority opinion. What man chose to take away he can restore, though he may need to call for, and receive, assistance from the higher powers. "We all get precisely what we ask for," says Huxley's Narrator,[45] and he speaks of the future as well as the past.

The thing that ultimately prevents the apocalyptists from taking a rosy view of the future—the really new thing in their philosophy of history, I might add—is their conception of "time." Implicit in most of the thought discussed in this paper, and fully explicit in theological and religious thought, is an eschatological conception of time akin to that of the *Revelation of John.* The "modernist" theology still so much in vogue at the turn of the century had asserted that God's "immanence" in the universe guaranteed the gradual raising of the human level and humanity's eventual "ascent toward

[45] *Ape and Essence,* p. 39.

the ideal of universal brotherhood." [46] Soured by the experience of the twentieth century, the apocalyptists, however, deny that the Kingdom of God can be realized except perhaps fragmentarily and temporarily, in the temporal world. "Is Time perhaps something which cannot possibly have its meaning within itself"? To this question, a key question for the apocalyptists, the German theologian Karl Heim answers categorically: "It lies simply in the nature of Time that everything which enters into the Time-form will, after a short period of blossoming, become withered, obsolete, rusty, consumed, exhausted." [47] Dean Inge, Karl Barth, Paul Althaus, and others take exception to Heim's "realistic" eschatology, but they agree with him that Truth is suprahistorical and that the full meaning of history is beyond history, beyond "time." On this view, history—future history as well as past history—becomes tragedy. Berdyaev said so in his first important essay on history, published in 1923: "The perfect state is impossible within history itself . . . Man's historical experience has been one of steady failure, and there are no grounds for supposing that it will ever be anything else . . . The significance of history is in terms of the antithetical principles, in their tragic conflict and decisive clash at last." [48] At the last, Berdyaev prophesies in his autobiography, the Lamb will triumph over the Beast, and the Beast will be shackled, not to eternity but to time—"for hell is that which remains in time." [49] The Oxford Conference of 1937, which brought together Christian theologians from all lands, echoed the Russian's double refrain of a kingdom that is not of this world, and of history as an unresolved struggle between Two Cities. The Lutheran theologian H. D. Wendland told the Conference that "each advance in man's rule of the world brings with it a fresh form of the demonic," and that the complete cancellation of the contrast between secu-

[46] See, for instance, R. J. Campbell, *The New Theology* (London, 1907), p. 63 and *passim.*
[47] *The New Divine Order,* pp. 61–2, 74.
[48] *The Meaning of History,* pp. 197–98, 204.
[49] *Dream and Reality,* p. 298.

lar and sacred history could come only at the end of time. The Catholic Christopher Dawson declared that the conflict between the Two Cities was as old as humanity "and must endure to the end of time." [50] It would be pointless to multiply further examples, except to demonstrate that this conception of "time" is by no means peculiar to the theologians. It is certainly implied, for instance, in the historian Toynbee's conviction that "man is born unto trouble," that suffering is in fact the prerequisite for "learning" and the spiritual advancement of the race. He therefore prophesies "a continuance of toil and trouble for as long as we can peer ahead into our future." [51]

Despite their conception of "time" the apocalyptists (except, of course, those bitten by the death-bug) do not, however, despair altogether of western civilization. "Fragmentary," if not complete "actualization" of the Kingdom is always a possibility in history, and no man is excused from laboring in the fields because he knows that until the "end" the tares will continue to grow together with the wheat. Admittedly, the times are bad, so bad that Joad (and others) think that perhaps man cannot advance "except help be given to him from outside." [52] Most would agree, moreover, with Schweitzer that because the restoration of civilization depends so much on the individual personality, the odds against it are greater than in any previous period of decadence. Yet David did defeat Goliath, and Toynbee tells us how the odds can be upset. He lists three means: in politics, work toward world-government; in economics, strike a compromise between socialism and free enterprise; "in the life of the spirit, put the secular superstructure back into religious foundations." [53] On the whole, the apocalyptists

[50] *The Kingdom of God and History,* pp. 154, 162, 216.
[51] "Can we Settle with Russia?" in *New York Times Magazine,* Dec. 2, 1951. See also his essay, "Christianity and Civilization," in *Civilization on Trial* (New York, 1948).
[52] *Decadence,* p. 419.
[53] "Does History repeat itself?", in *Civilization on Trial,* p. 39.

tend to minimize the institutional means, or perhaps one should say that they regard them as incomparably less important than Toynbee's third means. Dean Inge, in one of his latest books, reviews recent apocalyptic literature and rightly observes that it pins its hopes for the future primarily upon a change in the human heart and mind.[54] Inge does not mention Jaspers's *Man in the Modern Age,* but this book summarizes about as well as any the common conviction. "The most admirable institutions," "the most effective technique," says Jaspers, "can be used in conflicting ways. They are of no avail unless individual human beings fulfil them with an effective and valuable reality. What actually happens, therefore, cannot be modified by an improvement in expertise, but is exclusively decided by the being of man. Decisive is man's inward attitude. . . ."[55] In Jaspers's view individuals must somehow will to rise to a knowledge of their being and thus free themselves from the "dominion of apparatus." Less vague than this "existence philosophy" but of the same order of thinking, is Schweitzer's plea for the reunion of knowledge, power and ethics; Aldous Huxley's and Joad's "revival of mysticism"; Koestler's "cosmic loyalty with a doctrine acceptable to twentieth century man" which would act as a brake on expediency, but which unhappily cannot be manufactured in a laboratory.[56] Brunner states the explicitly religious point of view in his Gifford lectures of 1947–48. The real hope for a tolerable future, he declares, rests neither in "civilization" as such (science, technology, organization), nor in the "illusion" of universal progress, but in man's reorientation toward the invisible world which is "beyond" and "above" this visible world. This is a paradox: we can humanize life in this world "only when we know that it is not our primary but only our secondary task . . . In all times of Christian history it was those Christian men and

[54] *The End of an Age* (London, 1948), Preface and first chapter.
[55] *Man in the Modern Age,* p. 185.
[56] See Julien Delattre's remarks in *The Age of Longing,* p. 137.

groups of men who did not believe in progress who did the most to move the world in real progress." [57]

Thus, the majority of the apocalyptists try to steer a middle course between extreme pessimism and extreme optimism. But the balance, as I have suggested, tips towards pessimism—how else can we interpret their conception of "time," their lack of confidence in human nature and institutions and, in some instances, their death-wish? Their philosophy of history might be called the philosophy of the jagged line, to distinguish it from the philosophy of linear progress—the jagged line which records the ceaseless dialectic of the "divine" and "demonic" in history. There is considerable wisdom in this philosophy. The radically existential situation in which Europeans have been living for two generations has stimulated these men to discover historical insights which were perhaps not possible in either the eighteenth or nineteenth centuries; insights which can conceivably be utilized to construct a more balanced, if more sober, civilization. But these insights are often weighed down by a mood heavy with melancholy and world-weariness. If man can hope to "salt" and "leaven" the world, he should also be "sober in his expectation for and from this temporal world. He knows that it cannot transcend its limits of death and sin." [58] This statement might have come from the *Revelation of John*. In reality it comes from a twentieth-century theologian who, having witnessed terrible events, senses the approach of the four horsemen of the apocalypse and pins his hopes for the future upon another world.

[57] *Christianity and Civilisation*, II, 141.
[58] *Ibid.*, 142.

7.

The "Theology of Crisis"

Gustav Krüger

EDITORIAL NOTE: *The twentieth-century apocalyptic vision is no-where more vividly conveyed than in the crisis theology of Karl Barth and his school. Although Barth himself has mellowed some-what in the years since he astonished the world with his commentary on* Romans *and his sermons on the* Word of God and the Word of Man, *the movement he launched during the first World War altered the whole course of theological thinking in the interwar years and constitutes one of the principal sources of contemporary religious existentialism. Gustav Krüger was a prominent German church his-torian, a generation older than Barth, who gives us in the following article, drawn from lectures delivered at Union Theological Seminary in New York in 1926, an absorbing account not only of the main features of the new theology in its early years but also of its spiritual roots in the experiences of European man during the first World War. The article supplies, in addition, valuable insight into the leading theological trends of the nineteenth century, here labelled "modern theology," which Barth and his followers implacably opposed. Pro-fessor Krüger's concluding remarks, a critique of the Barthians from the point of view of this same "modern theology," have been omitted.*

I

SOME FORTY YEARS AGO I ATTENDED THE LECTURES OF A YOUNG Giessen professor whose growing reputation was attracting scores of young men of different countries and tongues to the little German university on the borders of the Lahn, until

135

then almost unknown in theological circles. The professor was Adolf Harnack, whom I am proud to call my teacher. During the very months I spent at Giessen he was putting the last touches to the great work which has since established his world-wide fame, the "Dogmengeschichte." In that book the origin and development of early Christian doctrine, which had long been the object of critical study on the part of eminent scholars, was delineated in such masterly fashion that further progress hardly seemed possible. But what especially attracted us in this work as well as in Harnack's whole attitude, was the fact that he was no mere antiquary, no anatomist, so to speak, dissecting a corpse, but on the contrary was keenly aware of the fact that the Christian Dogma of which he wrote was a living organism. He held it to be the duty not only of the historian, but also of the theologian, to free that organism of the dross which had adhered to it and which weighed so heavily on the minds of earnest Christians. It was the task of the scholar to show that certain doctrines, by means of which the Church of former days had endeavored to interpret the divine mysteries to its adherents, had in fact come into existence at a definite period, within a definite horizon, and out of a definite world-view, none of which had the least resemblance to our own. And that demonstration would make it impossible to consider such dogmas and formulas, themselves the product of history and therefore, like all historic things, transitory, as binding upon Christian thought under the wholly altered conditions of our day. It was indeed a step towards freedom. But it will be readily understood that in those circles which clung to the old interpretation of dogma, regarding its very letter as holy, Harnack's attitude was thought to be subversive, if not revolutionary, and that among such people he speedily became the best hated man in existence. In fact, when shortly afterwards he was called to Berlin, the dictum went forth that now there had been established at the capital that seat of Satan which St. John saw erected at Pergamos.

In following this path Harnack thought of himself only as

the disciple of a greater man, his teacher Albrecht Ritschl. That eminent theologian made it his life work to introduce a conception of the Christian religion which should be free, on the one hand, from the domination of the forms with which human hands had enveloped it and, on the other, from that attenuation to which the scriptural revelation had been subjected by philosophical speculation and rationalistic interpretation. Between the Scylla and Charybdis of orthodox theology on the one side and liberal theology on the other, Ritschl sought to point a new way, taking as his guides Kant with regard to form and Luther with regard to matter. His undertaking was so simple, while its aim and method were so convincing, that he could not fail to succeed. In fact, the ablest theologians at the German universities, and in their train the whole rising generation, came completely under the influence of his teaching. The "School of Ritschl" was everywhere talked of, and even in the United States that school exerted no little influence upon the development of theological science.

By a peculiar, though by no means fortuitous coincidence, the birth and propagation of this Ritschlian theology were contemporaneous with the rise of our new German Empire. Under the clear-headed leadership of a statesman of rare genius, the Germans of that day undertook to erect a state which should hold its own in the broad and rapid stream of modern life, freed from the ballast of antiquated tradition, and sustained by the enthusiasm of millions, who had no intention of continuing to be merely a people of "poets and thinkers," but meant to create for themselves, in the concert of Europe and perhaps of the world, that place which had hitherto been denied them. In one sense it may be affirmed that what Bismarck did for the German nation Ritschl achieved for German theology. And in this connection it is important to note how the idea of "Beruf" (vocation), in its bearing upon Christian ethics, was interpreted after the model of the *prefectio christiana* expounded in Melanchthon's defence of the Augsburg Confession. That idea was developed principally by Ritschl's most prominent successor, Wilhelm Herrmann of Marburg. The strong insistence on the moral and religious value of the citizen's calling, when practised in the fear of God and love of man; on the association with the "world" in all its aspects, which such a calling not merely permits but actually demands; on the leavening of civil life with a religion untrammeled by idle speculation about the Whence and the Whither, by metaphysics and eschatology; on the duty of taking one's stand squarely and courageously in the domain of reality—all this exercised a peculiar fascination upon a generation which felt itself called to coöperate in the establishment of a state consecrated to the interests of modern civilization. To reconcile religion and culture, the Ritschlian theology seemed to be exactly what was needed. I may refer once more to Harnack, who in his "Wesen des Christentums" (in the English translation, "What is Christianity?") by means of a survey of the historical development, addressed to laymen as well as students of theology, gave definite expression to this conception of the Christian religious life.

It cannot be denied that, from the first, this theory of Christianity was not free from the reproach of rationalism. Its antagonists—and it had some very fierce antagonists— soon discovered in it a recrudescence of the tendencies which had characterized the Enlightenment of the eighteenth century. Kant was a suspicious witness for the defence, and Ritschl's representation of Luther seemed to them a distortion. They lost no time in pointing out that Ritschl's theology came dangerously near to the positivism of August Comte, which especially disclaims any concern with religion. And finally, by renouncing every attempt to find a metaphyical basis for religion, Ritschl could not escape the charge that, like Ludwig Feuerbach, he had failed to avoid the danger of illusionism. All this seemed borne out by the fact that, however severely the Ritschlians, both master and pupils, might criticize Schleiermacher, they nevertheless held fast to that great German idealist, as the pioneer of modern theology, and consequently to his anthropocentric conception of the Christian faith.

These censures multiplied and became more pointed when the original Ritschlian theology was modified at the hands of the younger generation of Ritschlians (to which I myself belong), under the influence of the new point of view engendered by the study of the history of religions. That point of view resulted in what, before the war, we were accustomed to speak of briefly as "modern theology." This latter takes its stand on "historicism," that is, on what one of our leaders, the too-early deceased Ernst Troeltsch, defined as "the systematic historicizing of all our thoughts about man, his culture, and his values," a process which was begun by the Enlightenment and continued and to a certain extent completed by the scientific labors of the nineteenth century. In the course of time, this historicism involved Christianity together with the source of its revelation, the Bible—this last particularly, and to a far greater degree than Ritschl himself would have approved. Incidentally it had the effect of giving a merely relative value to the theological statements concerning Christianity and the Bible, and thus increasing those dangers to which I have just alluded. But nothing could check its triumphant march, and wide theological circles were forced to submit to it with what grace they could. From the standpoint of the Protestantism which clings to revelation, this victorious movement was divesting Christianity of its supernatural character. Perhaps those who had spoken of Satan's seat were right. Meanwhile every theological faculty had set up such a seat of Satan; for somehow or other all the faculties had capitulated to historicism, whether their members leaned to modern or to moderno-positive, to pietistic or to orthodox views.

Then came the war, and with it a reaction. Students of theology, and those who still looked forward to that vocation, were summoned to the field of battle. They fought and bled for honor, home, and country. And then they came back, with hearts stirred with longing, and with a veritable hunger for religion. They had experienced the infinite, the unspeakable; the heights of enthusiasm and the depths of dejection, the tremendous and the trivial, the sublime and the hideous, things to confirm their faith and things to provoke despair. Their souls were alive with a new impulse to deliver mankind from the demon of hatred. Consciously or unconsciously, they recoiled from that mechanical civilization whose horrible excrescences they had constantly witnessed during the dolorous years of the war, and to whose disastrous effects they had themselves been forced to contribute. Had they really gone to war for such a civilization? and in the name of religion? Could one preach war in Christ's name?—this war, that had achieved nothing but destruction and devastation, that had wrought the ruin of real culture, of all civilization worth the name, and had torn to shreds the "bands of pious awe" in both morality and religion? The stock phrases, the "suicide of Europe," the "decay of the West," which were given a scientific rendering in that work of Oswald Spengler so eagerly read all over Germany, were not without their effect on our young students of theology.

Like Faust, they "longed for revelation." And now, when they returned to the university and sat at the feet of their theological teachers, they were confronted with this historicism, which we in happier days had regarded as the very framework of theology, the meat and drink of science by which a whole generation had been kept alive. Instead of reviving, this historicism repelled them; instead of refreshing, it chilled them. That purely relative appraisement of every event in history which went hand in hand with it was as dust to souls thirsting for the absolute. What we older men had called science—the critical analysis of the books of the Old and New Testaments, the intensive study of the past of Church and doctrine, the systematic elaboration of the faith in dogmatics and ethics—all this seemed only to lead away from the one thing needful. And the attempt to reconcile modern civilization with living religion was of all things the most futile.

This might conceivably have happened without the war, but the decisive factor was certainly the war. Involuntarily we turn our eyes to the seventeenth century, the period of transition from orthodoxy to pietism. When the storm of the Thirty-years War was over and quiet once more reigned in the German provinces, then too it became apparent that the younger generation had wearied of confessional strife; that the bickerings of orthodox churchmen had lost their attraction; and that students were disinclined to seek instruction in long-winded exegetical and polemical lectures which apparently had nothing to offer the inner man. It is most illuminating to trace the development from the days of bitter controversy between Lutherans and Calvinists—as well as among the Lutherans themselves—down to Philipp Jacob Spener and August Hermann Francke, a development which led to a complete reversal in the conception of theological science and theological study. What then occupied decades is now struggling for accomplishment in the course of a few years. And no wonder, in an age that has witnessed a world war; a war in which, in an incredibly short time, more battles and more fighting occurred than in all previous wars combined.

Like Spener and the great Pietist leaders, our young theologians aimed to take as their point of departure the conception of Christianity held by the Protestant reformers. Of course they were dealing with a different antagonist. For they were no longer confronted by the Old-Lutheran or Old-Reformed orthodoxy. It was the exact opposite of that orthodoxy, the Enlightenment, which seemed to block their way. In the Enlightenment, or the palpable consequences of it down to the present day, they perceived the root of all evil. Because for it man is the measure of all things, and religion is a mere function of the human soul, hence something belonging to this world and purely subjective. That view is opposed by the "faith" of the biblical and Protestant tradition, faith in something given, objective, real—faith in the Word, the Word of God, who is above everything human and created; the Word that speaks to us out of the sacred documents of Christianity; the Word of which Luther affirmed that it is the *principium primum* and the source and cause of all things. Here God the supramundane, not man the intramundane, is the measure of all things. Nor should we speak of "God *and* man," in the sense of something intermediate between the two, but only of "God, *not* man." And our duty is to surrender ourselves enthusiastically to this God, before whom man, his culture, and his values are as nothing.

II

Before attempting to enlarge on these statements, I should like to mention a personal experience. It was in the autumn of 1920, at the Wartburg. A large company of religious-minded persons was assembled to listen to a lecture by a young clergyman, whose name, then almost unknown, has since become familiar to all groups of German theologians— Friedrich Gogarten. He spoke, in connection with the book of Spengler to which I have already alluded, on the "Crisis in our Culture," making the central point of his discussion the question whether religion is the soul or the crisis of that culture. After what I have said about this movement, the answer he gave will perhaps be obvious. But the older generation among his hearers—myself included—were not at the time quite clear on the subject. We separated with the feeling that we had heard something important, without being able to give an exact account of it. The five years which have since elapsed have made things more clear, and today we are confronted only with the question whether or not we can endorse the conclusion then expressed. But this very question is, under existing conditions, one which searches heart and reins, and on its answer principally depends, if I am not mistaken, the future development of theology in Germany. We have reached the point where we speak without further definition of a "Theology of Crisis." What we mean by it I will now endeavor to explain.

The views expressed by Gogarten in that lecture at the Wartburg owed their origin to the stimulus he had himself received from Karl Barth and the latter's great book on Paul's Epistle to the Romans. Barth is a Swiss, born at Basel in 1886, the son of a Calvinist minister who afterwards became professor of Theology at Bern. He studied in Bern, but principally in Tübingen and Berlin, and was strongly influenced by both Harnack and Herrmann, the very theologians with whom he later most disagreed. For ten years he was pastor in a little town in the canton of Aargau. In 1921 he was appointed professor of Reformed Theology at Göttingen, and since last autumn he has been teaching at Münster, in Westphalia. The book by which he is best known was written during his pastorate. In spite of its size, it has gone through several editions, and today it is among the most widely circulated and, what is more, most widely read theological works.

It is a commentary on the Epistle to the Romans; not after the pattern of these learned works bestowed upon us by the historico-critical period of theological science, but a discussion of the profoundest questions of revealed religion, based on St. Paul and with continuous elucidation of the latter's thought, and it may well be compared to the great works of the Reformers on the same subject. Barth approached his sublime theme in the same spirit as Luther. Like Luther, he did not mean to stay on the surface, but was resolved to penetrate "to the kernel of the nut, to the marrow of the bone and the wheat." We may leave to one side the question whether his interpretation of Paul is always correct. It might be assumed that something of his own spirit would inevitably creep in. What we are concerned to point out in the present connection is the great emphasis he lays upon the paradoxical nature of religion and of faith in particular as the organ of religion. Here Barth shows himself to be in agreement with the great Danish writer, Kierkegaard (died 1855), whose utterances he often quotes. Though undoubtedly influenced by Kierkegaard, he was originally of kindred spirit. You know the old phrase, *credo quia absurdum*. Employed in this way, it is merely the traditional abbreviation of the terse sentences of Tertullian: "The Son of God was crucified: I am not ashamed of it, precisely because it is something to be ashamed of. The Son of God died: that is perfectly credible, because it is absurd. He was buried and rose from the dead: that is certain, because it is impossible." In this "because" in place of the rational "although" lies that which, according to Barth also, is the very essence of religion. In God, in the knowledge of God, in man's relation to God—everywhere, this paradoxical nature of religion is apparent. Thus Barth can write: "Christ is himself the paradox. He is *the* possibility which has all the tokens of impossibility." Or again: "The possibility of belief can be comprehended only as impossibility." And perhaps his strongest statement: "Our experience is that which is not our experience; our religion consists in the suspension of our religion."

If we are not impatiently to brush aside these and similar statements—and they might be multiplied a hundredfold—as absurd or at best a mere dialectical playing with words, we must remember that for the men of highest rank in the domain of religion, for Paul, Augustine, Luther, and Calvin, the paradoxical, that is, that which conflicts with the apparent, was the very life-principle of religion. Religion is in fact the escapement in the clock or, to use Barth's words, the "great disturbance" in life, which as such must permeate all things. If it fails to do that, "if God does not alone remain—God, the unknown, the hidden, in his eternal power and deity the *only* strength of the strong—then all things have become as sounding brass and a tinkling cymbal." Barth thinks that he can explain Paul—and, one may add, Luther—best by constantly pointing away from God as revealed (*Deus revelatus*) to God as hidden (*Deus absconditus*); in fact, by seeing precisely in the revelation of God in Jesus Christ—another paradox—the complete concealment and disguise of God. For does not God become in Jesus Christ a genuine secret (μυστήριον, as Paul says), guarded from all inquisitiveness.

and religious impertinence? It is almost as if Barth dreaded the profanation of the God revealed through the cross of Christ, which, in the words of the apostle, was unto the Jews a stumbling-block and unto the Greeks foolishness.

If we bear all this in mind, we shall understand better why Gogarten, in answering his own question, could only say: Religion is not the soul of culture; it is the *crisis,* that is, the doom, of culture. Religion is anything but what the Enlightenment, idealism, and modern liberal Protestantism think it is, namely, the crown and fulfillment of true humanity. On the contrary, it is "the point at which not man's health, but his sickness (that is, sin, the thing which separates us from God) becomes manifest; where not the harmony, but the discord of all things begins to sound; not where culture is established, but rather where, together with its partner barbarism, it is most emphatically called in question." In conscious opposition to all who seek to bring harmony into the field of religion, Barth writes: "To be a religious man is to be a torn, a discordant, a restless man. Only he can be at one with himself in whom the great question of his oneness with God has not yet been awakened." He would actually "refrain from recommending religion as something desirable, interesting, or enriching, to innocent people who in their heart of hearts desire only to be at rest." With great frankness he expresses the opinion that "whoever honestly prizes his individual peace and quiet, or a well-tempered humanity, or the continuity of human culture, should, with Lessing, Kant, and Goethe, defend himself with all his might against the invasions of religion." To be sure, he must not flatter himself that he can keep religion out, for the "religious possibility" resides too deep in man for him to escape it entirely. "Western culture is certainly not the power to steel him against that possibility." On the other hand, culture— whether science, art, morality, or even religion itself, in its every-day sense—never leads to the "impossible" possibility of God. These may lead to all sorts of surrogates, for instance to the Church, and may indeed, as we shall see later, have their own uses, but to genuine religion they do not lead. "The reality of religion is man's horror of himself." When once a man has digested the truth of these words, he will be immediately convinced that culture is doomed, regardless of the degree of culture he may himself have attained, and no matter how in every-day life he is affected by it, whether positively or negatively, with acquiescence or with protest. Nor is there any need of a "last judgment" or (as Barth puts it) of a "brilliant or terrible finale," and "end of the world" through an historical telluric or cosmic catastrophe. Judgment is being passed at every moment. That "horror" consists in the recognition of the fact that at every moment we stand on the confines of all time, begetting in the truly pious the bold resolve to recognize and apprehend in the end (of the human) the beginning (of the divine). "Let man but tread his own path to the end, and he will stand before God."

When this revolution takes place within us, we reach an inward state utterly different from all that lies on *this side* of the "judgment." For between the temporal works of man and the eternal works of God, between this side and the other side, between culture and genuine religion, there is a radical difference. Yet that is not saying that life on this side is rendered impossible for us. Only we must bear in mind that, so long as we reckon values according to purely human standards, we are moving in a mental atmosphere which has nothing to do with religion. "Our consciousness of the distance which separates man with all his culture from God, does not involve our keeping the two absolutely apart. To be sure, if we humanize the divine in its relation to history and materialize it into some particular account of religion or salvation, God as such is sacrificed in the process. But when once we are clear about that, we perceive that every occurrence in the world of culture and history familiar to us derives content and meaning from the unknown God, and that every impression of revelation points to revelation itself." With this premise, and obviously following in the footsteps of Nietzsche, Barth can even defend the "uses of history." He holds that "seen in this higher light—the light which shines down from the divine upon the human—history speaks to life as its mistress (*historia vitae magistra*)," although "the value of God's communications remains unaffected by the course of human history."

This dialectical attitude towards religious problems enables Barth, as I have already hinted, to take a generous, or rather a tolerant position as regards the germs of genuine religion which may exist among Christians and non-Christians, in or outside the Church and the churches. He says somewhere, "We are ready to take our place cheerfully beside the Roman Catholic, the Orthodox Protestant, the Liberal, the adherent of the League of Nations, or anybody else, and to quiet him with the desired assurance, You are right—that is, with the disquieting proviso that you too are wrong."

These and similar ideas were elaborated by Barth in his remarkable commentary, not systematically—the subject did not allow that—but by combining them impressively with his exposition of Paul's thought, in lucid, animated, and at times even fascinating language. To the receptive reader his ideas are highly suggestive; and it is not for nothing that thousands and tens of thousands return to his book again and again. The critic, however, finds himself somewhat at a loss before it. Dialectics are very difficult to deal with. The arguments you were about to bring forward, your adversary always has disposed of in advance. And should you succeed in getting him into a corner, he will adroitly withdraw into the fortress of his paradoxes and from that coign of vantage laugh all attacks to scorn. Or else he may shrug his shoulders and deliberately refuse to answer.

Very properly my colleague in the chair of philosophy at Giessen, Professor Messer, concluded his summary of Barth's ideas, to which I am much indebted, with Barth's own words, "You are right—with the proviso that you too are wrong." I suggest that for the moment we content ourselves with this proviso, which Barth himself, following his paradoxical habit, has characterized as "disquieting."

III

But there is one question which we still have to face, and it is one which, in view of Barth's dialectics, seems more urgent than ever. That is the question, What is to become of theology with such an interpretation of religion as "the crisis of culture"?—of theology as a science, taught at the universities? This question Barth answered in a lecture to which he gave the title, "The Word of God the Subject of Theology." The lecture was delivered in 1922 to the same audience which two years earlier had listened to Gogarten, in a village church at the foot of the Elgersburg, another of the Thuringian castles, and the impression it then made is vividly before me even to-day. It has since appeared in print together with other treatises of his. The handy little volume, bearing the general title, "The Word of God and Theology," contains the quintessence of Barth's thought and would, in my opinion, well repay translation into English.

It is obvious that Barth could have no patience with the idea that the pursuit of historico-critical science, with which the theological faculties are mainly occupied nowadays, is the task of theology. I say, the task of theology; for Barth is far from wishing to hinder the occupation in itself. He is well aware that knowledge concerning the phenomenon of religion and the forms of its manifestation in history is indispensable to the historian, the psychologist, the philosopher, and therefore also to the theologian in so far as he is something of all these. But he cannot understand why such investigators should not be capable of acquiring and cultivating that knowledge by themselves, and without the assistance of theology. Or, he asks, is the so-called "religious sense" the private property of the historian or psychologist who happens to be also a theologian, so that the ordinary historian and psychologist is incapable of studying the documents of religion with the necessary devotion and expertness? If theology is to be merged in the science of religion, theologians have forfeited their right to any place in the universities. As a science, in the same sense as the other sciences, theology is merely a useless duplication of several disciplines belonging to other faculties. As theologians (such is Barth's thesis) it is our duty to speak of God even in the university. What for others is a mere note of interrogation somewhere in the background, a bare possibility, which they may recognize only as a "Grenzbegriff," as the impossible (note the paradox!), that theology must defend as the Answer. It must not speak with bated breath or whisper about God, but must speak aloud; not merely hint at him, but, being itself derived from him, must bear witness of him; not place him somewhere in the background, but, in defiance of all methodical presuppositions, must set him in the very forefront.

Yet we—the dialectician himself interposes—are men and as such cannot speak of God. For to speak of God, if it is to be taken seriously, would be to speak upon the basis of revelation and faith. The task of theology would be to declare that *God* becomes *man,* actually as the *Word of God.* For this "as the Word of God" is the only answer that is truly transcendental and for that very reason has the power to solve the riddle of God's immanence. Barth can think of three different paths which might conceivably lead to that answer, although he is certain that none of them will actually reach the goal: the dogmatic, the critical, and the dialectical. Orthodoxy chose the first, for which Barth does not blame her; indeed, he considers the powerful and vital supernaturalism which pervades the ecclesiastical creeds as preferable to modern broken-windedness. Yet he feels called upon to affirm that orthodoxy only succeeds in suppressing man's quest for God. The abrupt "There, believe that!" of the creeds accomplishes nothing. The second path was chosen by the mystics. In accordance with his fundamental ideas, Barth calls it "the critical path," because here man offers himself for judgment, in the endeavor to die as man, to surrender his

individuality, his personality, his selfconsciousness, to the
end that he may become a partaker of God. What renders
this path commendable, is the recognition that man really
does seek something he is not. Here God becomes man with
such energy that, so to speak, nothing is left of man. But
even so, one still cannot speak of God. For that *that* should
be God which would permeate a man while annihilating
him, is indeed, what the mystics and their followers *declare*,
but what no one is in a position to *demonstrate*, since along
that path we can get no farther than a negation. So there
remains the dialectical path, the path of Paul and the Reformation. This path Barth considers the best, because it
brings the strength of the dogmatic path, namely the positive
development of the idea of God, and that of the critical path,
namely the negation of the human, into relation with the
presupposition common to them both, the living truth, by
which alone affirmation and negation gain significance. That
God—the real God!—becomes man—actually man!—that
fact, following this path, is seen to be the vital thing, the
essential content of a genuine speaking of God. But the
dialectician knows well enough that on so narrow an edge
one cannot stand still, but must keep moving if he is to avoid
a fall. Above all, not even the dialectician can make himself
clear when called upon to speak, unless the desire for God is
already present in the person he seeks to convince. For what
he has to say is based on the asumption of that very truth
which he is striving to establish.

And so the conclusion of the whole matter is another paradox: "The Word of God is at once the necessary and the
impossible task of theology." It is necessary, because a return
to the lower levels, where you are nominally a theologian
but in reality nothing but a scientist, is as impossible to the
theologian as to take leave of theology altogether. But the
task is impossible, because only God himself can speak of
God. If therefore you say, "the task of theology is the Word of
God," you are simply proclaiming the defeat of all theology
and all theologians. So we must rest content with realizing

both facts: that we must and nevertheless cannot speak of God. And in so doing we shall give God the praise.

IV

I have presented these ideas at such length, firstly, because I think they merit it on their own account, and secondly, because an accurate acquaintance with them is required as a basis for our further considerations. At one point in his lecture Barth introduces an historical observation. He traces the pedigree which he claims for his theology. It ascends through Kierkegaard to Luther and Calvin, and on up to the apostle Paul and to the prophet Jeremiah, who, after he had been speaking of God for a quarter of a century, still felt compelled to exclaim, "Ah, Lord God! behold I cannot speak, for I am a child." And then Barth points out with special emphasis that the name of one theologian we might have expected is not included in the pedigree— Schleiermacher. "With all due respect to his genius, I consider Schleiermacher a poor teacher of theology, because he seems dangerously unaware of the fact that man as man is in need, in desperate need; unaware further of the fact that the whole fabric of religion, and not least of the Christian religion, shares in this need; unaware finally, that to speak of God is a totally different thing from speaking of man in somewhat lofty language." With these words war—uncompromising war—is declared against a point of view which was fundamental in scientific German theology, particularly socalled modern theology, during the nineteenth century, and which remains so to the present day. That point of view has its root in German idealism, that is, in the thought of the poets and thinkers of the classical period of German literature, for which the name of Schleiermacher has become, as it were, the symbol.

In so far as the thought of German idealism concerns the theologian, it can be summed up as a synthesis of religion and culture. Herder, towards the end of his life, expressed it in the fine formula, "to humanize Christianity and christianize humanity." This is the ideal which, under the influence of Herder, Goethe incorporated in the figure of Brother Humanus in "Die Geheimnisse," one of his profoundest poems, and which, so long as he lived, was never absent from his sublimest utterances on Christianity. It is the spirit of that humanistic Christianity which breathes throughout Fichte's wonderful sermon: "Guide to the Blessed Life." It is the conviction which inspired Schleiermacher when, in words of fiery enthusiasm, he called upon the educated among his countrymen to restore to religion the consideration they had been withholding. In earlier years we were taught that this idealistic conception of Christianity was directly descended from the Reformation. And it is certainly true that later German thought, especially of the classical period, cannot be imagined without the influence of the Reformation. But in reality idealism sprang from the Enlightenment. For it absorbed, as its indispensable premises, both the naturalism and the rationalism of the Enlightenment. And the supernaturalism and the irrationalism by which in turn idealism strove to overcome the Enlightenment, is not the same as that supernaturalism and irrationalism on which was founded the religious faith of the Reformers and on which historic Christianity was reared. It is true that idealism attempted to substitute a revealed religion for the natural religion born of the Enlightenment; but we must not forget that its revealed religion is something that originates in the inherent creative powers of the human soul. That being the case, not only is the idealistic conception of religion not derived from the faith of the Reformers, but it stands in direct opposition to it.

It is this truth that Barth and his associates are striving to disseminate. And in doing so, they direct their attacks especially against Schleiermacher, because in his great theological work he gave that systematic expression to the idealistic conception of religion and revelation which became authoritative for later generations. They attack him with a violence and pugnacity which does credit to their courage, although frequently lacking in the respect due to their antagonist. But we need not make too much of that. From the nature of such controversies, exaggerations and misunderstandings are inevitable. For them a great, a holy cause is at stake; they may be pardoned if they fail to spare the individual.

Their champion in this "new controversy over Schleiermacher" is Emil Brunner. Like Barth he is of Swiss birth, but he has remained in Switzerland, and for the past two years has been professor of systematic theology at the University of Zurich. The book which speedily placed him in the front rank of our younger systematic theologians bears the title: "Mysticism and the Word," with the subtitle: "The Contradiction between the Modern Interpretation of Religion and Christian Faith, as Illustrated by the Theology of Schleiermacher." On its title-page may be read a double motto; on the left a quotation from Goethe's Faust, "Gefühl ist alles; Name ist Schall und Rauch" (Feeling is everything, the name but empty sound and vapor); on the right a sentence of Luther's, *Verbum est principium rerum.* These quotations are well adapted to display the author's purpose. Schleiermacher's interpretation of religion is that of Faust, which is also that of modern theology. On the other hand, it stands in opposition to that of the Reformation and therefore to Christian belief. After what I have said about Barth, you will readily see why Brunner should select as a motto for the Christian belief of the Reformers "the Word"—the Word of God, the Word through which God reveals himself. Not quite so clear is his selection of the term "mysticism" for its antithesis. Brunner here deliberately takes issue with all those to whom mysticism is "nothing more and nothing less than the ultimate and most profound apprehension of religion as religion, the sublimation, as it were, of the religious in religion." For him—so runs his paradoxical antithesis— mysticism is "the most sublime form of the deification of nature, of heathenism, of the materialization of spirit." The justification for this startling assertion he finds in the close

relationship which, he thinks, exists between mysticism and
aestheticism. These two he calls twin sisters, their mother's
lap being what he is inclined to term "the musical world-
view." For "the primary element in music is feeling, bound-
less feeling, limited by no law, confined in no form, flowing
and surging like the ocean, immeasurable, mysterious, unconscious, and uncontrolled."

In this feeling the modern man "experiences" religion.
With pointed sentences Brunner shows how our modern
literature, in so far as it aims to be religious (and that is
largely the case), is dominated by this quest of "experience,"
and how theology endeavors to keep pace with it. The latter
"pours new wine into old bottles, or else it coins, out of this
new religious consciousness, new forms of expression and
seeks more adjustable, elastic, living symbols." The fact that
it seeks symbols and rejects definite ideas is characteristic
of this mysticism. "Compared with one's own original personal experience, belief which has a definite *what* as its object
—the discredited *fides quae creditur*—appears to the modern
pietist and theologian a mere petrifaction of that which once
had life." Yet the theologian's conscience is not entirely easy.
He vacillates between mysticism and faith, reinterpreting
and recasting the content of faith in terms of mystical experience. He is filled with secret longing for mysticism, but dare
not take the final step, and so contents himself with compromise. Meanwhile he has forgotten the "Word," the essential element of faith. Accordingly Brunner brings the accusation: "Mysticism works its most terrible havoc by destroying
the understanding of the Word; by substituting for the clear,
luminous revelation of God in the Word a 'musical revelation' born of intoxicated feeling. The Word is reduced to a
mere 'word,' a mere means of utterance, whereas it is actually
the creative spirit, the source of all spirit."

It is obvious that a theology marked by such exclusiveness
was bound to come into conflict with Schleiermacher's theology of harmony and synthesis. For did not Schleiermacher
insist that his philosophy and his theology (which he calls

dogmatics) were "determined not to contradict each other"? A general survey like this cannot undertake to show in detail how Brunner proceeds to prove that Schleiermacher's theology is anti-Christian. It will be sufficient to keep in view the fundamental problem, which in this case is: Reason and Revelation. It was no accident that Brunner selected that problem as the subject of his inaugural lecture upon taking up his professorship in Zurich. The lecture, which was the logical sequel to his book, was entitled, "Revelation as the Foundation and the Subject of Theology."

In his book Brunner had formally defined the task of theology as consisting in "ordered reflection on the origin, the meaning, and the connection of the truths in the maintenance of which faith consists." And he had repeatedly pointed out that, in direct opposition to mysticism, which lives on "the indefinite and indefinable," emphasis must be laid on reflection and its "daylight clarity." In the lecture this definition is set forth in more general terms. Recognizing, in the presence of his academic audience, the necessity of justifying theology as a science, Brunner begins by putting his finger on that which lies at the root of all scientific achievement. All science lives on the vitality of enquiry, on the intensity and depth of the problems it faces. All research originates in the consciousness that what we do not know is precisely what we desire and ought to know. And the deeper we bore, the nearer we come to the question of questions, namely, the questionableness of our knowledge. It is the mission of theology to keep alive within us the remembrance of that questionableness and to provoke the *reflection* it demands. This mission she has in common with philosophy, which latter, for the very reason that it takes for its problem the presupposition of every other science, namely the validity of knowledge, has always been regarded as the fundamental science. Theology is ready to travel the same road with philosophy for a considerable distance. In particular, like critical philosophy, she takes care to avoid all false leads out of the labyrinth such as are offered by metaphysics (after

the Aristotelian pattern) or by speculation (after the Neo-
Platonic fashion). She rejoices when philosophy agrees to
recognize morality as the foundation of all theory and the
consequent primacy of the practical reason over the theoretical reason. But there their roads part. There is one thing
which philosophy, though bound on principle to cast doubt
on all things, dare not do; it dare not lay hands on reason
itself. It will not and cannot attack the instrument with which
it operates. Theology, on the other hand, believes it possible
and necessary to discard that instrument. When boring down
to the deepest questions, a point is reached where even the
practical reason does not avail, because even the practical
reason knows only postulates. At that point one is confronted
by the question which concerns our very life, a question so
urgent that it turns into an accusation and the failure to
answer it brings condemnation—this question: Can you
justify yourself before the highest court that will sit in judgment upon you, the court which you call God? Man and
reason furnish no way over the gulf which yawns at this
point, no answer to that question, no deliverance from that
accusation.

The answer to this question can come from God alone,
through his invasion of the world-order established by himself. To try to think this out, to grasp it with our reason, is
madness. But what if this divine invasion be construed not
as a thought but as a deed, not as an idea but as an event?
What if God emerged from his silence? if the divine Logos,
as actual Word, spoke to us in time? if God revealed himself?
Christian faith is the assertion that that thing has happened,
and the task of theology is to make it comprehensible. The
Word of God, to quote Barth, is the task of theology. But the
Word of God became flesh in Jesus Christ. To that event, to
that moment in history, faith points as the spot where eternity
became time and time eternity. And there faith finds the
answer to the question which man and reason cannot answer,
and the solution of the life-conflict which man's power can-

not solve—the justification of the sinner, the divine promise of an eternal and perfect goal. It is Christ.

This idea of revelation Brunner has worked out with the utmost precision and with almost passionate ardor. I give a few examples from among many agitated passages: "Revelation is something that happened only once, here and only here, then and only then; it is He and only He." "God alone is God, and man is never and in no sense God too; and there is no transition from one to the other." "The God of the Old Testament is unquestionably the presupposition of the Gospel revelation." "There is no point where the finite merges into the infinite, for *finitum non est capax infiniti.*" "Therefore revelation is not a continuation of nature or creation, not the blossom or kernel of humanity, not the culmination of evolution . . . but the interruption of continuity, the intrusion of the utterly dissimilar—in a word, it is the miracle." Revelation is "the paradox against which nature and reason rebel, to the thinker foolishness, to the moralist a stumbling-block. It is *the* paradox, *the* contradiction in thought (Denkwiderspruch), not merely *something* paradoxical, *something* contrary to reason." In short, we must not oppose rationalism with irrationalism, which merely disregards reason, but with anti-rationalism, which slaps it in the face.

You will agree that he could not have expressed himself more plainly. And perhaps you will share my admiration for the courage of the young man who dared to propound such ideas to a company of scholars of which the large majority were of a wholly different way of thinking. Brunner's conception of revelation is, I do not hesitate to say, directly opposed to that of German idealism, and consequently to that of modern theology. For it is characteristic of the latter, as Brunner himself correctly states, that it holds revelation to be vouchsafed to us whenever we are able to perceive in the visible the symbol or image of the invisible; whenever in the depths of the human soul that mysterious identity of the contemplated divine with the contemplating human spirit is attained; whenever in human consciousness the door is opened to the divine Being; in short, when religious experience and revelation, the human consciousness and the divine consciousness, are immediately united. Call to mind the words of Kant about the starry firmament that moves us to devotion, or Goethe's adoration of the sun as a revelation of the Highest. Think how we feel ourselves lifted into higher spheres when the first notes of Beethoven's Eroica strike upon our ear, or when hundreds of jubilant voices resound in the glorious Sanctus of Bach. Enter Faust's study and with him open the Bible:

> We pine and thirst for Revelation,
> Which nowhere worthier is, more nobly sent,
> Than here, in our New Testament.

According to Brunner, all this is mysticism, panaestheticism. The difference between the two conceptions of revelation is obvious.

8.

The Scientific Outlook
in 1851 and in 1951

Herbert Dingle

EDITORIAL NOTE: *The new theology of Barth and Brunner was a revolution demonstrably inspired by historical events. The revolutions in scientific thought since Copernicus and Newton have followed an internal logic of their own, largely unrelated to developments in the outside world, although they often influence thought in other fields in their turn. In the article which follows, Herbert Dingle contrasts the view of the physical universe held by scientists in the middle of the nineteenth century with the scientific outlook today, after the revolution in physics carried out by Einstein, Planck, Bohr, and Heisenberg. In 1851, the year of the Great Exhibition at the Crystal Palace, the world was made of matter, which obeyed certain hard, clear, fixed laws, and moved at specified speeds in specified courses. Today, as Professor Dingle points out, scientific knowledge—in the Victorian sense—has dwindled to nothing. With the help of modern philosophy of science the contemporary scientist realizes that he knows, strictly speaking, nothing at all about the "real" world. Many sensitive thinking people see in the alleged failures of physics only another indication of man's finitude and estrangement from being; for others, including Professor Dingle himself, the result is a new sense of freedom of human religious enterprise. Science and religion, he argues, need no longer worry about either one "proving" or "disproving" the other. His article was first presented as a lecture at the Royal Institution, London, in March, 1951.*

"A THOUSAND YEARS IN THY SIGHT ARE BUT AS YESTERDAY when it is past." On this scale, which recognises the proportions no more than the unit measures of astronomical time-keeping, we may place the year 1851 at 11 o'clock yesterday morning and the present moment shortly after dawn today. The day so near its culmination when the Great Exhibition displayed and concealed its glories woke to life in the seventeenth century, with the heliacal rising of Galileo, shortly to be followed by the sun of Newton. The day that succeeded it opened in cloud, through which rays from the sun of Einstein are now beginning to light our way. But we do not get a new sun with each new day. The old one returns,

> repairs his drooping head,
> And tricks his beams, and with new spangled Ore,
> Flames in the forehead of the morning sky.

The sun of Einstein is the sun of Newton, and we, awakened and refreshed, seeing the shadows shortening instead of lengthening, nevertheless walk by the same light as did those who began the scientific pilgrimage yesterday morning.

That, in substance, is what I want to say. And now, since the Astronomer Royal holds high office in this Institution, I must return from eternity to time and fit it into one of his mean hours.

What I am concerned with this evening is not the actual state of scientific knowledge today and in 1851, or the actual or possible applications of it to practical affairs, but the scientific outlook, the ideas of what they were and are doing held by those responsible for the creation of that knowledge as well as by the general public. All, therefore, that I need say about the visible content of science in 1851 is that it was firmly grounded on the mechanical ideas of Newton, which seemed to be justified and exemplified by every new advance, and that it accorded perfectly, and apparently inevitably, with the general scheme of things that formed the scientific philosophy of the time. That philosophy is our main consideration, and it would be very satisfactory if I could bring before you some firsthand statements of it by those whose thoughts and actions it directed. That, however, is just what I cannot do. It was fundamental and it was universal, but it was so deep-seated that only on the rarest occasions did it appear in explicit statements. *The Proceedings of the Royal Institution* first appeared in 1851. One can read the early volumes and find excellent accounts of the progress of science in various fields, but no account at all of what science was conceived to be or what its discoveries signified. I must therefore rely for the most part on what seems to me to be implied rather than stated by the scientific literature of the mid-nineteenth century, restricting my references largely to the outstanding, if not the only, work that made the philosophy of science its theme—Whewell's *Philosophy of the Inductive Sciences.* This work was first published in 1840. A second edition appeared in 1848, and there were further editions after the Great Exhibition. Whewell, of whom it was said that science was his forte and omniscience his foible, was not a typical scientist, but he cast his net wide. Supremely confident in his own judgment, he was nevertheless preserved from the more serious consequences that befall such philosophers by the fact that he had previously written a *History of the Inductive Sciences.* There is no easier way to construct a completely self-satisfying philosophy of science than to be ignorant of history, as our own time amply demonstrates. Whewell at any rate wrote with knowledge, and he did succeed in making articulate the instinctively-held convictions of the time.

The basic assumption of the scientists of 1851 was that there was lying before them a world of material objects, moving about in space and time. Their task as scientists was to study this world by direct observation, by the use of instruments, and by experimental arrangement of conditions so as to facilitate observation and measurement. None of these processes was conceived to change the world in any way. Whether it was observed or neglected, known or unknown, understood or not understood or misunderstood, it remained the same independent world that had existed before there

were minds to apprehend it, and would go on existing and
operating in exactly the same way if all life ceased to be.
There was, in fact, a fundamental dichotomy between the
material world on one hand, and, on the other, human minds
with their hopes and fears, despairs and aspirations, exulta-
tions and agonies, disappointments, convictions, illusions and
everything that makes intelligent life what it is. None of these
things was any concern of science. They did not exist in the
sense in which the material world existed. They were ephemeral, incalculable and, from the scientific point of view,
negligible.

It is important to realise the strength and the essentially
metaphysical nature of this belief in the existence or reality or
substantiality, or whatever you care to call it, of matter, because in these days of return to the strictly empirical basis of
science, those more at home with the modern outlook (fortunately for my purpose now, they are not numerous) might
not realise exactly what it meant. It implied that any particular piece of matter—say a stone—though it was made
evident to us by its qualities—its hardness, colour and so
on—was nevertheless not compounded of those qualities but
was some underlying entity of which they were merely accidents. This essential stone indubitably *existed,* and although,
if pressed, the scientist might have found it difficult to say
exactly *what* existed, or what *existence* meant, or why he was
so sure that the stone existed, in fact he rarely if ever was
pressed, and so he had no reason to call his assumption into
question. Whewell expresses the matter very clearly:

> The Idea of Substance . . . is involved in all our views of external
> objects. We unavoidably assume that the qualities and proper-
> ties which we observe are properties of *things*;—that the adjec-
> tive implies a substantive;—that there is, besides the external
> characters of things, something *of which* they are the characters.
> An apple which is red, and round, and hard, is not merely
> redness, and roundness, and hardness; these circumstances
> may all alter while the apple remains the same apple. Behind
> the appearances which we see, we conceive something of which

we think; or to use the metaphor which obtained currency among the ancient philosophers, the attributes and qualities which we observe are supported by and inherent in something: and this something is hence called a substratum or *substance,* that which stands beneath the apparent qualities and supports them.

But "substance" is clearly metaphysical; only these inessential qualities are observed. How, then, are we to know from them that a substance exists in any particular case? Clearly there must be at least one specially accredited quality for this purpose, and Whewell found this in weight. We need not concern ourselves with the arguments by which he establishes its uniqueness to his own satisfaction, because we are now trying to understand, not to justify or to condemn, the philosophy he is expressing. We merely note, therefore, that the weight of a body (or its inertia—Whewell was prepared to accept this as an alternative) was exempt from the liability to deceive that besmirched the honour of qualities in general. The senses might be misled in any other way, but when they apprehended the descent of a balance-pan they were infallible.

This, of course, was not only Whewell's belief; it is implicit in the writings of almost any scientist of the time. But it is interesting to pause here and notice the quite unconscious divergence between the beliefs that would have been expressed if called for, and those that actually provided the criteria by which discoveries were judged. In 1846 the existence of the planet Neptune was first predicted by its weight and then observed visually. The event caused a tremendous sensation, and everyone acclaimed the triumph of the mechanical philosophy. But what actually convinced astronomers of the reality of Neptune—the detection by its weight or the detection by its power of reflecting light? Suppose all the mathematical calculations had been confirmed but the planet could not be seen: would the discovery have been celebrated then? Or suppose there had been no perturbations of Uranus, but the image of a weightless object had been observed in the telescope: would its existence have been denied? It cannot be questioned, I think, that what convinced everyone of the reality of the new planet was the fact that it showed just those qualities of roundness and colour that were treated so slightingly by Whewell, and not its exhibition of the intrinsic property of weight which was supposed to be the guarantee of existence. I mention this here because it is part of my thesis that the men who carried on the scientific tradition established in the seventeenth century did so truly and faithfully, but thinking all the time that they were doing something else. The revolution that came in the twentieth century was simply the overthrow of that false notion of what science was and is; science itself has pursued the same undeviating course from Galileo through Newton and Einstein to our own time.

Let us return, however, to what the mid-nineteenth century scientists thought they were doing. They looked out upon a real external substantial world of material bodies whose content was measured by its mass or weight. It was not a static world; its constituents moved about, interacted with one another, and made themselves known to an observer either by impinging on his body or by sending emanations towards it through an intervening material medium. The information thus provided gave clues—often very indirect—to the eternal and unchanging principles that were firmly believed to underlie the behaviour of the world. One had to be careful, however, because it was possible to have experiences, sometimes indistinguishable in themselves from sensations caused by the external world, which in fact were not so caused. These were to be ignored. They were called illusions or hallucinations or phantasies, and the word implied not merely that they were of a different character from "real" sensations, but also that they were beyond the pale of serious consideration; they were to be distinguished only to be cast aside. From the authenticated real sensations one had then to infer what went on in the real world. This, when found, had to be expressed in the form of *laws*, i.e. statements, usually mathematical, from which, given certain characteristics of the state of the world, or a specified part of it, at any particular moment, one could deduce its state at earlier and later moments. The world was thus regarded as exhibiting, with the passage of time, a succession of states, each connected with its predecessor and successor by what were regarded as unbreakable links of absolute necessity. This was referred to as the principle of cause and effect.

To complete the picture, we must note a general acknowledgment of some Supreme Power, and men of very different theological beliefs agreed in holding that the substantiality of matter demanded a Creator, and the law of cause and effect a Designer, to make them intelligible. Huxley, for instance, speaks of the "Divine government"; Whewell of the "Creator and Governor of the universe"; Herschel of the "Great First Agent"; Grant, who in 1851 was completing his *History of Astronomy,* of the "Supreme Being"; and so on. This seems to have been thought of as having something to do with religion. But these majestic names corresponded to nothing that the scientist was discovering, and the Entity represented by them was not available for the solution of scientific difficulties. It served mainly to dignify perorations and to provide that curious relief from an unfathomable mystery which comes from ascribing it to another one.

The scientific quest, then, may be summed up as the search for the universal, inviolable, causal laws that governed the course of events in the real external world. The general character of the laws was known; they were descriptions of the operation of forces—or, in general, agencies—on a world of inert ponderable matter. The matter could be observed; the agencies had to be inferred from the observations. A great part of the work had been done by Newton. His successors had added to his laws of mechanics laws of heat, of light, of sound, of magnetism and electricity, and all these had either been reduced, or were believed to be reducible, to the fundamental mechanical laws. The completion of the process was in sight, and the next generation or so would see the whole round world in every way bound by causal chains about the feet of Newton. It was the eleventh hour of scientific progress, and it brought with it appropriate emotions. "We range with Science," wrote Tennyson, "glorying in the time."

Contemplating this situation in the perspective afforded by the passage of a hundred years, we are perhaps most struck by the fact that those who occupied it thought that it was the culmination of the scientific revolution inaugurated by Galileo and established by Newton. Actually it was nothing of the kind. The essence of that revolution was the substitution of the examination of experience for speculation about the external world. In the eighteenth and nineteenth centuries scientists went on examining experience, but imagined that they were still learning about an external world. But in fact such a world had nothing at all to do with scientific practice; it was an idea unconsciously carried over in thought from the previous centuries. When Galileo rolled spheres down an inclined plane and derived the law of descent, the law said nothing at all about the spheres. It gave a relation between the reading of a measuring rod and that of a water clock; no reference to a sphere entered into it. The size, colour, temperature, and every other quality of the sphere were quite irrelevant; even its weight—especially its weight, for that was the point at which the new procedure broke most obviously with the old. It had previously been held that heavy bodies fell faster than light ones; Galileo showed that weight did not enter into the matter. And Galileo's independence of the substantiality of the external world was equalled by Newton's independence of causal laws. "To derive two or three general Principles of Motion from Phænomena," he wrote, "and afterwards to tell us how the Properties and Actions of all corporeal Things follow from those manifest Principles, would be a very great step in Philosophy, though the Causes of those Principles were not yet discover'd." His own great achievement, in fact, was precisely of that kind.

To find the origin of the nineteenth-century philosophy of science we must go back beyond Galileo, and we shall then find it wherever we look, for it dates from the beginning of man's realisation that experience is not essentially chaotic. To take merely one example of each of its two main elements, we find Avicenna, early in the eleventh century, criticising the alchemists on the ground that although they might change all the *qualities* of lead into those of gold, the *essential nature* of the substance still remained that of lead. Avicenna's "essential nature" was Whewell's "substance." "Cause" again is analysed minutely by Aristotle, and the existence of a First Cause deduced. All this, which the seventeenth-century scientists exchanged for the study of experience, the Victorians enshrined in the heart of their thinking, and while making unprecedented strides in the correlation of experience by following the new scientific procedure, they automatically translated their achievement back into the terms of a barren philosophy and praised Newton for what he had disclaimed.

The result of all this was that they were completely deceived about the extent and nature of their achievements. They thought they were approaching the end of their task of discovering the causal laws that governed the world of material substance: actually they were at little more than the beginning of their task of understanding the world of experience. Thinking they knew almost everything, they in fact knew next to nothing. Take the experience of an ordinary day, and consider how much of it they had brought within the scientific scheme. In the first place, about a third of it never entered their heads as either deserving or admitting of understanding. Though dreams had been known to change the course of the world's history, and were indubitably experiences, they were not parts of the material world, and so were denied "reality." The enlightened scientists of that time did not know why they preferred eggs to bacon for breakfast; why an intelligent man like Mr. Smith could put that Conservative bill in his window when the Liberals were so obviously the right Party; why it should be raining again when the weather seemed so settled yesterday; what nice

young Mr. Brown could possibly see in that silly Miss Green;
why they should be going to catch a cold when they had
carefully avoided all draughts; why this was such a bad year
for apples; why, in fact, anything at all that happened in the
ordinary course of events should happen as it did. Their
knowledge was almost wholly confined to what could be
observed in circumstances so extraordinary that they never
existed at all in the natural course of things. They needed
carefully constructed instruments, a laboratory strictly
guarded from outside interference, and workers trained by
long and specialised practice before anything could be observed that revealed the supposedly universal and inescapable causal laws. Everything that made ordinary familiar
occurrences differ from laboratory events was a disturbing
influence, to be cleared out of the way before one could observe the handiwork of the Great First Cause. The reason why
the Victorians thought they had solved most of their problems was that they had succeeded in persuading themselves
that the difficult ones were unimportant. When you have
banished everything from the universe except the contents of
a scientific laboratory, it is easy to range with Science, glorying in the time; there's nothing to stop you.

   But fortunately the scientists, though they bowed the knee
to Baal, went on worshipping Jehovah in their hearts. Their
practice was that of Galileo and Newton, though their philosophy was that of the ancients, and sooner or later an in-
congruity was bound to show itself. It appeared first in the
theory of heat. Soon after the time of which we have been
speaking, the real, substantial, material object had been
recognised as an aggregate of minute identical molecules
moving about and constantly colliding with one another.
The molecules were not, in fact, observed; like gravitational
force, they were invented, in true scientific fashion, as a medium for expressing what was observed. But the nineteenth-
century scientists could not think in terms of experience.
Their molecules were unimaginable without the hall-mark
of substantiality, so they immediately became bits of matter

and were automatically subjected to causal mechanical laws. What those laws were, however, was mysterious. If the molecules obeyed the ordinary mechanical laws of motion it was difficult to account for the variety in the specific heats of bodies. If they did not obey those laws, how could one discover what laws they did obey? The scientists, at least temporarily baffled by this problem, turned their attention to what could be discovered with the knowledge they did possess, and soon realised that this was quite a lot. They could account for the gas laws, the phenomena of diffusion and transpiration and viscosity; they could predict surprising things like the independence of the thermal conductivity of a gas on its density, and achieve a number of other results of the greatest interest, and all without knowing in the least how a single one of their molecules behaved or what principles governed its movements. The molecules could, within very wide limits, do what they pleased; the measuring instruments would give the same readings in any case. It was as though men were learning all about the redness and roundness and hardness of the apple without knowing anything at all about its substantiality or the eternal, immutable laws by which the Great Creator and Designer had left his impress on the universe.

There should, of course, have been protests—reactions of the strongest indignation at this prostitution of the capability and godlike Reason that had been given to men for higher ends. But there were not. So complete was the break between what the scientists were doing and what they thought they were doing that, on the contrary, everybody was delighted. Men's unconscious scientific instincts were satisfied by the progressive correlation of experience, and the demands of their conscious philosophy were met by the confident but quite unfounded hope that somehow all this would lead in time to an understanding of the real, eternal world of molecular movements. It would be an understatement to call the molecules a Mrs. Harris: they were the holy St. Harrises, worshipped with greater and greater adoration the more they hid themselves from sight. "Though in the course of ages," wrote Maxwell in 1873, "catastrophes have occurred and may yet occur in the heavens, though ancient systems may be dissolved and new systems evolved out of their ruins, the molecules out of which these systems are built—the foundation stones of the material universe—remain unbroken and unworn." But if anyone had ventured to say, "Show me the foundation stones, that I may tread on them," what he would have been shown would have been a demonstration that no matter how you treated a given quantity of gas, a certain function of the readings of thermometers, pressure gauges and metre rods, when applied to it in certain ways, remained constant. *That* was what remained unbroken and unworn. The real, eternal, substantial molecules were figments of the imagination. Such as they were, they were broken with ghastly effect at Hiroshima, but the relation between the measurements was not altered.

This divergence between scientific achievement and the estimation of scientific achievement has grown continuously from that time onwards, until now it is well nigh complete. The more we have learnt about the relations between our experiences, our observations, the less we have been able to say about the supposedly real entities whose actions we have been said to be observing. The simple molecules of Maxwell have become the electrons, protons, neutrons, positrons, π-mesons, μ-mesons, and goodness knows how many more such mysteries, of present-day nomenclature. Maxwell could at least say that his molecules were hard, elastic, isotropic, and a few other things; all we can say about our foundation stones was summed up in a phrase by Eddington; "Something unknown is doing we don't know what." In another connection, Artemus Ward is reputed to have said: "The researches of many eminent scientific men have thrown so much darkness upon the subject, that if they continue their researches we shall soon know nothing." In the matter of the substance of the real, material universe, this ultimate accomplishment has now been literally realised: we do, in fact, know precisely nothing at all.

This path to the revelation of the Victorian misconceptions, as I said, began to diverge from the highway of thought not long after the Great Exhibition of 1851, but it is only in our own time that it has led us to a point from which return to the substantial material world is clearly seen to be impossible. Progress has been gradual, the ultimate particles, while losing more and more of their accessibility, still retaining their hold on our formal belief until almost the present day. But while the process was going on, another quite independent line of research shattered the whole fabric of material substantially at a single blow. Einstein's special theory of relativity first came before the scientific world in 1905. It showed, first, that there was no sense in which we could say, as an independent fact of nature, that a body had any particular state of motion. We could regard it as stationary or as moving in any direction with any speed; the choice was entirely ours. Secondly, the theory showed that all the quantities with which we were concerned in physics—the masses, weights, volumes, shapes, temperatures, colours, and so on, of bodies—were dependent on the motions of the bodies. It followed inevitably that all these things also were at our choice; there was not one single characteristic of one single constituent of the substantial material world that was not subject to our caprice to evaluate it as we would. Everyone has now for many years accepted the theory, but, so tenacious are we of our prejudices, that there are few who realise how completely incompatible it is with any form of materialism. But let us take a single example, and confine ourselves to the so-called fundamental property of matter, its weight—or, since what we measure with a balance and call weight is really mass, to the one property of mass. Imagine two bodies which, when they are lying beside one another, relatively at rest, are exactly alike in every respect—say, two identical copper spheres. When weighed on the same balance in the same laboratory, they are found to have the same mass. Now let one of them, without being otherwise altered in any way, be set in motion with respect to the other. Will their masses still be the same? Everyone who accepts the principle of relativity will agree that they will not. Which will have the larger mass? Again, all relativists will say: "That which is moving." But which one is that? Again our relativists will reply: "Which you choose." If, then, I choose to say that A is moving and B at rest, than A is the more massive. If, without doing anything at all to the bodies, I then change my mind and say that B is moving and A at rest, then B immediately becomes the more massive. It is thus entirely a matter of your or my caprice which of the two bodies contains the more of the eternal, independent, substantial reality of the universe, and you can make one choice and I another with perfect propriety, while a third person can choose to have the masses equal if he will.

This argument is extremely simple and quite inescapable, and, like the culmination of the study of fundamental particles, it completely destroys the doctrine that what science is examining is an independent world of matter. We still use the language appropriate to such a notion, but it has become metaphorical, and the real subject of our studies and our discoveries is simply our experience. Looking back, we can see clearly enough that it has always been so. The quantities occurring in our equations are the numbers we observe on the scales of our instruments when we perform certain operations with them. It is a gratuitous addition to suppose that they are properties of some metaphysical stuff that we invent to adapt our thinking to the habits of childhood. Up to recently the addition has been more helpful than harmful; now it has become more harmful than helpful. It is like the carrot held in front of the donkey. So far it has served its purpose. It has made him run heroically and achieve what would have been impossible without its allurements. But now he is getting hungry, and it seems curiously ineffectual in meeting the new need. He is beginning to realise that the road he had been following is not, after all, that which leads to assimilation of the carrot but has been determined by quite other agencies and is directed towards quite another goal. The sooner he learns to focus his eyes on a point beyond the carrot, the sooner will his desires find satisfaction.

To those who succeed in taking the new view, the spectacle of the scientific adventure becomes transformed. We are not, as the nineteenth century thought, near the end of a description of a material world. We are little past the beginning of an understanding of the unity in diversity of our experience, and see an unlimited vista of fresh relations waiting to be understood. The change is fundamental and inescapable, but prejudice dies hard, and it is far from being generally realised. The language of the old material philosophy survived Newton and it is surviving Einstein, though it is now strained almost to breaking point. The philosophy of science is not a popular subject, and for the most part scientists, knowing that they are acting rightly and producing results, give little thought to the meaning of their practice. They are content to let their findings seem nonsensical. Some of them even deprecate such thought, as a distraction from the important business of getting something done. They are willing to see truth for ever on the scaffold, wrong for ever on the throne, so long as the scaffold goes on swaying the future. This attitude is understandable, and if anyone holds such feelings strongly he is undoubtedly right to avoid the philosophy of science; he has little faculty for it, and his contribution could be spared. But unfortunately the prosecution of science is not the whole of our activity in this vale of tears, and if we wish to see life steadily and see it whole we must take account of fields of action in which a true understanding of what science is doing is of the utmost importance. We may ignore such fields, but they will not ignore us, and unless our ideas are clarified concerning the nature and possible scope of science we are likely not only to find the science of the future becoming more and more unintelligible, but also to wake up too late to the fact that there will be no more science for us to try to understand.

One of the most prominent elements of present-day thought is the so-called philosophy of dialectical materialism. It appears to have originated in a combination of certain economic doctrines, deduced from information available at the middle of the nineteenth century, with the fashionable philosophy of the time—that of Hegel. But the idealistic flavour of Hegel's ideas was little to the taste of the early dialectical materialists, and they substituted for it the current scientific philosophy of a fundamentally real material world which I have been describing. The result was a system in which the basic substance, so to speak, was nineteenth-century matter, and the dynamic was the Hegelian dialectic which played in the world of social and economic affairs a role roughly corresponding to that of Newtonian forces in the world of mechanics. It was an ingenious system, and it assumed its full share, if not more, of the mid-nineteenth-century confidence in the indubitable rightness of its fundamental principles. All that future history could do was to demonstrate their working; it was powerless to alter them or set them aside.

Anyone who has studied nineteenth-century science can see how conformable this was to the existing scientific philosophy, and anyone who studies twentieth-century science can see how uncomformable it is to ours. Yet the curious fact is that a number of present-day scientists—some of them even physicists of high eminence—embrace the doctrines of dialectical materialism with an enthusiasm suggestive more of the loyalty of a football partisan than of rational conviction. They claim also to find support for it on scientific grounds, and indeed go so far as to say that it is itself a scientific philosophy—the only legitimate one—though of course without the liability to modification that scientific theories are usually held to enjoy. It is appropriate therefore to ask those who advance this view how they reconcile their doctrines with the facts I have been describing—the gradual recession of the substantial material world into complete inaccessibility, and the dependence of the supposed measures of its properties on our arbitrary choice; for they are, of course, aware of these facts and might be expected to have something to say about them. That, however, appears not to be the case: if one is foolish enough to ask such questions he is left to answer them for himself. As an earnest seeker after truth I have looked in the writings of our scientific dialectical materialists for enlightenment in this perplexing situation, but I have found none at all. When the discussion takes such a turn that the subject of relativity comes into the reader's mind, he can almost see the shocked face of the author start up from the page and hear him say with righteous Victorian horror, "O no, we never mention her!" And, sure enough, one is soon drawn back to the internal struggle that goes on in a piece of ice when the temperature rises—a subject that is treated in a manner which the most profound student of the caloric theory could hardly improve upon.

What is the meaning of this strange silence? The question would be of merely academic interest were it not that the false idea that dialectical materialism is a tenable philosophy is a most serious menace not only to the future of civic freedom but also to the future exercise of scientific thought and practice. With the former danger I am not here concerned, but with the latter I am, and I therefore appeal to those scientific men who hold that dialectical materialism has any living importance for us today, to take these specific facts that I have been describing and show us how they can be reconciled with it. Until they do so it is impossible for anyone acquainted with the actual situation to see this strange pseudo-philosophy as anything but a preoccupied and bewildered ghost, wandering aimlessly among the antimacassars and aspidistras and panting for the heavy lavender-laden air in which alone it can breathe freely. Ghosts are interesting things and worthy of serious study; it is when they are thought to have the properties of living beings that they become terrible.

Of the many aspects of the change from the nineteenth to the twentieth century outlook that would well repay consideration, I can mention only one or two. In general terms we may say that the Victorians looked on the progress of science as a process of accumulation. Knowledge once acquired remained for all time; fresh knowledge was added to it, but without changing it in any way.

> Let Knowledge grow from more to more.

> Slowly the Bible of the race is writ,
> And not on paper leaves or leaves of stone;
> Each age, each kindred, adds a verse to it.

The process would go on until God had made the pile complete, and it was then near enough to completion to show the essential character of the structure of the universe; further additions would improve the symmetry without altering the general plan. Our view today is very different. Certainly experience grows from more to more, and must do so as long as time endures and records are preserved; but the picture of the whole which we form in our attempt to express its interrelations undergoes unceasing transformations—it is a kaleidoscope rather than a fixed mounting structure. Progress in scientific conceptions is like a view gradually emerging out of a drifting mist on which a changing light is playing. We observe what happens when α-particles are projected towards a gas, and our picture of the atom suddenly changes from the likeness of a billiard ball to that of a solar system. We add to our knowledge of the actual solar system the fact that light is deflected by the Sun, and immediately the lines of gravitational force that previously held its members together disappear, and each planet is seen to travel freely along its own groove. We can no longer say, The world is like this, or The world is like that. We can only say, Our experience up to the present is best represented by a world of this character; I do not know what model will best represent the world of tomorrow, but I do know that it will coordinate a greater range of experience than that of today.

There is another aspect of the new outlook that is of the greatest importance. When we take experience itself as the subject-matter of science, we can no longer maintain the fundamental distinction between sensations and other experiences that seemed so obvious in the nineteenth century. Sensations were then naturally marked out as valid clues to reality because they were revealed by the action of the real external world on our sense organs. Macbeth's dilemma about the reality of his dagger, which he could see but could not feel, was no dilemma to the nineteenth-century playgoer. If the dagger had been real he would have felt it; he didn't feel it; therefore it was not real and therefore it could be ignored. It didn't occur to the scientists of that time that, "real" or not, Macbeth certainly had the experience of seeing it, and that experience called for scientific study just as much as one accompanied by the corresponding experience of touch.

But the instinct that led the physicist to act scientifically in spite of his unscientific thoughts was no less active in the physiologist and the psychologist. The illusions and hallucinations and dreams that were dismissed with such contempt from the world of reality were nevertheless studied and became the source of far-reaching generalisations of which today everyone realises the importance, whether or not in their present form they are likely to survive further study. The word "delusion" to a modern psychologist carries the same measure of significance as the word "reality" to a spectator of the Great Exhibition. And it is unquestionable that such experiences are significant. Hitler's delusions have caused immeasurable suffering and given a new direction to the course of events all over the world—quite a respectable performance for things that didn't exist. Moreover, in the realm of mental phenomena relations are found which would have been thought fantastic in the nineteenth century. Mr. Smith's neighbours, and Mr. Smith himself, would have been astonished to learn that his predilection for the Conservative Party had less to do with its political programme than with the fact that a hated schoolmaster had once spoken approvingly of Mr. Gladstone; and Mr. Brown would have smiled in contempt if told that what he perceived in Miss Green was not superior intelligence and beauty but a reminiscence of a forgotten nurse who had been kind to him in infancy. We are forced to recognise that, at bottom, all experiences are equivalent from the scientific point of view. We classify them, and in each class construct a model universe that expresses their relations with one another. The experiences that satisfy certain tests of what is sometimes called "objectivity" are correlated by the conception of what we call the physical universe, comprising nebulae distributed in space-time. Other experiences, satisfying other tests and therefore classified differently, are correlated by the concept of what we call mind, comprising such notions as the unconscious, the ego, the id, or whatever other structure is preferred. But no grounds now remain for giving one higher scientific status than the other, or for denying the possibility of a relation because it would violate our preconceptions.

This is particularly important in clarifying the relations between science and religion. The disputes of the past—and a particularly violent example broke out soon after 1851— were able to arise because both sides agreed in accepting the presuppositions we now see to be inadmissible, but differed on minor details. It was common ground in the evolution controversy that one had to start with the assumption of a substantial material world in which certain events had occurred according to causal laws. What was disputed was the relative weight of different kinds of evidence concerning what had happened—on one hand, rational inference from existing events; on the other, the authority of the Scriptures. But the real conflict lay deeper than either side realised. What the scientists were unconsciously fighting for was freedom for their scientific process of finding relations between experiences; and what the religionists were unconsciously fighting for was the validity of their spiritual experience. On the scientific side it was one more example of an instinctive rightness of behaviour coupled with a complete misconception of what they were rightly doing. For let us suppose they were in fact seeking, as they thought they were, for the causal explanation of the existing state of the physical world. Then clearly they could not have rejected Philip Gosse's theory that God had made the world, by one creative act, exactly as it would have appeared had it actually been the scene of slow evolution. For that would have involved but one hypothesis of a perfectly legitimate kind—namely, that of a single exhibition of power, intelligence and will, all qualities familiar in ordinary experience and differing from their human manifestations only in degree. Instead of that they preferred numberless hypotheses of alternations of physical conditions in different parts of the world, their imagined effects on living creatures, the inheritability of those effects, and so on. A simple application of Occam's razor would immediately have severed this fantastic growth and cast it into the fire. Why then, was Occam's razor not used? Simply because the scientists were not really seeking for the causal explanation of the variety in the organic world, but for rational relations between their observations. Gosse's theory would have left the various observations of fossil bones and casts, their occurrence in the geological sequence of rocks, the effects of selection among domestic animals, and all the rest, as so many independent and unrelated products of the creative act, whereas the evolution theory knit them together into a single rational structure. In their hearts the scientists wanted correlation, not explanation, and so they did for the organic world what Newton had done for the solar system— related its phenomena by a single principle and left the causes to be found out.

The religious opponents of the theory likewise had another than their ostensible motive. They did not object to the cor-

relation of observations and had no quarrel at all with Newton. They were not urging a supernatural as opposed to a
natural order of things, for Gosse's explanation made no
greater appeal to them than to the scientists. They accepted
without question the motion of the Earth and the non-
existence of the firmament, in spite of biblical statements to
the contrary. None of these questions, about which most of
the argument gathered, touched the core of their fears. What
they—or at any rate the most sincere of them—really
dreaded was that the discarding of the cosmological ideas
with which their faith had become so closely intertwined
would entail also the stigmatising of their religious experience
as an illusion; that, for example, the rejection of the Thir-
teenth Book of St. Augustine's *Confessions* would involve a
rejection of the Tenth Book also. We can still partly—but I
think only partly—understand what the word "illusion"
meant to a Victorian. No inner certainty that an experience
was a fact could, in the average man, survive the conviction
that it had no origin in the real world. Only a spiritual genius
could retain his faith in such circumstances.

The whole controversy is now largely a thing of the past;
it excites little, if any, feeling among thinkers of the present
day, whatever their chief interests may be. But that is not because the questions so bitterly argued have been settled. It
is rather because those concerned to uphold the validity of
religion have realised that the matter has not the importance
for them that their grandfathers thought it had. They have
seen that it is possible to concede the geologist's time-scale
and the gradual evolution of species without in the least im-
pairing the foundations of their religious beliefs, and accordingly they have now no incentive to interfere with the scientist's correlation of his observations of fossils. From the
modern point of view, from which experience appears as the
starting-point, the initial datum, of our considerations, and
not as a derivative of an imagined real material world, the
experiences that have given rise to the physical and biological sciences are seen to be different from, but, for scientific

purposes, co-equal with, those that have given rise to the faiths for which men have died. The correlation of the former, though by far the more advanced, has not yet come within sight of conceptions sufficiently generalised to be capable of embracing the latter.

But again in this field we observe the phenomenon we have noticed before, that the formal philosophy of our men of science lags behind the necessary implications of their practice, and we still have the same old ghosts of Victorian misconceptions haunting the structure of modern scientific philosophy. In a recent popular series of broadcasts, for example, the speaker, in summing up his conclusions on the nature of the physical universe, remarked that "it seems to me that religion is but a blind attempt to find an escape from the truly dreadful situation in which we find ourselves." What the "dreadful situation" was he did not explain, nor did his tone suggest that he was in fact overcome with dread. Indeed, the conformity of his language to his ideas contrasted somewhat unfavourably with that of the ancient Hebrew writers whom at the time he was patronising: one did not get the same impression of absolute conviction born of living experience. But the chief point of interest is the utter lack of awareness of what scientific progress has been revealing during the last hundred years. To hear religion described as a blind attempt to escape from the conclusions of astronomical research is to hear a blind man, rising from the study of acoustics, pronounce his opinion that optics is an attempt to escape from the truly dreadful jazz band across the way. The cases are precisely parallel. Such nonsense is intelligible only on the assumption that the speaker has not yet realised that science begins with experience, but still presupposes the old substantial material world that reveals itself only to the animal senses.

It should be possible, when these fantasies have been outgrown, for science and religion to advance in harmony and even with mutual assistance, but I think it would be unduly optimistic to suppose that no further conflict between them will arise. When the religious experience is recognised as a genuine phenomenon, the scientific psychologist, inevitably seeking to correlate it with other phenomena, is most likely to bring it into relation with psychological states some of which are now regarded as abnormal or even pathological. It is scarcely to be expected that men with little scientific curiosity, but to whom their religion is the most precious thing in life, will view without protest what they cannot but regard as a degradation of the highest they know. It seems to me that this is the most likely ground of the conflict of the future. It will, of course, rest on a misunderstanding. Science has no concern with the intrinsic value of any experience; its object is only to find relations between one experience and another. The word "pathological" has no significance for it—or at any rate not the chief significance that it has for those with a preconception of what is to be regarded as a healthy state. The scientist, for example, cannot be expected to overlook the fact that experiences that follow over-indulgence in certain liquors are likely to be related to experiences that follow under-indulgence, or fasting. That does not in the least mean that the intrinsic value of one experience may not be infinitely greater or less than that of the other. The vibrations of Caruso's vocal chords bore the closest possible scientific relation to those of Mr. Frank Sinatra's—a relation which it would be folly to overlook—but the non-scientific music-lover is not likely to hail this discovery with delight. The highest wisdom lies in recognising both the relations and the very different values of the things related.

The discarding of an old prejudice and the cultivation of a new outlook are not matters that can be completed in a moment. One first catches a glimpse of a new way of regarding things, and begins to see a few outstanding features of his surroundings in a new light. But he does not immediately realise that the whole scene has been transformed. Deep-seated beliefs remain, incompatible with the new outlook though they may be, and only gradually begin to take on a strange appearance and arouse misgivings. For a long time, like Copernicus, to whom the heliocentric doctrine never suc-ceeded in showing the unreality of the celestial spheres, he unconsciously maintains two inconsistent attitudes, and in all good faith harbours beliefs fundamentally at variance with one another. The Victorian presuppositions established themselves so firmly in the minds of our immediate ancestors that not even the example of the founders of modern science and the faithful observations of their principles by their suc-cessors can enable us yet wholly to escape the influence of the false notions. It must be left to the future fully to realise the emancipation that we can at least see to be inevitable.

9·

The Decline of Political Theory

Alfred Cobban

EDITORIAL NOTE: *One of the peculiarities of twentieth-century thought is what Alfred Cobban calls "the decline of political theory," by which he means the decline of reasoned and systematic efforts to provide a normative science of politics in the great tradition of Aristotle and Locke. We have many competent specialists in political behavior who describe the political process and analyze power relationships; we have a number of ideologies produced by politicians and propagandists for mass consumption; but nothing like classical political theory. In the post-1945 era, of course, even ideologies find few adherents in the industrially advanced countries. It is the age of the expert, the technocrat, the man who does what is expedient and explains his actions later. If the failure of such ideologies as socialism and fascism may be laid to disillusionment with government by ideologues of the type of Stalin and Hitler, the decline of political theory obviously has deeper origins, not only in changing socio-economic conditions but also in the inability of science and philosophy to provide that correlation between fact and value which political theorists of the classical eras could take for granted. Professor Cobban studies some of these underlying causes of spiritual drift in our century and ends on a note of cautious optimism. The signs of a possible renaissance in political thought are detected in a recent article which continues from the point at which Cobban leaves off: see Dante Germino, "The Revival of Political Theory,"* Journal of Politics, *XXV (August 1963), 437–60.*

POLITICAL THEORY IS NOT A PROGRESSIVE SCIENCE. AT LEAST, anyone who puts, say, Aristole's *Politics* beside the political writings of the twentieth century could be excused if he thought that progress in the subject was imperceptible. A cynic might even argue that everything that is worth saying on political theory has already been said *ad nauseam,* and draw the conclusion that it is time we gave up such wearisome reiteration. But this view would be false, because if political ideas do not progress, their formulation certainly changes. The conditions of social life alter, sometimes more slowly and sometimes more rapidly, in the last few centuries at an increasingly dizzy pace; and as they alter, the words we use, and the ideas they convey, lose old meanings and acquire new ones. For this reason a continual restatement of political principles is both necessary and inevitable—as long, that is, as the tradition of political thinking, which is one of the peculiar characters of Western civilization, remains alive.

It is a tradition with a history of some two and a half millenia, though with one considerable break. Century after century the political ideas of the Western World have undergone progressive modification. The interplay of idea with institution has changed now one and now the other, and the flow of ideas has been punctuated at intervals by the synthesis created by a great political thinker. No such synthesis has appeared in our own day or for some time past, but this is not surprising. Great political thinkers cannot be produced to order, and we need not wail and beat our breasts because there is no contemporary Burke or Bentham. If a general tendency to cease thinking about society in terms of political theory were to be observable, that would be a matter of greater significance than the mere fact that there are no intellectual giants in the field of political theory today. I propose to suggest that there *is* such a tendency.

The view that our cherished political ideas may be capable of dying will naturally meet with opposition, yet there is nothing impossible in such a development. Political ideas are not immortal, however we try to identify them with eternal

values. Conscious of our own mortality, we cling all the more
to the belief that there must be something presiding over our
destinies which is eternal. There may be, but it is not likely
to be the little gods of our own creation, whether we call
them Imperial Rome, or Divine Right of Kings, or even
Democracy. The belief in the permanence of such ideas is
only another form of the sophism of the ephemeral—the
faith of Fontenelle's rose, which nodded its head and proclaimed in the wisdom of a day that gardeners were immortal, for no gardener had ever died within the memory
of a rose. Ideas grow and decay, change into new forms and
are reborn. It would be a cause for amazement if the process
of continuous transformation were to come to an end while
political thinking, as it has existed since fifth-century Athens,
still survives.

But does it survive? Conceivably political theory at the
present day may *not* be undergoing one of its many metamorphoses, passing through a chrysalis stage before emerging in a
new form. It may just be coming to an end. This has happened in the past. Once before in the history of Western
civilization a great age of political thought came to an end.
The development of Greek political ideas reached its climax
in the writings of Plato and Aristotle. In the Hellenistic age
attention began to turn away from political theory and into
other fields. For a time, with the rise of the National Law
school of thought and the elaboration of juristic conceptions
by the Roman lawyers, it might have been possible to regard
the process as still one of growth and development. But in the
Roman Empire politics turned into the struggles of court factions and military dictators, and political thinking as the
Greeks understood it ceased.

The experience of the Greco-Roman world is not without
relevance to our own time. Some at least of the conditions
which accompanied this earlier decline and fall of political
theory are repeated today. It is a commonplace that state
activity is irresistibly expanding. More and more of the activities of society are falling under the control of bureaucracy

and therefore are to some extent outside political control. Great military machines are being created, to the support of which more and more of the wealth of society has to be diverted. These are as yet, it is true, the servants and not the masters of the civil power, but so the legions were in Rome for a long time. This is an age of revolutions, like the age of Marius and Sulla and Caesar, and revolutions are apt to end in military dictators; in more than a few countries they begin with them as well. The knowledge of this tendency is perhaps one reason why it has hitherto failed to operate in Soviet Russia. In Nazi Germany also the Army was never able to challenge the party successfully.

Possibly in the new form of party organization a technique has been found for averting military dictatorship and the rule of pretorian guards to which the Roman Empire degenerated. But the substitution of the party machine for the military machine is not necessarily a great improvement. It means the rule of a small oligarchy, with political life concentrated in the internal struggles of its factions. Both bureaucracy and party seem also in practice to involve the emergence of a superbureaucrat or party chief, or both rolled in one, in whom ultimate power is concentrated, and who is himself semideified as the incarnation of the state, like the Roman emperors. Since the majority of the population are naturally outside the chosen circle of bureaucracy or party there is also a need, as long as a degree of political consciousness survives in any part of this excluded majority, for a machinery of repression, a system of delation and espionage, political police, concentration camps or prisons and the rule of universal suspicion—such as Tacitus described in dreadful detail in his imaginative account of the last years of Tiberius, and Camille Desmoulins borrowed for a description of France under the Terror.

It may be said that this picture represents only half of the world, and that is doubtless so. But are some of these tendencies completely absent anywhere? Contemporaries naturally notice differences. Historians, looking back on an age, are often more struck by similarities. The most fundamental trends in any period are those which exist at the same time in the most diverse and apparently opposed camps. If I were asked what are the deepest underlying tendencies of our age I should look for those which are common to both sides of the Iron Curtain. I should look for something which communist Russia and capitalist America have in common. At bottom, it seems to me that there are more similarities than either side would be very pleased to admit, and that they are sufficient to make the parallel with the ancient world a fair one, though obviously it must not be pushed too far.

The parallel is also noticeable with respect to the decline of political theory. In the period when Caesarism was rising, the ideas associated with the old Roman conception of *libertas* were falling. The connection between new conditions of society and the decline of political thinking may be obscure, but it would be dangerous to suggest that there is none. The rule of *senatus populusque romanus* led to anarchy when an empire had to be governed instead of a city. Rome was faced with the choice of abandoning the political principles by which it had achieved greatness, or seeing the Roman world degenerate into a chaos of warring states. Its solution was the Empire, in which, however, the classic political theories of the city-state could find no place, any more than the institutions by which they had achieved some measure of realization. For political theory to exist, it seems to me, there must be an active political life. One does not expect to find it flourishing among Australian aboriginal tribes, in the Russia of Ivan or Peter, the Paraguay of the Jesuits or the empire of the Caesars.

Are there signs—I do not say more— that our own political ideas may be coming to their end as those of the ancient city-states did? It would be absurd to suppose that one wants a continual stream of new political ideas, or old ones new-fashioned; but I suggest that there has been rather a long interval since there was last any original political thinking. It is necessary to go back to the eighteenth century to find it.

This, I admit, is a sweeping statement, which it would require considerable space to attempt to justify.

But let me present one consideration. The dominant political idea in the modern world is democracy. Most of the contradictions of contemporary politics find their place under the democratic umbrella, but broad as that is they jostle one another, and moreover the umbrella seems to be leaking badly. And where are the political theorists of democracy today? Instead of a rational theory it has become a sort of incantation. It is the "open sesame" of political treasure hunters everywhere. The world is full of would-be Aladdins chanting "democracy." The masses, at least in those countries which have no experience of democracy, are waiting in a state of mystic faith on the revelation that the word is to produce. Where at least the idea has been known longer, expectations are not so high. Is it unfair to suggest that there is even a certain degree of disillusionment, a feeling that the traditional conceptions of democracy do not answer our greatest problems?

Liberal democratic principles ceased to evolve in the nineteenth century: in general, the world of practice is apt to be a generation, sometimes a century, behind the world of original thought. But the nineteenth century failed to refashion and think out anew, for the benefit of its successors, the ideas that it was living on. It provided, admittedly, an intellectual ancestry for nationalism and Fascism and communism, but that is another story. Liberal democratic principles ceased to evolve then, but the world did not stop at that point, and it has become a very different place since. Meanwhile democracy, for lack of thought, has ceased to be a living political idea. It has become a shibboleth, and not even serviceable as such. A password is no good when all the hostile camps use it indiscriminately. For the most part it has ceased to be discussed seriously and in relation to the concrete problems of practical politics. It has largely become a meaningless formula. Politicians, like the princess in the fairy tale condemned to the oracular utterance of frogs, seem scarcely able to open their mouths without some platitude flopping out, wet and flabby and slightly repulsive, but is this political theory? If it is, no wonder that practical men prefer to ignore it. Coins can remain valid currency even when they are worn quite smooth. Political ideas need periodical recoining if they are to retain their value.

It may be said that this is not a fair argument, that practical politics has always been conducted on the basis of platitudes. A Burke was the exception, his fellow member for Bristol, whose political principles were summed up in "I say ditto to Mr. Burke," the norm; but at least he had a Burke to say ditto to, and besides Burke a great body of informed and serious public discussion existed on the rights and wrongs of political behavior. Where will the average politician find a discussion of theoretical questions on the same level today?

Of course, there have been writers in the last few decades who have had something siginficant to say about the contemporary political situation, but the same conclusion about the decline of political theory seems to emerge from a study of their work. I am thinking of such writers as Ferrero, Bertrand de Jouvenel, Russell, E. H. Carr, Reinhold Niebuhr, Lasswell, Hans Morgenthau and others. The thing that impresses them most about political life is the state as power. They envisage power as a kind of electric force, now diffused and now concentrated, which not merely runs through society but is its very essence. "The laws of social dynamism," says Lord Russell, "are only capable of being stated in terms of power." The wretched individual atoms of which society is composed are massed together, hurled violently about, disintegrated by power, which they did not create and cannot control.

Traditional political theory, in so far as it has failed to recognize this fact is regarded as no more than a beautiful fairy tale. To quote Reinhold Niebuhr,

> It may be possible, though it is never easy, to establish just relations between individuals within a group by moral and rational persuasion and accommodation. In inter-group relations this is practically an impossibility. The relations between groups

must therefore always be predominantly political rather than ethical, that is, they will be determined by the proportion of power which each group possesses at least as much as by any rational and moral appraisal of the comparative needs and claims of each group.[1]

According to Niebuhr the tragedy of the human spirit is "its inability to conform its collective life to its individual ideals." This is the reason why men "invent romantic and moral interpretations of the real facts, preferring to obscure rather than reveal the true character of their collective behavior." In other words, it is the dilemma of "moral man and immoral society." Man, when he became a social and political animal, sacrificed his individual morality to the egoism that is the accompaniment of social life. The complaint is not a new one: it was the theme of Rousseau's *Discourse on Inequality.* But for the modern thinker, unlike Rousseau, there is no resolution to the tragedy of society. Humanity is caught in a cul-de-sac. In such a situation absolute pessimism is unavoidable. There is no possibility of creating, as Rousseau set out to do in the opening chapter of the *Contrat social,* a society in which justice can be allied with utility and power with freedom. There is no hope of establishing rational or ethical control.

In a different way the same conclusion was reached by Ortega y Gasset. He wrote:

> we live at a time when man believes himself fabulously capable of creation, but he does not know what to create. Lord of all things, he is not lord of himself. He feels lost amid his own abundance. With more means at his disposal, more knowledge, more technique than ever, it turns out that the world to-day goes the same way as the worst of worlds that have been; it simply drifts.[2]

All this is degrees of pessimism below Machiavelli. The author of the *Prince* saw society at the mercy of arbitrary power,

[1] *Moral Man and Immoral Society* (New York, 1933), pp. xxii–xxiii.
[2] *The Revolt of the Masses* (London, 1932), p. 47.

but believed that somehow out of evil would come good; the tyrant would serve social ends that a better ruler might not be able to fulfill. We have lost the innocence of a Machiavelli now and do not look for moral good to be born of political evil. Political pessimism is deeper than it has been perhaps since St. Augustine wrote the *De Civitate Dei*. Indeed, for a century and a half pessimism has slowly been infecting the intellectual world. That is a process I have no space to trace, though it has, I believe, a close connection with the decay in political ideas that has been contemporaneous with it.

The decline of political theory may thus be regarded as a reflection of the feeling that ethical values have no place in the field of social dynamics and power politics. This, I believe, is the real significance of "the revolt of the masses": it means the rise to control of those who live their lives without theory, to whatever class they may happen to belong. Another term for it is the rule of the expert, I mean the technician, the *Fachmann*, to use the German word for an especially German disease. Twenty years ago Ortega y Gasset saw what it meant. "Anyone who wishes," he said, "can observe the stupidity of thought, judgement and action shown to-day in politics, art, religion and the general problems of life and the world by the 'men of science,' and of course, behind them, the doctors, engineers, financiers, teachers and so on." [3] The politician who merely repeats platitudes is no worse than his own experts; he is not to be singled out for criticism. And how can he be held responsible for failing to translate political theory into practice if there is no theory to be translated?

There is another way of looking at the decline of political thought. Professor Toynbee sees our civilization going the way of previous civilizations, and consoles himself with the idea that the death of a civilization may be the birth of a religion. Ferrero put it differently. Mysticism, he said, is a form of escapism from the horror of illegitimate power. One seems to remember the early Christian invocation: "The poet has

[3] *Ibid.*, p. 124.

said, 'O lovely city of Cecrops,' wilt thou not say, 'O lovely
city of God'? " And a modern poet repeats the cry:

> Man, frustrated and sleep-forsaken,
> Gloom-regarding from inward sight,
> Sees the city of God unshaken
> Steeply stand in unworlded white;
> Sees, adrift from his faith-lost learning,
> Sun-remote from terrestrial thought,
> Power, envisioned by earth's discerning,
> Peace, by mortal aspiring wrought.[4]

A nobly phrased restatement of an ideal that appeared to
men in a former time of troubles, but one that belongs to a
nonpolitical age. Religious revival *may* be a way out, but it is
not a political way. And will it be the resurgent idealism to
give substance to our hopes, or merely a narcotic to our dis-
contents? The religious approach to political problems is also
not without its dangers. The Nazi Revolution of Destruction
gained greatly in force by being able to drape itself with the
robes of chiliastic aspiration.

In this analysis—though that is to dignify a brief indication
of some contemporary tendencies, as I see them, with too am-
bitious a title—I may seem to be bent on a pessimistic interpretation of the modern world; but what I have said so far is
only a one-sided view of the current situation. To take it as
the whole truth would be to despair of the political community prematurely. If it is true that political theory has ceased
to develop, is this a sign that political life is in fact coming to
an end and that we are entering a nonpolitical age, as the
ancient world did? Here one must appeal to a broader view
of the facts. The differences are far greater than the similarities. If there are signs that the world is moving in the direction
of universal empire, there is no reason to believe that it will
reach that goal before the present age of catastrophes has
been long continued. Bureaucracy is not yet the major reality

[4] Siegfried Sassoon, "Ode," in *Vigils* (London, 1935).

of government in any Western country; nor are pretorian guards or political parties yet our masters rather than our servants. In short, there seems no reason to believe that if there has been a decline of political theory this is the necessary result of the appearance of a social and political situation in which it no longer has any valid *raison d'être*. If this is so, the only alternative explanation is to suppose that it is declining because of some internal condition, and not because of the inevitable pressure of objective fact. Perhaps something has gone wrong with political thinking itself. I believe that it has, and that it is even possible to suggest a diagnosis.

If the decline of political theory is to be explained by some inherent misdirection in contemporary thinking about politics the remedy might appear to be to work out, on abstract grounds, the proper way of thinking about politics. This method has certain attractions. It can be used to justify practically any form of political theory that appeals to us; because naturally the conclusions we arrive at will be determined by the assumptions we start from, and we are not in much danger of starting from assumptions that do not appeal to us.

However, I propose not to adopt this line of approach. Fortunately, we have not to *invent* political theory; that was invented long ago. If there is a right way of considering its problems, I think we should be modest enough to believe that it might possibly be the way of all the greater political thinkers of the past; that is, if there is a way which so many, and such diverse, theorists have in common. I think there is. In the first place we have the simple, obvious fact that they all wrote with a practical purpose in mind. Their object was to influence actual political behavior. They wrote to condemn or support existing institutions, to justify a political system or persuade their fellow citizens to change it: because, in the last resort, they were concerned with the aims, the purposes of political society. Even Machiavelli does not merely describe the way in which things are done, without also indicating the way in which, and to what ends, he thinks they *ought* to be done. At the opposite extreme, Plato's *Re-*

public may represent an ideal to which the human race—perhaps happily—cannot attain, but in his mind it was no mere Cloud-Cuckoo-Land of fantasy.

Political theory in the past, I suggest, was essentially practical. The political theorist, in his way, was a party man, and party men themselves used not to be afraid to season their practice with the salt of theory. One of the striking differences between political discussion in, say, the eighteenth century and at the present day is that politicians have on the whole ceased to discuss general principles. This is not stated as a criticism, but as a fact which needs explaining, and I think one clue to the explanation has already appeared. The study of political theory, I have just said, was formerly the work of men intently concerned with practical issues. It has become instead an academic discipline, written in various esoteric jargons almost as though for the purpose of preventing it from being understood by those who, if they did understand it, might try to put it into practice. It has entered the high realm of scholarship, and, as Whitehead has pointed out, some modern forms of scholarship, at least, reproduce the limitations which dominated thought in the Hellenistic epoch. "They canalize thought and observation," he says, "within predetermined limits, based upon inadequate metaphysical assumptions dogmatically assumed." [5]

Political theory has in this way become disengaged from political facts. Even worse, it has become disengaged on principle, as it has seldom if ever been in the past. The academic political theorist of today may study the great political thinkers of the past, but in the name of academic impartiality he must carefully abstain from doing the kind of thing that they did. I put it forward as a hypothesis that this may conceivably be one source of the decline of political theory.

The view that the connection between political theory and practical politics is a condition of the survival of theory deserves a more elaborate discussion than it can be given here. But if it were to be accepted, then there is an important corol-

[5] A. N. Whitehead, *Adventures of Ideas* (London, 1933), p. 151.

lary to be noticed. The implication is that the issues with
which political theory has been concerned in the past were
not chosen arbitrarily, or as a result of some theoretical argument, and that theory was able to come to grips with the
practical world because its discussions were determined by
the actual conditions and problems of the day. For example,
John Stuart Mill lived in an age when new social problems
called for measures of state action which conflicted with established ideals of individual liberty: his thought derives its
value from the fact that he devoted himself to the task of
attempting to reconcile the two demands. Bentham's life-
work was to establish a theoretical basis for the legislative and
administrative reforms that were urgently needed in *his* day.
Burke, faced in Great Britain, America, Ireland, France with
a challenge to the existing bases of political allegiance, attempted to provide an alternative to the new democratic
principle of the sovereignty of the people. Rousseau, conscious of the moral collapse of divine-right monarchy, offered
a new justification for the rightful powers of government.
Montesquieu, earlier, had seen the defects of absolutism, but
his alternative was a return to the aristocratic organization
of society, and the limitation of all power by law. Locke provided a political theory for a generation which had over-
thrown divine right and established parliamentary government. Hobbes and Spinoza, in an age of civil wars, maintained that sovereignty meant all or nothing. And so we
might continue, till we reached in the end—or rather the
beginning—Plato and Aristotle, attempting to prescribe
remedies for the diseases of the city-state. Among recent political thinkers, it seems to me that one of the very few, perhaps
the only one, who followed the traditional pattern, accepted
the problems presented by his age, and devoted himself to
the attempt to find an answer to them was Harold Laski.
Though I am bound to say that I do not agree with his
analysis or his conclusions, I think that he was trying to do
the right kind of thing. And this, I suspect, is the reason why,
practically alone among political thinkers in Great Britain,

he exercised a positive influence over both political thought and action.

If political theory *has* become generally disengaged from practice, and if this is one cause of its decline, it will be worth while asking why this has happened. The bias of the academic approach away from action is not a new thing, and it can hardly provide an adequate explanation by itself. An answer which goes a little deeper can be found, I think, again by a comparison with traditional political thought. The object of this was to arrive at the judgment that one form of political activity was better than another. Academic impartiality between what it believed to be good and bad it neither sought nor attained. Because its aim was to influence action, it had to consider the forces that move men, and these are not the products of abstract analysis but of the passions. And since not all passions could be regarded as conducive to a good end, it had to be the passions under the guidance of ethical motivation. In other words, politics was essentially a branch of morals, or ethics. It is not my object here to discuss the problems of ethical theory. What I want to do is to suggest that modern political theory has largely ceased to be discussed in terms of what ought to be; and the reason, I believe, is that it has fallen under the influence of two modes of thought which have had a fatal effect on its ethical content. These, and they have come to dominate the modern mind, are history and science.

The historian naturally see all ideas and ways of behavior as historically conditioned and transient. Within itself, history has no standard of value but success, and no measure of success but the attainment of power, or survival for a little longer than rival individuals or institutions have survived. Moreover, history is the world studied under the category of what is past: however much we may proclaim that all history is contemporary, its nature is to be a field into which practice cannot penetrate. The paradox of history is that though its writing is a contemporary action, with practical consequences, the historian puts this fact in the back of his mind and tries to behave as though it were not so. By itself, in political theory, history can produce only the crudest Machiavellianism. If all historians are not little Machiavellis, it is only because they take their political ideals from some other source and carry them into their history. This is, fortunately, almost unavoidable, though it might sometimes be a good thing if they were a little more conscious of the ideals they are in fact applying and inculcating through their histories. This is yet another problem which can be raised but not discussed here. It is sufficient to say that at least there is a tendency among modern historians to regard the passing of ethical judgment as an illegitimate process against which historical discipline should be a safeguard. In so far as it is a successful safeguard it is also one against thinking about the problems of political theory at all.

The influence of historical thought did not stop at this. History acquires more positive, and more dangerous, implications, when it is made into a philosophy of history. This was particularly the achievement of Hegel and Marx. The dominant trend in both Hegelianism and Marxism was to associate ethics with the historical process—by which I do not mean the grand pattern of the universe, which I suspect was not revealed even to Hegel or Marx, but the little corner of the fabric which came under their immediate notice, the few strands which they took for the pattern of the whole. Even if Hegel and Marx themselves did not intend this result, in those who followed them there was an uneasy slip from saying, "This is what will be," into saying, "This is what ought to be." The result was to base moral judgments on temporary and limited historical phenomena. Hegelian and Marxist politics, therefore, have had the ultimate effect of setting up a politics devoid of ethical foundations. In this way they played an important part in creating a breach between modern political practice and the traditions of political thinking in the West.

The influence of history over the modern mind is, however, challenged by that of science. Particularly in the forms of mathematics and psychology, science has influenced political thinking practically from the beginning; though of course the scientific bases on which earlier political theories were sometimes built are about as closely related to modern science as the voyages of Sinbad the Sailor are to modern geographical discovery. This did not prevent Plato and Aristotle from being great political theorists. It is only in recent times that a general belief has grown up in the possibility and desirability of studying politics by the methods that have achieved such remarkable results in the natural sciences. This belief is embodied in the new common term, political science. I do not ask, is political science possible? It must be, it exists. But what is it? The object of science is to show how things happen, and why, in the nexus of cause and effect, they *do* happen. There is no reason why political phenomena, as well as any other phenomena, should not be treated in this way so long as we do not mistake the result for political theory and expect it to answer questions which in the nature of things it cannot answer. What I mean is simply that it is not the function of science to pass ethical judgments. That statement can hardly be questioned. I imagine that any scientist would indignantly repudiate the suggestion that his scientific thought entered into the category of what ought to be. The political theorist, on the other hand, is essentially concerned with the discussion of what ought to be. His judgments are at bottom value judgments. The kind of opinion he offers is that one line of political action is ethically preferable to another, not merely that it is more efficient, whatever that may mean; and surely we have seen enough in our day to know that the difference between political systems is not merely a difference between relative degrees of efficiency.

In case I am thought to be unjust to the political scientist, let me give what seems a fair description of the way in which he envisages his task. It is fallacious, says a recent writer, to suggest that the only way of understanding politics is to participate in it: we do not teach the principles of geometry by a manual training course in carpentry. Political science is a body of knowledge, which must be taught and learned like any other body of knowledge. What this definition neglects is the fact that the degree of moral disinterestedness possible in natural science is impossible in the field of political theory. The political scientist, in so far as he wishes to remain a scientist, is limited to the study of techniques. His subject may be compared to eighteenth-century German cameralism, which was a political theory by bureaucrats, about bureaucrats, for bureaucrats. Mostly, what is called political science, I must confess, seems to me a device, invented by university teachers, for avoiding that dangerous subject politics, without achieving science. Taking it at the highest valuation, political science can give us guidance of the greatest possible importance in achieving the objects we want to achieve; it cannot help us to decide what those objects should be, or even what they are. And to believe that we are all agreed on them and therefore do not need to discuss them is surely, in the light of contemporary events, the wildest utopianism. In the last resort science, like history, leaves us, as Ortega y Gasset put it, to drift: we have a magnificent technical equipment for going somewhere, without anywhere to go.

The image of political life which emerges from the prevailing tendencies in political thought is not a pleasing one. The state appears as a ship in the sea of politics, with no port of embarcation or destination inscribed on its papers, manned by a pressed crew, whose whole endeavor is devoted to the task of keeping the vessel afloat in uncharted waters, with little to help them save their own traditional seamanship, and the records of earlier captains and crews who have for all time been tossed on the seas in the same endless, meaningless motion. A depressing picture, I think, perhaps dreamed up by some remote philosopher who has seen the ships scudding by from the lanternroom of a dead lighthouse, dead because he has carefully extinguished the light.

Luckily we need not take the picture too seriously: it is only an analogy, and analogies are the camouflage of loose thinking. The sea is, of course, the sea of politics. But the state is itself the community as a political organization, the bond that holds it together; the life it lives is also politics. And how is the ship distinguishable from the crew? The state is no mere wooden artifact inhabited by men; it *is* men as political animals. And sea, ship and crew move on together for they are the same. How can we envisage ourselves as inhabiting the ship of state in the sea of politics when the ship is ourselves and the element it moves in our own political being, and *we* rouse the storms and *we* still the waters?

One thing is missing from the picture. It is missing from contemporary politics also. This, as I have said, is the idea that the ship is going anywhere. A sense of direction is lacking, a feeling of purpose. That, I think, is what the decay of political theory means in ordinary terms to the ordinary man. Does it matter? If we were all of us, all our time, porkers not even from the sty of Epicurus, perhaps it would not: our purpose would be set by something outside ourselves, and it would be just as well that it should not be revealed to us in disturbing detail. Such, of course, may be the facts of the case; but rightly or wrongly the human mind demands something more than living from trough to snout. In the absence of a more or less rational theory to justify its sense of political obligation and the rightful powers of government, it will fall victim to an irrational one. If it cannot have, say, Locke on *Toleration,* it will have, say, Hitler on *Mein Kampf.* That is what the decline of political theory means in practice.

One last word. The analysis I have made is perhaps moderately pessimistic; but it is not intended to lead to the conclusion that in political thinking we have reached the terminus, the end of that line. The reasons that I have given for its decline are in themselves even encouraging, since there are signs that they may be only temporary aberrations. Historians are in revolt against philosophies of history: ethics is sapping the lack of morale of professors of history. Hegelian politics is already dead. Marxist politics is increasingly revealed as a dialectical apologia for the pursuit of power for its own sake. The inadequacy, in relation to the broader issues of political society, of the scientific study of administrative methods, constitutional devices, electoral statistics and the like—I hope it will not be thought that within their own field I am attempting to deny the value of the techniques of political science—is gradually becoming apparent.

For a century and a half the Western democracies have been living on the stock of basic political ideas that were last restated toward the end of the eighteenth century. That is a long time. The nineteenth century did pretty well on them, but provided no restatement for its successors. The gap thus formed between political facts and political ideas has steadily widened. It has taken a long time for the results to become evident; but now that we have seen what politics devoid of a contemporary moral and political theory means, it is possible that something may be done about it. After a generation's experience of drifting directionless on a stormy sea the need of recovering a sense of direction, and therefore control, is beginning to be felt. And if political theory revives, if the idea of purpose is reintroduced into political thinking, we may take up again the tradition of Western political thought, and in doing so resume that "continuous transformation of morals into politics, which still remains politics," in which, according to Croce, lies "the real ethical progress of mankind."

10.

Existentialism—Christian and Anti-Christian

Helmut Kuhn

EDITORIAL NOTE: *The last three articles in this anthology examine from different points of view the character and impact of the existentialist movement. Broadly defined, existentialism may be seen, in William Barrett's phrase, as "the philosophy of Europe in this century." Even more radically than the apocalyptists, the cyclical philosophers of history, and the neo-orthodox theologians of the Word of God, the existentialists give expression to twentieth-century European man's alienation from science and culture, conventional religion and morality, politics and the dream of progress. They alone seem to speak with absolute candor of the meaning and meaninglessness of total war, total states, and the total organization of human life by science, technics, bureaucracy, and the mass media of persuasion. At a deeper level, they come face to face with the spiritual nothingness which lies waiting at the end of man's historic search for truth. When all metaphysical, theological, scientific, ethical, and political structures of thought have been weighed and found to weigh nothing, what then? To this colossal "what then?" existentialists both in the anti-religious and the religious camps address themselves with a toughness of mind unparalleled in the history of modern thought. The article below by Helmut Kuhn introduces existentialism as a movement and explores its roots in the thought of Søren Kierkegaard.*

I. The Existential Disturbance

WHAT REALLY IS EXISTENTIALISM? WHILE FEW PEOPLE ARE prepared to give a confident answer to this question, this

movement which is so puzzling to our contemporaries has
yet been very successful with them. As evidence we may point
to the mark which it has left on contemporary speech. We
may now talk of an "existential" thinker or an "existential"
mode of thought with a fair chance of making ourselves understood and without committing ourselves to any particular
philosophical creed. By the epithet "existential" we mean
to describe a thinking animated and supported by the personal life of the thinker. There is implied the rejection of
abstract speculation with no bearing on life. All thinking,
or, at any rate, all thinking in philosophy and theology—this
mode of speech suggests—ought to be "existential," or else
it will be irrelevant and worse than that, harmful. For it
evades the test of life. In Paul Bourget's novel, *The Disciple,*
a philosopher with relentless logic draws conclusions which
obliterate the principles of civilization. This subversive philosophy does not prevent its author from living the inoffensive
and civilized life of a scholar. His disciple, however, takes his
master's conclusions to heart—with disastrous consequences.
Thought reveals its seriousness, sublime or terrible, only
when it is existentially comprehended and appropriated.
Ideas worth the name clamor for incarnation in lives and
deeds.

The test of life, in the majority of cases, consists in the trial
of suffering. Existential, we repeat, is called a thinking "animated and supported by the life of the thinker." We may
now rectify or rather amplify this formula by asserting: an
existential thinking is one which supports the thinker, especially at times when he is desperately in need of support. We
believe this and that, we cherish hopes both for ourselves and
for mankind, we have our philosophical ideas and hold to
our theological principles. But in the depths of our minds a
suspicion lurks that all this might be fair weather philosophy.
To find out whether there is the gold of existential seriousness
in our beliefs, they must be tried in the crucible of affliction.
Then, what seemed high-minded conviction may stand revealed as levity, and what seemed brave optimism, as callous-
ness. For this is the worst thing about our fair weather ideas:

the day of our fair weather may strike others with the terrors of a tornado, and our happy-go-lucky philosophy add insult to their injury. It is irritating to hear a well-fed man lecture his hungry neighbor on "Man shall not live by bread alone. . . ." There are many with us, in this country, in Europe, China, India and all over the world, whose misery silently refutes the brightly colored structures of thought which our complacency erects. Simple human decency requires us to be "existentially serious" in our thinking.

In the sense in which the word "existential" is used in the preceding paragraphs everyone hopes to be an existential thinker. It would be especially shameful for the Christian, who professes faith in the Cross, to confuse God, "Maker of heaven and earth, judge of all men," with the purveyor of a progress evidenced by expansion of the market. One day the market will contract, progress will go in reverse, and our idol, the giver of progress, will become involved in the general deflation of values.

All this, as a broad statement concerning the nature of human beliefs and convictions, may appear unobjectionable and even commonplace. However, the insistence on existential seriousness, justified though it is, readily lends itself to abuse. A criterion of the validity of theories is employed which itself is extraneous to all theory. It consists in the "test of life" or the "trial of suffering." It tests ideas not by examining their adequacy in relation to the objects to which the ideas refer. Instead it is interested in the way in which they are held by a living person. It tests their subjective authenticity rather than their objective truth. But how can we use in our arguments a criterion which, by its very nature, is extraneous to theory and argument? How can we transfer the "test of life" into our philosophical or theological disquisitions?

The abuse which the concern for existential seriousness invites consists in talking about this seriousness and mouthing the tremendous words of "tragedy," "despair," "anguish," and the like as though such language offered insurance against "existential refutation." A little reflection should be sufficient to show that a tragic theory of life can serve as an evasion of tragedy just as well as an optimistic theory depicting our world as the best of all possible worlds. To object to a theory that it lacks existential seriousness is tantamount to resorting to personal aspersion instead of using fair argument. Dr. Samuel Johnson may have been right in affirming that David Hume "had a vanity in being thought easy." [1] But as far as so personal an argument can be countered at all, David Hume's repartee—the sceptical serenity upheld by him on his death-bed—was not inferior in persuasiveness to the pious censure of his antagonist. Following the great lexicographer's example we may with equal plausibility (and with equal lack of conclusiveness in regard to any particular case) suspect that some of our modern existentially-minded and fiercely sombre writers have "a vanity in being thought heavy." Surely, flaunting a cheerful philosophy in the face of a suffering world shows lack of sympathy and sensitiveness. But it is also a dastardly thing to attack other people's hopes and happiness by claiming a monopoly on both suffering and the wisdom which, allegedly, results from it. In fact, the affectation of sorrow, because more deeply knowing, is more reprehensible than the affectation of light-heartedness.

Once more, by "existential" we denote a quality of thought and, at the same time, a demand which everyone, regardless of his philosophical or theological affiliations, should make upon himself. The term conveys an invitation to anxious self-scrutiny. But its usefulness in constructing a philosophy or theology is highly problematic. And from controversial use it ought to be excluded altogether.

II. The Existential Negation

We are now prepared to leave the philosophically neutral forecourt of a general existential disturbance and cross the threshold into Existentialism proper.

[1] *Boswell's Life of Johnson*, Oxford University Press, 1934, II, p. 117.

In maintaining that the "test of life" or the "trial of suffering" is extraneous to all theory, we seem to be on safe ground. Yet precisely this affirmation is challenged by Existentialism. Existentialism may be defined as that school of thought which undertakes to incorporate the trial of suffering in its philosophical or theological structure. Since the counterpart to suffering on the level of thought is despair,[2] we may rephrase our definition by describing Existentialism as a philosophy which tries to win certainty through despair. Various premonitions of this idea are found in a number of thinkers, especially in Blaise Pascal and F. H. Jacobi. But its true originator is Søren Kierkegaard. Accordingly, contemporary Existentialism in all its diverse manifestations is a Kierkegaard renaissance.[3] Jean-Paul Sartre, the dominant figure in post-war French Existentialism, a determined atheist, seems at an infinite distance from Kierkegaard, a Christian, though a very disquieting one. But in spite of the disparity of religious conviction Sartre builds his philosophical structure in *L'Être et le Néant* (Paris: Gallimard, 1947), around a number of concepts borrowed from Kierkegaard. The same is true of Karl Jaspers and, to some extent, also of Martin Heidegger, the two main figures in the German Existentialism of the 'twenties and 'thirties. In order to study the basic pattern of Existentialist thought we must turn to the fountain-head of the movement, the long forgotten and suddenly remembered Kierkegaard.[4]

The existential disturbance which started Kierkegaard on his impassioned search was total in scope. With him the suspicion of disingenuousness fell upon the whole enterprise of

[2] The German word *Verzweiflung* expresses more adequately the intended meaning: not so much a loss of hope as a condition in which doubt has destroyed all certitude.

[3] Gabriel Marcel is the one exception to this rule. In his *Journal Métaphysique* (Paris: Gallimard, 1927) he developed an existentialist philosophy before becoming acquainted with Kierkegaard.

[4] For a more elaborate treatment I may refer to my book, *Encounter with Nothingness: An Essay on Existentialism* (Hinsdale, Illinois: Henry Regnery, 1949).

philosophical-theological interpretation. *Philosophia perennis,* western man's attempt to wrest from the mystery of existence reliable though fragmentary truth about God, the world, and man, appeared to him an artful evasion—an escape from the persistent demands of existential seriousness. He called into question not this or that idea but the very principle and tradition which had produced and nourished the life of ideas. Thus he placed the appeal to existential self-scrutiny into the center of thinking, setting himself up as a modern Socrates.

Kierkegaard hardly realized how radical a revolution he advocated. What is here called "tradition" or "traditional metaphysics" was largely concealed from him by the vicinity and imposing bulk of Hegel's philosophical edifice. This latest and by no means typical embodiment of metaphysical thought seemed to him the avatar of speculation itself. Wrestling with Hegel he was forced to adopt his adversary's language. But through Hegel, he hit the wider and more deeply laid foundations of all metaphysics, carrying a long step further Kant's attack against the metaphysical-theological tradition. Yet even this statement falls short of expressing the radicalism of Kierkegaard's "great refusal." What we describe as "traditional metaphysics" is, aside from its historical sources, an embodiment of common sense brought to bear upon the large issues of human life and experience. Against this "natural metaphysics" Kierkegaard leveled his criticism. The "unnaturalness" of this critique— its going "against the grain"—seemed to this critic a badge of truthfulness. So one need not be a student of Plato, Aristotle, or the schoolmen to be shocked by Kierkegaard's negations. Administering this shock was part of his Socratic mission.

It is natural for thinking man to study the world as it is offered to his senses, and to try to find meaning in it. Meaning involves order and regularity, but not every order is meaningful. The order demanded and sought by the human quest must be such as to include man, the seeker. In it a place must be assigned to him—one which he can either miss or fill properly. His craving would end in frustration, could he not obtain a glimpse at least of such a humanly intelligible order. Once espied, it becomes amenable to different interpretations: either as a self-caused and self-sustaining reality, a cosmos in the pagan sense of this word, or as a creation, pointing to God, its maker and sustainer. In any event the interpretation, as the discovery of meaning, will be of utmost practical or "existential" significance to the interpreter. He will have arrived at an understanding of himself through the world, and his knowledge will be an initiation to wisdom. Thus largely viewed, Plato, Aristotle, St. Augustine, St. Thomas, Leibniz, and Hegel, in spite of enormous differences of method and principles, are seen to pursue the same purpose. By all of them the principle of Classic Rationalism is maintained: they view human reason as an organ for the disclosure of meaning. And it is the denial of this principle, involving as it does the denial of man's "natural metaphysics," on which Kierkegaard's thought, and that of Existentialism generally, hinges.

Unless we bear in mind this Great Negation and its shattering effects, Existentialism will seem an insoluble riddle. For Kierkegaard the negation grew out of the Romantic malady—the irony of disillusionment and *Weltschmerz*. In our own time two national catastrophes, the German defeat of 1918 and the collapse of France in 1940, were instrumental in reviving Kierkegaard's experience in modern minds. Because of the double object of the negation—reason in the traditional as well as in the natural sense—the approach to the negation may be either sophisticated or naive. The outstanding example of the former approach was furnished by Martin Heidegger. Assisted by his disciples he undertook, with sombre enthusiasm and penetrating insight, critically to destroy the principles of traditional metaphysics.[5] This was in the decade following the First World War, and for

[5] Cf. Karl Löwith, "Les implications politiques de la philosophie de l'existence chez Heidegger," *Les Temps Modernes,* II (14 Nov. 1946), p. 346.

one so occupied it became possible to mistake for a recovery that which was actually the final step towards the German catastrophe and the beginning of the end: Adolf Hitler's rise to power. After the cataclysm of 1945 the ground was cleared for a naive approach. Hans Zehrer,[6] writing in the years of deepest misery, took his departure from the "man in the barrack," the German refugee from the eastern provinces, a figure of utter bereavement. Once he had a home, a wife, children, land, cattle. Now he has only what he can carry with him. Deprived of his world and yet alive, he asks the agonized question: what is the meaning of it all?

In discrediting reason as an organ for the disclosure of meaning, Kierkegaard's chief interest was not merely to point out the inadequacy of specific metaphysical conceptions. This is what Kant did in attacking natural theology. But Kierkegaard went beyond the Kantian criticism. Supposing that reason succeeded in furnishing an interpretation of the world, he argued, its very success would defeat its purpose. The meaning so discovered could not possibly be a meaning for man. Meaning as conceivable by reason involves a system in which contradictions are harmonized into a consistent whole. But man lives and moves and has his being in the sphere of conflicts and contradictions. Metaphysics would hoist him onto the seat of the spectator. But being a finite, concrete person rather than a disembodied spirit, he is precluded from playing so lofty a part. No spectator's lodge for him—he belongs in the arena and must do his thinking in the mêlée. For this reason metaphysics is harmful in addition to being deceptive. It is the existential evasion *par excellence*. Little man would screw himself to a height from where he believes he can take a bird's eye view of things. If he succeeded, he would cease to be human.

So far Kierkegaard's argument—which is also the platform of Existentialist thought. The question whether the argument is sound should not be hastily answered. Those who follow suit blindly forget that the problem raised—the

[6] *Der Mensch in dieser Welt* (Hamburg, Stuttgart: Rowohlt, 1948).

question, really, how finite man can be rational or how reason can be human—has been alive in metaphysics from its inception. Metaphysics seeks an answer to this question by showing that man does not occupy a completely fixed locus in the order of things. He has a margin of liberty; he may either rise or sink. Philosophy, viewed as existentially real, is ascent. The stimulant behinds its ultimate questions is a mystery rather than a problem,[7] and its method[8] is an itinerary of the mind towards God rather than a logical contrivance. In Hegel this timeless existential movement of thought became travestied into temporal progress, i.e., history. So Kierkegaard had a good case when he refuted Hegel's conception of reason. But he was wrong in thinking he had confounded reason. In the Existentialist court reason is not given a fair hearing.

We return to our definition. Existentialism, we suggest, is thought which endeavors to become self-authenticating by including the trial of suffering within its own domain. This thought begins with a negation. It denies reason's power to provide meaning. But since we cannot live without meaning, the result is despair. Such is the trial of suffering for the thinking mind. No thought is authentic unless it has traversed despair, the Existentialist claims, and he offers himself as an expert guide through those bleak regions.

III. The Existential Drama

An evocative expression of thought is one that, in addition to communicating arguments and conclusions, creates a frame of mind in the hearer or reader. Rhetorical and homiletic speech is evocative, and so is devotional theology. Philosophy has developed its own evocative style whose great models are Parmenides' poem and Diotima's speech in Plato's *Symposium*. This philosophical evocation is the linguis-

---

[7] The concept of "mystery" in contradistinction to "problem" has been developed by Gabriel Marcel, *Être et Avoir* (Paris: Aubier, n.d.).

[8] It is well to remember that method (μεθοδοs) originally means "pursuit."

tic expression of the idea of intellectual ascent: the hearer is
to actualize in his mind a thought-process which is, at the
same time, a life-process. Existentialism, using the traditional
method of evocation, inverts it. Rather than a love-guided
ascent to vision it teaches descent into the frigid terrors of
despair. It does so with no evil intent. For in spite of the
gloom in which it is wrapped it has its own optimism. It is
even under suspicion of sometimes playing with terrors and
light-heartedly courting a fearful temptation. In Existentialism it is hopefully assumed that falling man, once he has hit
the bottom of negation, will rise again, by rebound, as it were.
And there is the further suggestion that he can rise in no
other way. The inner movement to be initiated by the Existentialist argument describes a curve, descending first to a
nadir and then, after passage through the critical moment,
its "peripety," rising sharply to a height above rational
expectation. This dynamic pattern may justify our speaking of an "Existentialist drama." The stage is within, and
protagonist and antagonist are one and the same person.

The "dramatic" situation is created by the Existentialist
negation. Meaning as discoverable by reason is obliterated,
and the things which surround us and intrude themselves
upon our consciousness form neither a cosmos nor a creation.
They are no text to be deciphered. They have no tale to
tell. The relationship of unrelatedness which thus obtains
between man and surrounding reality is best described by
the term "estrangement." [9] Accordingly the stranger is a
symbolic figure whose aimless trail runs through Existentialist fiction as exemplified by Franz Kafka's *The Castle,*
Albert Camus' *The Stranger,* and Jean-Paul Sartre's *The Flies.*
Be homeless, an uprooted one, be a stranger! This terrifying
imperative is the preamble of the Existentialist drama.

That this demand is formulated in reaction against the
diametrically opposed and equally intolearble demand, "Be
at home in the world! " need not here be insisted upon. It is

[9] For a classic expression of estrangement see S. Kierkegaard, *Repetition*
Princeton University Press, 1941), pp. 114–115.

more important to note that the destruction of a false and impertinent sense of familiarity ("nature at our beck and call") results in a keen and philosophically enlightening awareness of the concrete individual as different from "things." The Cartesian and post-Cartesian assimilation of the human self to things sub-human is brought under attack, and a fresh sensitiveness to the unity of the person—mind incarnate rather than mind and body—is cultivated.[10] At this juncture a much quoted definition of Existentialism becomes intelligible. It is said to be a philosophy according to which "existence is prior to essence." Essence, in this formula, stands for that all-comprehensive order within which everything is determined as "such an one." From this order of determining "essences" or "natures" man alone is exempt, the Existentialist affirms. Instead of being determined by the essence or nature of "man," he as existing determines himself. He is free. With this Existentialist declaration of human freedom the progress of the existential drama towards a crisis is precipitated.

It is among the chief purposes of Existentialist evocative exposition to make man realize his own freedom. But the freedom of which we are to become aware is very unlike the freedom of choosing the better of two alternatives on the basis of rational deliberation. Freedom of choice presupposes a standard to determine the preference, a fixed idea of the good. But under the dispensation of estrangement no signs of good or bad are imprinted upon reality. There is no essence of "the good." Accordingly the freedom whose consciousness

[10] There is a group of Existentialists whose chief interest is directed towards an understanding of the concrete person and the uniqueness of the I-thou relationship (including man's relationship to God) and who have hardly any dealings with the "existentialist drama." Martin Buber (*Between Man and Man* [New York: Macmillan, 1948]; cf. *Journal of Philosophy*, XLVI, pp. 75–79) and Gabriel Marcel are the chief representatives. In this country, H. Richard Niebuhr moves in a similar direction ("The Ego-Alter Dialectic and the Conscience," *Journal of Philosophy*, XLII, pp. 352–359; cf. *Journal of Religion*, XXVI, pp. 203–214).

grows out of despair and estrangement precedes and renders possible the freedom of choice. The original freedom is that of the stranger who has no business to attend to, no appointment to keep or duty to discharge, for nobody has a claim on his affection. Dropping the simile, the Existentialist's freedom is to be conceived as commitment to nothing. For only meaning can engage and *ex hypothesi* there is no meaning. The awareness of this freedom is an encounter with nothingness—an experience suffused with *Angst* (dread or anguish). Nothing in particular is dreaded by this dread, for since nothing is prized nothing can really be feared. Yet dread persists. Through it, existing man perceives his bottomless freedom. As we sustain this anguish the descending curve of the inner movement reaches its lowest point. The crisis is at hand.

A peculiar imagery, invented under the influence of mysticism by Kierkegaard and persisting in contemporary Existentialism, serves both to picture and evoke the crisis of despair.[11] Man is seen as placed at the brink of an abyss—the abyss representing Nought (the void in which all meaning is lost) as well as freedom in the sense just defined. He then is seized by giddiness, an emotion in which two opposite tendencies are confusingly blended. Giddiness makes him withdraw with horror while, at the same time, a sweet and sinister fascination bids him step nearer and let himself fall.

The series of images comes to an abrupt halt. That which follows is unpicturable. We may experiment with a variety of imaginary sequels. We may imagine either a devout ending or a tragic one. In the first case the sufferer would be carried across the abyss by the hands of grace and landed on the firm ground of faith. In the second case, his vertigo would hurl him to destruction. Or even a humorous version could be imagined, modeled on Shakespeare, *King Lear*, IV, 6, where the cliff from which the blind Gloucester leaps turns out to be a beneficial lie. But none of these endings recommends itself as more plausible than the others. Imagination

[11] Cf. J.–P. Sartre, *L'Etre et le Néant*, p. 69.

falters, and the hesitation thus felt is indicative of an inconclusiveness of thought.

In the densest night of anguish, at the very moment when all support is withdrawn to the perplexed and troubled mind, all certitude blotted out, the lights of truth extinguished by the enveloping Nought—then, out of the midst of the vortex of despair, a new certainty is miraculously to arise. Be it so. But we, living and thinking this side of the chasm which separates us from the promised land of faith,[12] can form no clear expectation as to the nature of the assurance which is to come to us. By definition the expectation is empty, i.e., expectation of the unexpected. This reflection may well cause alarm. Is the happily negotiated passage through the crisis of despair a reliable mark of authenticity? We may really have been "made wise by suffering" ($\pi \acute{a}\theta \epsilon \iota \ \mu \acute{a}\theta o s$), to use the well-known formula of ancient tragedy. Or we have only escaped from the passive despair of nihilism into the active despair of fanaticism. Then our new certitude, dearly though we paid for it, is actually the ignominious flight from the intolerable truth of nothingness. . . .

Such is the quandary into which the Existentialist argument maneuvers us. It is a revealing fact that at this point where the precise nature of the rising move, the resuscitation from the spiritual death of despair, comes under consideration, Existentialists divide into two sharply distinguished camps: the theists and the atheists, or the Christians and the "Titanic" thinkers.

The Christian, Kierkegaard, interpreted the saving move as the seizure of religious truth "by virtue of the absurd." For him the discomfiture of reason became the triumph of faith, and the central Christian mystery, Incarnation, confounded in his view the claims of rational metaphysics. A curiously inverted apologetic resulted: instead of representing faith as acceptable to reason, its intellectual offensiveness was insisted

---

[12] For only in this rôle, as ailing from the doubt which the Existential negation has inflicted upon us, are we addressed by the evocative analysis of the Existential Crisis.

upon. In our own time, Karl Barth's Existentialist theology shifted the emphasis from the paradox of Incarnation to the hearing of the Word of God by man prepared for this communion through crisis. But by and large this was still a development of Kierkegaard's answer.

According to the secular Existentialism which, like its Christian partner, developed in the wake of the First World War in Germany, the crisis of despair is to open our eyes to an insight which, by its origin, is safe against Existential Negation. For Karl Jaspers[13] this insight was a transrational, symbolic knowledge. In the "exaltation" (*Aufschwung*) which follows the "shipwreck" of the intellect, meaning is espied under the form of symbols (*Chiffren*). But the truly creative mind of the movement was Martin Heidegger. By means of a new intellectual sensitiveness which he owed to the "phenomenological" method of his master, Edmund Husserl, he developed the grandiose though fragmentary picture of man's finite world[14] as revealed to anguish in the face of Nothingness.[15] After the Second World War Jean-Paul Sartre, the most resourceful of Heidegger's disciples, developed his own dread-inspired and noughtcentered world-picture. With him, atheism, disclaimed by both Jaspers and Heidegger, became a point of doctrine. He put man in God's place as the creator of values.

The contrite sacrifice of the intellect *versus* the proclamation of man's emancipation from divine authority—so great a disparity of results may well set us on our guard.

IV. The Divine Being and the Human Nought

"Except a man be born again he cannot see the Kingdom of God" (John 3: 3). "That which thou sowest is not quickened, except it die" (I Cor. 15: 36). "Therefore we are buried

---

[13] *Man in the Modern Age* (London: G. Routledge, 1933).

[14] This "world" is neither cosmos nor creation.

[15] *Sein und Zeit*, 1. Teil (Halle: Niemeyer, 1927); *Was ist Metaphysik?* (Bonn: Cohen, 1929).

with him by baptism into death: that like as Christ was raised up from the dead by the glory of the Father, even so we also should walk in the newness of life" (Rom. 6: 4). These familiar words urge upon us the question: does Existentialism spell out in the language of philosophy the religious truth, "Die so that you may live"? Or does it rather express the defiance of man delivering himself from divine tutelage?

The crisis through which the Existentialist leads is an encounter with nothingness. In answering the above questions, everything depends upon the interpretation of "Nothing." "Nothing" may be understood as an ultimate datum of experience out of which, as a point of departure, "world" is arrived at. This is the "Titanic Nought." Again, "Nothing" may be taken to mean our own, the human being's nothingness (man separated from God is nothing). Then, through a *coincidentia oppositorum*, i.e., the coincidence of utter deprivation and ultimate superabundance, God, too, will *appear* to us as "Nothing." This is the "Religious Nought."

The "Titanic Nought" is the product of the secularization of two closely allied theological ideas: the hiddenness of God, and the total depravity of man. This may be illustrated by the sequence of three quotations. First, Martin Luther: "It is God's nature to make something out of nothing. Hence he who has not yet become nothing, out of him God will not yet make anything." [16] An echo of this great sentence is heard in Kierkegaard, but with the overtones of a Titanism, which the writer himself rejects: only by understanding himself inwardly, he notes in his *Journals,* can man rid himself of that destructive irony "which bids true understanding begin with ignorance in the same way in which God created the world out of nothing" (August 1, 1835). In Sartre, at last, man creates himself out of nothing: "There is no human nature, because there is no God to conceive it. . . . Man is nothing else but what he makes himself." [17]

The Nought of the "Titanic" Existentialist is to the Divine

[16] Quoted from Zehrer, *op cit.,* p. 13.
[17] *L'Existentialisme est un humanisme* (Paris: Nagel, 1946), p. 22.

Nought of the Mystics as total darkness, caused by the absence of light, is to temporary blindness, caused by an excess
of light. A contemporary mystic, whose language is influenced by Existentialism, writes: "The soul with a thrill of
joy becomes conscious of that blessed nought which allows
her to see nothing, either in herself or in all things, but the
sole work of her Creator." [18] Seen from the point of view of
this more inclusive Christian experience the Existentialist's
tryst with Nothingness is intelligible—as a temptation. The
temptation of Father Donissan in Georges Bernanos' *Sous le
Soleil de Satan* may serve as an example: "One who, clinging
with both his hands to the top of the mast, suddenly loses his
equilibrium and sees yawning below—no longer the sea but
the whole siderial abyss, with galaxies foaming in travail
billions and billions of miles away, beyond that immeasurable void which his fall is about to traverse—this unfortunate
could not feel in the hollow of his breast a more absolute
vertigo. The intrepid man, as though bent and torn away by
the tremendous appeal of the Nothing, sees himself lost beyond recovery. And yet, even at this moment, his dominant
thought was still dull defiance." Temptation may be viewed
as included in the plan of salvation, and it is possible that
the generation now living is singled out before others to
sustain "the tremendous appeal of Nothingness." But a
temptation should not be courted.

Crisis, to be sure, is an integral part of the Christian
scheme of life and thought. But the question is whether this
crisis is actually to be conceived as having its center in the
intellectual life; in other words, whether it is primarily a
crisis of certitude. This seems doubtful. Perhaps a line should
be drawn between despair and *Angst* ("dread")—two conditions which Existentialism tends to confuse. Despair belongs
together with defiant self-assertion. *Angst* pairs off with
humility. The Stoic fortitude that goes with despair—a

[18] Paul Claudel, *Présence et Prophétie* (Fribourg en Suisse: Librairie de
l'Université, 1942), p. 26.

militant virtue prized above all others by Existentialists—
is all too wary of fear; whereas we surmise that "at this present time the living Christ is, so to speak, in the Garden of
Gethsemane." [19]

[19] Gertrud von Le Fort, *Die Letzte am Schaffott* (München: Ehren, 1931),
    pp. 30–31.

11.

Existentialism and Existentialisms

Mikel Dufrenne

EDITORIAL NOTE: *The thought of such formidable philosophers as Heidegger, Jaspers, Marcel, Sartre, and Merleau-Ponty cannot be exhausted in a single article. Professor Kuhn's essay stressed the "human" appeal of existentialism, and its intimate connections with theology, themes which were especially compelling when the movement first caught the attention of the general educated public in the aftermath of the second World War. But existentialism is more than a spiritual revolution: it is also a penetrating inquiry into some of the oldest problems in metaphysics. In their labors the leading existentialist philosophers take up the pursuit of truth in a new way, but they do pursue truth, and in so doing they have much in common with the philosophers of the Western tradition. In short, existentialism is not confined to "existential" dramas and confrontations. It is also a rigorous philosophical movement which, indeed, may well be accused at times of an excessive aridity of manner and method. Mikel Dufrenne here reviews existentialism as a philosophy and contrasts the major existentialists on a number of crucial issues from the perspective of the mid-1960's.*

INSTEAD OF EXISTENTIALISM, WE SHOULD SPEAK OF EXISTEN-tialisms. If we were to go into the history of contemporary philosophy, I might show that there is a perpetual internal fight among the group of philosophers who are given the label of Existentialists, and, what is more, that none of them claims to be an Existentialist: for instance, Heidegger says he cares only for ontology, and he disavows Sartre; Sartre disavows himself when proclaiming himself a Marxist in his last book; Sartre and Merleau-Ponty, who were, as long as Merleau-Ponty lived, good friends, disagreed on philosophical as well as political issues. Nevertheless, my contention is that to speak of Existentialism means something, but that every one of the so-called Existentialists treads now his own path in his own direction.

I. The Main Aspects of Existentialism

Existentialism had a definite meaning twenty years ago, in the time of distress, when, through war and torture, freedom and civilization were at stake. In order to show what it meant, I will refer mostly to Sartre, the first Sartre, although the second Sartre, as we will see, is not so different. But we must think of it as a genuine and difficult philosophy, and not merely as an attitude suggested by an historical situation, nor as a collection of literary themes. As a matter of fact, I would like to emphasize that many pseudo-existentialist themes do not necessarily belong to Existentialism. Such are the themes of the absurd, of nausea, anxiety, of the exaltation of freedom for freedom's sake. Many of these themes have been popularized by Camus; it is only too bad that Camus is not a philosopher, nor even a very profound thinker. Many of these themes have also been developed by Sartre; but one should keep in mind that Sartre does not approve of them: in his first works, when he discovers freedom as the essence of man, he wants to show in which traps reflection about freedom may fall, and which bad uses of freedom action may make. If Roquentin is nauseated, if Mathieu is haunted by anxiety, it is because they refuse to commit themselves by assuming their freedom; if hell is the others, it is because we expect from the others what they cannot give us. If Goetz is torn between the Devil and the good Lord, it is as long as he hesitates to be a man among men. If negative attitudes may be a way of freeing thought from some prejudices and also of expressing the fact that the emergence of consciousness is unpredictable and unjustified, because the for-itself is not its own fundament, those attitudes are never the last word of existentialist ethics. Now this ethics is grounded on a philosophy, and we must examine some main notions of this philosophy.

a) Existentialism suggests existence. Existence is traditionally, with essence, a category of being. So Existentialism is put forward as a philosophy of being, an ontology, distinguishing itself from the more shy (or more reasonable) philosophies which deal only with knowledge or language. It returns to the Aristotelian conception that the eternal object of philosophical research is Being *qua* Being. It also rediscovers in its own way, according to Sartre, the famous ontological proof: the idea that essence entails existence, or that an existent can only have a being—nature or essence—on the condition that it has being, that it be. So existence comes first. But the originality of Existentialism consists, instead of using this proof in favor of a supreme being, in distinguishing two types of being, or two ontological regions, both different and reciprocally conditioned: the in-itself, the opaque and inert being whose essence implies existence, and the for-itself, the transparent being of consciousness, whose existence posits the essence. Where does this distinction come from? From the fact that, by a natural shift of meaning, one passes from Being to the beings, to the existents; and there are for those existents two ways of existing, depending on the relation, within themselves, of existence to essence: the in-itself is what it is, it has somehow too much essence, but it has it only on the condition that it exists; and it is also as if it had no essence, because a consciousness is required for that essence to appear and to be determined, so that in a way the in-itself receives its meaning or essence from the for-itself. Conversely, the for-itself has not enough essence, because it gives this essence to itself, it has to be what it is, but also on the condition that it exists. And so the word *exist* has two meanings, depending on whether it designates the existence of a thing or of a free subjectivity, the fullness of being or the unsubstantial absolute of a subjectivity. It is generally for characterizing subjectivity that the word existence is employed; but we must not forget that, as Sartre says, "consciousness is born supported by a being that is not itself" [1] and which exists also. Existentialist ontology is at first a dualistic one. It keeps and transposes on its own level the distinction of object and subject made by the theories of knowledge. Why? Because it is a phenomenological ontology: it is inspired by phenomenology.

b) Existentialism starts from a reflection on the phenomenon. It carries out spontaneously the reduction which for Husserl is the condition of any philosophical thinking. It discovers the wonder: things appear to us, they show themselves. Every thing is given; if some things are hidden, they still can be given and are homogeneous to the given. There is no other world, no behind-world. Even the world of logical or mathematical objects, the world of universals, belongs to the only given world, because these objects also are given as the meaning of the signs, words or symbols we construct. Must we identify appearing and being? Here Sartre diverges from Heidegger. For him, *what* the thing is, that appears: the essence is not concealed behind the existence, it is read on the object as its meaning; doubtless this reading never comes to an end, because the essence, as the principle of the series of appearances, is infinitely removed, but this infinite is homogeneous to the finite and immersed in it. On the other hand, *that* the thing is, that the phenomenon entails a being of the phenomenon, that does not appear. The appearing drives us back to something which is its condition and which does not appear. Appearing is appearing *of* and appearing *to*. Appearing of means that appearing presupposes a being which appears. Sartre says: "That which appears does not exist *only* insofar as it appears . . . it is in itself." [2] The phenomenon of being requires a being of the phenomenon. This being is the

[1] *Being and Nothingness*, p. lxi.
[2] *Ibid.*, p. lxii.

ground for appearing, and it is coextensive to the phenomenon without having the status of a phenomenon. So Existentialism avoids the temptation of idealism, and rediscovers the
ontological proof: there is Being. On the other hand, what
appears appears to: to a consciousness which exists only as
consciousness of something, and which is therefore an unsubstantial absolute. There is another dimension of being, whose
nature consists in opening itself to appearances and revealing
being: such is the for-itself, which exists only in relation to
itself and to the world. This opened existence, light and transparent, is not nothingness, it is rather negativity, through
which nothingness happens to being.

c) And hence proceeds the main theme of Existentialism:
the peculiar fate of subjectivity. Existentialism represents
the perpetual revolt of subjectivity against systems, any
system which objectifies and enslaves it. Such already was
Kierkegaard's protest against the status ascribed by Hegel
to man, man as a pawn for history or a tool for logos. Kierkegaard wanted to be left alone in his quest for God. But there
are many other accesses to the self-assertion of subjectivity.
There is the ethical feeling of man's dignity, of the absolute
value of a rational being. This claim is itself a consequence of
Kant's discovery of the transcendental subject, an autonom-
ous subject which is not governed by laws of nature as in
Hume, but which imposes laws to nature and gives to itself
its own law. Husserl says also that consciousness is constitu-
tive, sense-giving. Other philosophers emphasize other aspects of subjectivity, its power to promote values, as in
Nietzsche, or, in Marx, to humanize the world and to overcome the alienation which man at first is sentenced to. But
what Sartre is mostly attentive to is the Husserlian notion of
intentionality: consciousness is merely the naked power of
aiming at something; in opposition to the massive, opaque
and inert in-itself, it is nothing, nothing but the being to
which the world is present. Subjectivity as consciousness has
no being; it is negative and asserts itself through negations
by which it gives sense to the in-itself because, as Spinoza

said, any determination is negation. And this negativity is the soul of freedom: subjectivity is primarily free.

That means also that man is not featured in a theological or cosmological program, he is not a means for any end, because he is himself the end, being such that he posits the ends. When Existentialism is Christian, it is ready to admit that man is not created *ad majorem Dei gloriam,* and that in any case he is as necessary to God as God is necessary to him. But Existentialism is more willingly agnostic: man must invent his own way; there he is, for nothing, and his birth is unjustifiable: mere contingency, whose sign is the facticity of the body.

d) The body. It is precisely this theme of Subjectivity that carries us into reflection on the human condition, where the for-itself is conceived as being-in-the-world. The necessary connection of for-itself with in-itself becomes, when the for-itself is understood as a concrete subject, and the in-itself, enlightened by the for-itself, is understood as the world, the relation between man and world. Being-in-the-world is not being a thing among things, it is bringing sense to the in-itself, so making that world be. The world as I live in it has myself as an absolute center of coordinates because I am involved in it and my presence to it is contingent. For consciousness to be sense-giving does not imply that it is a transcendental consciousness, impersonal and pure, and somehow creative, as in traditional idealism; on the contrary, consciousness is giving only because it is committed to the world, compromised by it, embodied. The incarnation of man means that the duality of in-itself and for-itself is overcome in at least one place: in man. The for-itself, as we said, is everywhere negation, even of itself: its freedom consists in refusing any determination in order to invent itself. What it negates is the in-itself that it is, and this in-itself is the body. Doubtless the experience I have of my body is not the same that others have; for myself, as Sartre says, "I exist my body." For others, I am a body, and this body is an object; for me, it is the instrument of my communication with the world. But it is true also that my body, such as I live it, is an object, with the density of the in-itself: the body is both a body and a soul.

We have evoked the other. Existentialism attaches great importance to my relationship with the other. In fact, many societies are more concerned with controlling the relationships between the group members than with dominating nature by science or technology. Being-in-the-world is being a man among men. Man calls for man: he meets him, but he also looks for him. He needs the other, not only to live and make the species live, but also to assert himself, to get recognition, as the child by his parents or the artist by his public, and to enter into collaboration, since his freedom is finite and wants to be carried over to the freedom of others. Man tends towards common ends, he aims at humanity.

Then he needs also society and culture. Through institutions he is given a status and a style of life. He tends to identify with his culture, even when he denounces and fights it, as with effort he denounces his own body. And culture is for him like another body: he lives in it and it lives in him. From this point of view some studies by American cultural anthropologists have an existential flavor.

Now society has a history. Man is a historical being because he is gifted with a memory which retains the past and a will which opens the future. And we meet the same paradox with history as with the body: man both is determined by history and makes history, even if he is unaware of it. So he remains an irreducible singularity, an unassignable freedom.

e) How can we grasp this relationship of man and world? First of all—and this will be the last theme I consider—by exploring the primitive experiences where this relationship manifests itself. Phenomenology, said Husserl, must be archeology. Husserl's concern was mostly to reveal the *doxa,* the naive opinion which *episteme,* clear knowledge, is founded upon: coming back to the source of all knowledge, one understands better how science is constituted; rational evidence has its roots in sensible evidence without losing its privileges. For Existentialism, the stress is on ontology rather than epistemology; its main concern is to show how man, from the very beginning, gets along with the world. Hence the interest in analyzing perception, emotion, feeling, anything which is immediate, as well as primitive civilizations, savage arts, magic. It is also on that level of immediacy that one may find the first manifestation of freedom: spontaneity. Spontaneity, the first form of liberty, is not sufficient because it has not yet asserted itself as a power of liberation, but happy because it harmonizes with the world and blossoms like a flower. I do think that the theme of innocence might have been more emphasized by existentialism; it has not been taken into consideration because existentialism has been more attentive to the tragic aspects of negativity, and also because it is deeply concerned with ethics: freedom for it implies responsibility and, as Simone de Beauvoir says, "If man wants to save his existence, what he only is capable of, his original spontaneity must raise itself to the level of a moral freedom, by taking itself as an end through the unveiling of a singular content." [3] We come back again to the idea that Existentialism is an ethics, maybe the only genuine one, if it is true, as de Beauvoir says, that "in a metaphysics of Transcendence evil reduces to error . . . and Existentialism only, as well as religions, actually takes evil into consideration." [4]

II. The Divergent Progeny of Existentialism

The themes we have evoked are the core of Existentialism. But they do not constitute a whole philosophy. As soon as they are given some development, they explode in diverging directions, probably under the influence of presuppositions which depend on the personality of each philosopher. Let us now summarize some of these trends.

a) *Gilson.* The notion of being is obscure in Sartre's ontology. Existence is not univocal; it is torn apart between too much and not enough; in both cases it is contingent, neither

[3] *Pour une morale de l'ambiguité,* p. 46.
[4] *Ibid,.* p. 48.

grounded nor grounding. There is a world, there are men,
that is all we can say. The only task for philosophy is to describe the relationship between man and world, and to call
man to himself. But some philosophies would prefer existence
to be justified and to appear as a fundament. Such is Gilson's
philosophizing. He congratulates Existentialism for having
rehabilitated the notion of existence against the temptation
of essentialism, and for having established that the knowledge of essences dissimulates the true problem, which is the
rooting of essence in existence. But he condemns Existentialism for having considered existence as a fact and not as an
act. We must, says Gilson, consider the pure act of existing
as the act of a supreme Being; anything which exists partici-
pates in this very act, which is both creative of itself—God
is *causa sui*—and creative of all creatures. Such is Aquinas'
existentialism, where ontology leads to theology. But it seems
to me that this idea of an act of existing is ambiguous; it
makes of existing the privilege of a being, and it transforms
the given into a giving. If existence is an act, there is a fact
of this act, but this act is not a fact. No being is capable of an
act except if it does not exist fully, if it does not coincide with
itself. If there is an act of existing, it belongs to man, not to
God. On the other hand, Gilson can introduce the idea of
God only by jumping from the idea of being to the idea of *a*
being. When he says that we must "posit existence at the root
of being," he no longer thinks of being as existence, but of a
being which exists. And as a matter of fact, he adds that
"since both essence and existence enter into the structure of
the real being, and since the primacy of existence asserts itself
in the being, this primacy is not a primacy of existence upon
being, but *in* being." [5] So existence is subordinated to being,
and being is a being. Possibly, Existentialism is responsible
for this misunderstanding, because it distinguished two types
of being and so invites us to pass from being to beings. And
maybe this confusion is unavoidable if it is always a being

[5] *L'Être et l'essence,* p. 323.

which is and if the problem is always to know what is and how it is.

b) *Heidegger.* But precisely here is a philosophy which endeavors to do justice to Being as such, I mean as distinct from the beings or the essents (essent is the word coined by a translator of Heidegger to translate *Seiend* as opposed to *Sein*). Heidegger was a student of Husserl, and he has inspired Sartre and Merleau-Ponty. But he does not accept being called an Existentialist for two reasons: because Existentialism tends to mistake essent for Being, and because it gives too much credit to human subjectivity. Let us look at those two points. Heidegger's fundamental question is: Why are there essents rather than nothing? And his fundamental assertion is the distinction to be made between essents and Being. To be sure, any essent is; but its being is not *a* being. And the philosopher must be concerned with Being, while unauthentic knowledge—the positive knowledge—is only concerned with essents, their nature or their essence. Theology itself is oriented towards the essent, the supreme essent, and not towards Being. But how can we seize Being, if not because it discloses itself?

Heidegger also starts from phenomenology: there are phenomena, something reveals itself. We may distinguish the phenomenon of being and the being of the phenomenon: this distinction has been borrowed from Heidegger by Sartre. But Sartre is interested in the phenomenon of being, because it requires the presence of a for-itself: it is for a consciousness that the phenomenon is a phenomenon. He is also interested in the being of the phenomenon because it teaches us the priority of being: there is a phenomenon only if there is some being. But as soon as the phenomenon drives us back to a being which shows itself, being is again mistaken for an essent. Now Heidegger is primarily interested in the phenomenon of being: this phenomenon is precisely Being itself. Being is not what appears, or to whom it appears, it is appearing itself: the essent shows itself, and this showing-itself is Being. Being is the presence, the horizon, the light, a light which lies neither in the sun as its source nor in the eye as its end, but which suscitates and justifies both the sun and the eye. If there is a meeting or an agreement between subject and object, such as phenomenology describes, it takes place in the space opened by this light. Being is conceived as so pure, in order not to be mistaken for an essent that it is nothing, as light is nothing. It is nothing disclosed and nothing hidden: it is the disclosure, the glory of the essent when the essent appears. This disclosure is truth as the Greek *a-letheia*. "Truth is inherent in the essence of Being. To be an essent—this comprises to come to light, to appear on the scene, to take one's place, to produce something." [6] In that sense we are in the truth, and this being-in-the-truth defines man.

But Being is not completely defined by the appearing, and it can also dissimulate itself. This dissimulation does not produce a secret to be found, as things are concealed in the nighttime after sunset: darkness itself is a phenomenon, it shows itself and so it is as clear as light. Being is not a hidden God to be found beyond the world. It is rather in the very unveiling that Being is veiled, because in making the essent appear it lets itself be forgotten; it is like a trap: what appears makes us forget the appearing. That is why the history of philosophy is, from the pre-Socratics on, the history of a progressive carelessness about Being: man is always tempted to reduce Being to essent.

So—and this is my second point—the ontological question requires from the philosopher what Heidegger calls a care for Being. In other words, appearing cannot appear but from a point of view. This point of view is the being-there (*Dasein*). Being-there means being in space, but mostly being in time, in a moment of time: *Dasein* is essentially historical. This *Dasein* is embodied in man, and that defines man. Man is the being which is haunted by the problem of Being, even when he forgets it, and which has an anticipating comprehension of Being. Man is the being which weaves and unfolds time;

[6] *An Introduction to Metaphysics,* p. 102.

time originates in man. "There is no time when man was not, not because man was from all eternity and will be for all eternity, but because time is not eternity and time fashions itself into a time only as a human historical being-there. But a necessary condition for his being-there is that he understands Being." [7] Man is the being which can tell Being. Being needs language and is in some ways language, for language also is revealing and may reveal only because Being primarily reveals itself. So man in his profound essence is the speaker, and as such committed to the service of Being.

But precisely because he ascribes to man this exceptional status, Heidegger refuses a philosophy of subjectivity or a humanism. For him, philosophizing cannot start, as in Descartes, from subjectivity, nor from the phenomenon as a correlate of a transcendental consciousnes, as in Husserl: it must start from Being. And it must also forget all information provided by human sciences which are only concerned with man as an essent. Man is to be defined in function of Being and as servant of Being, in an endeavor to grasp its ontological emergence. Heidegger tries to go back to the very origin, the ontological origin which is itself the origin for chronology.

This is not easy. His effort gives his philosophy the style of an oracle and makes it close to poetry. And this philosophy takes a more and more mystical character, because it gives more and more initiative to Being, although refusing to identify Being with any God. Consequently, dealing with man, it goes farther and farther away from anthropology; it tends to forget that, if man has a metaphysical vocation, it is insofar as he is man, an incarnated and socialized being, coming before the bar of anthropology, so that nothing that anthropology discovers about him is immaterial. Maybe ontology should call for humanism instead of denouncing it as illusory and misleading.

c) *Sartre.* There is a philosophy which wants man to accomplish man in this world: it is Marxism, especially in the modern version of it proposed by Sartre in his last book

[7] *Ibid.,* p. 84.

devoted to a philosophy of history and society. Many readers
have been wondering whether Sartre did not thus deny his
first book, and whether Marxism is not incompatible with
Existentialism. I do not think so. The second book is more
a deepening than an agonizing reappraisal of the first one.
A "critique of dialectical reason" substitutes for a "phenomenological ontology": what does that mean? The words dialectical reason evoke Hegel and Marx, the word critique,
Kant. Kantian critique is a path of access to the discovery of
subjectivity as a mode of being; in his own critique, Sartre
does not renounce the fundamental idea of his ontology: that
man is the future of man because freedom is irreducible. Only
the vocabulary changes: Sartre speaks of man rather than
of for-itself, of praxis rather than of consciousness, of matter
rather than of in-itself. But the praxis is always conscious and
self-conscious, and it always manifests freedom; matter as
in-itself is both the opposite and the product of freedom, it
both suscitates and limits freedom; in the end self-consciousness, which becomes self-awareness of praxis, is always the
principle and the model for intelligibility. The lexicon
changes because phenomenology seems from now on inadequate: it considers only the immediate and the abstract, it
does not provide sufficient means to deal with the central
problem of ontology, that is the problem of the relationship
between in-itself and for-itself, or between freedom and
situation, by which is defined being-in-the-world. Doubtless
Being and Nothingness had already examined the relationship
between freedom and facticity; it had analyzed my body,
my environment, my fellow men, but in the same way as my
past or my death, that is, as elements of my situation with
which I am directly concerned. But now Sartre wants to
think of being-in-the-world as being-in-life and being-in-
society: the socio-historical dimension is an essential element
of man's situation.

In order to understand these aspects the situation, Marxism is useful. For Marxism is a dialectic materialism. Materialism implies both an ontological thesis: matter is given

first; and an epistemological thesis: knowledge grasps reality. Those two theses are implicitly present in *Being and Nothingness*. The ontological proof is the assertion of the priority of the in-itself; the idea of an intentional consciousness prepares the idea of the veracity of knowledge. Materialism introduces, nevertheless, a very important new idea: the idea of scarcity as a determining factor of all of history, a radical evil. As for the term dialectical, which is new in Sartre's vocabulary, it carries with it two ideas: negativity and totality. Being is torn off by negation, or, what comes to the same thing, the immediate is mediated by determinations, but negation is itself negated, and the opposition is overcome: dialectics is this transcending motion which is a perpetual motion. *Being and Nothingness* already had found a place for negativity: the title of the book says it. And already the negation was conceived of as circular: the for-itself constitutes itself as the negation of the in-itself which also negates it; similarly, in the struggle of consciousnesses, as Hegel said, each consciousness aims at the other's death—this theme was developed in *No Exit*. But if there was no exit, no end for this fighting, it is because there was no dialectic to allow for the emergence of a totality. In the same way, in the ontology, dualism could not be overcome, and Sartre said that "it is immaterial for ontology to consider the for-itself articulated in the in-itself as a duality or as a disintegrated totality." [8] True, Sartre is less concerned in his last book with this metaphysical problem than with the anthropological one. Now, the main purpose of the concept of totalization is to throw some light on society and history. But we must carefully distinguish totalization and totality. Totality, if achieved, would mean the end of history, the return of a state of inertness and meaninglessness. Unfortunately, there are totalities: groups, institutions, closed societies, as Bergson said; and everywhere they come up against man. Besides that, the first alienation proceeds from matter: working is the first form of totalization, of synthetic organization of the

[8] *Being and Nothingness*, p. 624.

in-itself; and the matter which the praxis works on comes up against man, so that totalizing man is totalized by the matter he has totalized. So the Chinese, centuries ago, were pauperized by their own deforestation; and Spain, in the sixteenth century, suffocated under the burden of gold its trade accumulated. Now totalization constitutes also the objectivity of the social. The social is intelligible because its origin lies in human praxis; society is both the product of freedom and the place for alienation. And Sartre describes the various forms of this alienation: class or race struggle, colonialist oppression, capitalistic ferocity. History is not a happy one. And it has been said that the *Critique of Dialectical Reason* is a theory of evil.

Nevertheless, it is also an ethics. Sartre, as in all his works, calls for freedom. For, if the starting point of dialectics is in matter as materialism requires it, the spring of dialectics is in man, as the intelligibility of dialectics proceeds from the fact that consciousness is self-consciousness. Man everywhere has the initiative, even when he makes himself inert in order to act upon inert nature, even when he produces inert totalities where he alienates himself. There is no alienation but *for* a freedom. And *from* a freedom. For evil does not proceed only from the inertness of matter, or from the scarcity of goods, or from the weight of totalities, but also from the violence and the cruelty of men: to understand torture, we must have recourse to sadism or the will to power. Here the analyses of *Being and Nothingness* are welcome again: man's negativity often manifests itself as violence. Often, but not always: Sartre knows it, since he also evokes that brotherhood which prevails among the poor, the slaves, the rioters. And we might add that man may have with nature peaceful and friendly relationships. Some kinds of praxis, which do not socialize man, are happy: the praxis of the craftsman, of the peasant, of the artist. Dialectical motion may be comforting.

d) *Merleau-Ponty.* Here I would like to mention a last direction taken by Existentialism. Everywhere, up to now, we have seen philosophies endeavor to return to fundamentals, to the source: be it the act of existing in Gilson, Being in Heidegger, the dialectical motion which unites matter and praxis in Sartre. In Merleau-Ponty, as in Sartre, the fundamental is a relationship, the relationship between subjectivity and the world which defines being-in-the-world and which is manifested at its best in perception. "I am the absolute source," but this source is itself situated and given to itself: Man is in the world. This idea is not ignored by Sartre; but in *Being and Nothingness* Sartre is so intent on asserting the freedom of the for-itself that Merleau-Ponty accuses him of being "cogito-crazy." This was before the publication of the *Critique of Dialectical Reason*. But even after this book, there remains a distance between Sartre and Merleau-Ponty. Merleau-Ponty stresses perception, not praxis or sociality. Perception manifests the harmony between the perceiving and the perceived; it is somehow prior to them: *esse est perceptio*. Perception is the absolute beginning, the origin of conciousness, the emergence of sense. And Merleau-Ponty checks it by practicing the archeology which Husserl recommended: at the root of any human behavior, of any human creation—language, art, technics, science, politics—he discloses perception, this unreflective and spontaneous relationship between man and world. So that there is sense everywhere, in history or in events as well as in things, and this sense always at first appears in perception. Intentionality, rather than merely being a structure of consciousness, carries both consciousness and world; consciousness aims at the world, and the world answers to its aiming. Man, says Merleau-Ponty, "is this perceiving subject which, through the opacity of feeling, is intent on things which he has not the key to, but which he carries with himself the project of." [9]

Now, if I may mention myself, I would say that the work I have undertaken is a comment on this sentence. To say that man carries the project of the world is to say he is equipped with a priori, he assumes the transcendental. But the transcendental reveals itself in the empirical, as the meaning of

[9] *Phénoménologie de la perception.*

the empirical. The world must answer to man, and the a priori can be read in the object as what constitutes this object. So the harmony between world and man is the fundament on which thought and history are built. But are we not led back to Leibniz? For philosophy is tempted to dig out farther and to look for something beyond the fundament which I call the ground, something which generates the fundamental relationship. Might this ground be Heideggerian Being? No, because it must itself be an essent, or rather the totality of essents. Neither is it a God like the leibnizian God, separated from the world he creates. This ground is rather Nature, *Natura Naturans,* as Spinoza said: the unfathomable power of reality, the reality which can and maybe wants to appear, but which appears only to man and produces man in order to appear. But as soon as we say that, as soon as we speak of a Nature before man, we posit man, and we come back to the fundament. Nature is unthinkable. That is why the philosopher leaves the floor, and is tempted to give it to the poet.

12.

Demythologization—Crisis in Continental Theology

Peter L. Berger

EDITORIAL NOTE: *The theology of Karl Barth, discussed above in the article by Professor Krüger, was, especially in its formative stages, a theology shot through with existentialist insights largely derived from Kierkegaard. But in the last quarter-century theologies and systems of religious thought have taken the center of the stage which go further than the early Barth, and still further than the later Barth, in the direction of an existentialist world-view. The thought of Paul Tillich and Martin Buber owes much to modern existentialist philosophy. Pre-eminent among the existentialist theologians, however, is Rudolf Bultmann, a one-time follower of Barth, a distinguished New Testament scholar, and the leading force in Protestant thought in Europe since the second World War. The Bultmann controversy discussed below by Peter L. Berger brings into sharp focus the predicament of modern Protestant faith and, to a degree, the test to which all forms of supernatural faith are being put in our century.*

THERE CAN BE LITTLE QUESTION THAT, SINCE THE END OF World War II, the controversy over Rudolf Bultmann and his program of demythologization (*Entmythologisierung*) of the Christian message has occupied the center on the stage of continental Protestant theology. Ripples of the storm have touched theology on this side of the Atlantic as well and aroused keen interest if not participation. On the continent the Bultmann controversy has placed theology in a clear and present crisis. What is at stake is much more than a novel attempt of transcending the old formulations of liberalism and orthodoxy, both classical and "neo." Protestantism on the continent, especially in Germany, found itself in a state of exhaustion after the struggle with Nazi paganism. The great religious renascence hoped for in the fervor of that struggle failed to materialize, at any rate in the proportions antici- pated. The unity of the Confessing Church dissolved before the new pagan invasion from the East, while the power of Catholicism, both cultural and political, seemed stronger than ever. There emerged a new urgency to the qualifying phrase which Bultmann ominously used in his original essay to point out the significance of his program—"if church and theology are to continue existing at all."[1]

Bultmann's essay on "New Testament and Mythology," which touched off the controversy, was written during the war from within the circles of the Confessing Church in Germany. Time and place are highly significant. By the time the war was in full swing, the German church struggle was, to all intents and purposes, over. Much of the fervor which had characterized its early stages had disappeared, and a certain modus vivendi had been established between the Protestant churches and the Nazi state. With the silenc- ing of the early witnessing fervor, there was a new problem of communication in countless individual situations. What did the Christian still have to say to his fellow men? Especially, what did the Christian in uniform still have to say to his comrades, caught up with him in the apocalyptic events of the last days of the Third Reich?

It is under the aspect of communication that the demy- thologization controversy must be understood, both at the time of its inception during the war and in the years since

[1] Rudolf Bultmann, "Neues Testament und Mythologie," in Hans Werner Bartsch (ed.), *Kerygma und Mythos* (Hamburg, 1948), I, 25.

1945. It is an almost desperate attempt on the part of a hard pressed Protestantism to speak out and reach its contemporaries. It is born of the same concern which motivated Dietrich Bonhoeffer when he spoke of the need for Christians to accept modern man as free and mature, and to speak to him as such. How can the Christian communicate the message of the New Testament to this strange creature, modern man, for whom the sky has become empty, an occasion for aeronautics instead of wonder? Can this communication only be established by a return to a mythological sky full of gods? Or can, perhaps, the Christian message be understood by modern man without such an intellectual *salto mortale* back into mythology? If so, the Christian message must be freed from its mythological elements, must be *demythologized.* This became all the more important as Protestantism faced not only modern man flying his machines through an empty sky, but the massive mythological structure of Catholicism on the one hand and the fantastic "neo-mythology" of Rosenberg's "Myth of the 20th Century" on the other. The postwar situation has done nothing to lessen the urgency of this need for communication.

Bultmann's Position

Bultmann's program of demythologization is based on a certain conception of mythology on the one hand and of the mythological character of the New Testament on the other. While the latter is, at least in part, the result of Bultmann's exhaustive exegetical work, it also depends on the conception of mythology which Bultmann holds. This conception is not the result of exegesis, but of a philosophical position anteceding the scientific work, determining its significance and placing it in a certain perspective from the viewpoint of communication.

Mythology is defined by Bultmann as a pattern of thought in which the "otherwordly" is represented as acting within the world, in which God is represented in human terms, as, for instance, when God's remoteness from the world is represented as distance in space.[2] It is a translation of transcendence into the terms of immanence. In its essence, mythological thought understands reality as an interpenetration between the world of men and the world of divine beings. Not only does the divine break into and interfere with the events of nature, but the human personality itself is open to constant influence from another world, by gods and demons, magic and sacrament. The mythological view of reality is the one which antedates the modern view, shaped by science, which understands the cosmos as a closed system of causalities. It also antedates the modern view of man as personality, which, whatever its relationship with the causalities of nature, is also closed to alien and mysterious forces acting upon it from a world beyond.

Bultmann maintains that, from this definition of mythology, the world of the New Testament is a mythological one.[3] The world is divided into three stories, as it were: heaven, hell, and earth, each the location of specific supernatural forces. Earth itself is not only the location of everyday reality in the life of men, but the scene of struggle between the forces of heaven and hell, God and the devil. Human events are interpenetrated by these forces, as is the human being himself.

The mythological character of the New Testament, however, lies not only in certain cosmological features which may be laid aside by theology as *adiaphora*. The very content of the Christian message of salvation, the *kerygma* itself, is couched in mythological language. The preexistence of Christ, his incarnation as a human being, his crucifixion as offering atonement on behalf of sinners, his resurrection as the victory in a cosmic struggle, redemption through Christ as the removal of the curse of sin inflicted upon humanity by Adam, Christ's ascension to heaven and enthronement on the right hand of God, his return on the clouds at the end of history, the resurrection and judgment of the dead, the

[2] *Ibid.*, p. 23.
[3] *Ibid.*, pp. 15 ff.

presence of the risen Christ in the community through the spirit and in the sacraments—all these are mythological concepts, mythological thought patterns, mythological language. As such they form part of a view of the world which modern man is incapable not only of accepting but even of grasping. They are, in Bultmann's words, "finished" (*erledigt*), and, if Christianity depends for its existence upon them, then Christianity itself is "finished."

Man is not capable of freely choosing the view of the world with which he is to live and within which he is to think. This view of the world is given to him by his historical situation. Thus modern man, even if he wanted to think in mythological terms, is bound to the view of the world which science has given him. Therefore, it is impossible to ask modern man to accept the mythology of the New Testament. He may try to convince himself that this can be done by the kind of *sacrificium intellectus* performed by a modern Catholic when he accepts the dogma of the Assumption of Mary, but this is fundamentally deceiving oneself. The various attempts in our time to resurrect mythological thinking, such as the "neo-mythologies" of the Nazis or of various occultist groups like the Anthroposophists, only prove the fact that this type of thinking is moribund in the modern world. And, as Bultmann points out, even occultism today presents itself in the guise of a science. "It is impossible to use electric light and radio, to call upon modern medicine in case of illness, and at the same time to believe in the world of spirits and miracles of the New Testament." [4]

What follows from this? If Christianity is to be meaningful to modern man, it must be demythologized radically, at its heart as well as on its fringes. It is impossible to continue the process of the old liberalism, which, in full retreat before scientific thought, sacrificed this and that part of the message, gave in a little here and a little there, always in the hope that the heart of the message could be defended. Nor is it possible to follow any of the restoration movements back into orthodoxy, with its adherence to mythology in the teeth of mod-

[4] *Ibid.*, p. 18.

ern thought. One must either reject or accept the mythological view of the world as a whole. This must be done clearly and unambiguously. For the Christian preacher this is a question of honesty before his congregation. It is this radical approach to the question which gives those qualities of freshness and excitement to Bultmann's position.

However, Bultmann cannot go along with the old liberal attempt to demythologize the New Testament by interpreting the Christian message in terms of ethics or some type of mystic experience. This would mean abandoning the *kerygma* along with the mythology, and would constitute the real end of Christianity. The *kerygma* must be maintained, but it must be communicated to modern man in a non-mythological form. That is, the *kerygma* must be understood and interpreted existentially, as containing truths concerning man's existence in the world and before God. Bultmann believes that his program of demythologization is capable of doing this.[5]

Bultmann maintains that this procedure is called for by mythology and by the New Testament themselves. Mythology, while containing a cosmology, has a fundamental existential concern, which must be uncovered and interpreted. As to the New Testament, the very contradictions in it, such as the conception of man as fallen under bondage to demonic forces and, at the same time, called to decision, make demythologization necessary. This procedure is also maintained to be in accordance with the fundamental insight of Reformation thought that the Christian is always concerned with the *Christus pro me,* the Christ, not of an abstract and impersonal history in the past, but the Christ in the history of my own existence.[6]

[5] *Ibid.,* pp. 27 ff.

[6] Bultmann makes the distinction between *historisch* and *geschichtlich,* the facts of the New Testament being "historical" in the latter, existentially relevant, sense. Thus, the resurrection may be "historical" without the myth of the empty tomb. This is one of those occasions when one would like to make translation obligatory to all writing in the German language!

This interpretation is then carried out with the help of categories derived from existential philosophy, particularly that of Heidegger.[7] The New Testament is understood as offering a certain interpretation of existence in the world, which is existence in impermanence and toward death. In this world man is lost, cast into bondage under fear, in need of redemption. When man lives in accordance with the flesh, he lives unto himself alone, he tries to overcome his condition of forlornness by reliance on the self alone. He is closed within himself—as Luther put it, his heart is bent back upon itself. Contrasted with this condition is the life in faith and in the spirit, which frees man from the bondage to his past and opens him up toward God and the world. Faith in the Christian *kerygma* makes man free of this world by confronting him with the transcendent God. The things of this world become deeply insignificant and, by establishing distance between himself and the world, the Christian becomes free for the future. This life in the spirit, however, in contrast to gnosticism or mysticism, is not the entering upon a new psychic experience, such as occurs in ecstasy. It is always an act, a decision and, at the same time a free gift of God's grace, never to be possessed, never to be verified by any natural process, always to be chosen anew in each instant of time. Thus the Christian life is not to be understood in terms of supernatural relations and events. In its entirety it is located within the world. It can never be verified in terms of the miraculous, can never be taken out of the natural context of human existence.

The question then arises logically as to what the relationship of this Christian life is to Christ. Can there be Christian existence without Christ? If Christianity is essentially a certain understanding of existence, can it not be dissociated completely from Christ and the New Testament? Indeed, has this not been already done by modern existentialism, by the philosophies of Heidegger, Jaspers, Kamlah? Bultmann himself is far from complacent about this point: "I think one

[7] Bultmann, *op. cit.,* pp. 28 ff.

should be terrified by the fact that philosophy on its own has seen that of which the New Testament speaks." [8]

Bultmann grants that the Christian understanding of human existence can also be grasped philosophically, without Christian faith, though he points out that modern existentialism would be impossible without the New Testament, Luther, and Kierkegaard. However, he maintains that Christianity, in contrast to existentialism, maintains that more is needed for redemption from man's condition of forlornness than an understanding of this condition. Man cannot redeem himself by himself. Every act he performs is caught within his forlornness. Man can be freed only by an act of the transcendent God. This is the meaning of Christ—the act of God's love in freeing man from his forlornness, his life in death. In the *kerygma*, the proclamation of the risen Christ, the opportunity is given to man to accept this act of God through faith. It is this reliance upon God's act in Christ which distinguishes Christian faith from any existential philosophy without Christ.

The problematic of this position is obvious and was so to Bultmann from the beginning. It would appear that the line between the secular-existential and the Christian-existential understanding of man becomes uncomfortably thin. Moreover, it would seem that a limit is hereby set to the demythologization program. To speak of an act of God through Christ, in any meaning which goes beyond man's consciousness of this act, would seem to fall back upon an irremovable hard core of mythology. In the original essay Bultmann cannot do much more than confess his uneasiness about it: "Whoever maintains that any speaking of action on the part of God is mythological, must certainly call the speaking of God's act in Christ a myth." [9] Bultmann can only point to Kamlah, who, for reasons of his own, is willing to concede that one can speak of divine acts without becoming mytho-

[8] *Ibid.,* p. 35.
[9] *Ibid.,* p. 43.

logical. However, no attempt is made to reconcile this with Bultmann's own conception of mythology.

The act of God in Christ is now itself demythologized.[10] In essence, the act is understood as taking place *hic et nunc* in the meaning of *kerygma* and faith. The Easter faith in the resurrection is no longer faith in an historical event some 2,000 years ago, fixated in the myth of an empty tomb, but concerns the God who meets me as the Christian message is proclaimed to me. "Christ, the Crucified and Risen, meets us in the Word of proclamation, nowhere else. Just the faith in this Word is in truth the Easter faith." [11] Eschatology is thus demythologized from a cosmic to an existential meaning. Cross and resurrection are no longer cosmic events in a mythological universe, but acts of God in my own existence.

If demythologization frees the individual Christian from having to engage in a game of mental acrobatics with regard to the mythology of the New Testament, it also has a liberating effect on Christian theology. No longer must the theologian be in a constantly defensive position before the advance of biblical science. He need no longer worry over the next discovery, the newest manuscript. The Christian message is placed on a plane where scientific analysis can never touch it. Even if one were to take the extreme example of possible scientific discovery, the Easter faith of Bultmann would be unshaken: if one can imagine that a set of motion-picture cameras had been trained on the burial place of Jesus on Easter morning, and if all these films were suddenly discovered by an archeologist, and if they show nothing at all, or perhaps if they showed some of the disciples rolling away the stone and taking off with the body under cover of darkness—all this would yet leave intact Bultmann's Easter faith and, presumably, God's act in that faith.

In this way Bultmann also feels that he is maintaining the true paradox (*skandalon*) of Christianity, in Kierkegaard's

[10] *Ibid.,* pp. 43 ff.
[11] *Ibid.,* p. 50.

sense. The paradoxical faith demanded of the Christian is not that he swallow the mythological view of the world found in the New Testament. On the contrary, the paradox consists in the full acceptance of all that history, psychology, and sociology can tell us about the natural causes of Christianity, in the development of the Church as much as in that of the individual Christian—and then, nevertheless, to have faith in God's act through Christ. It is an acceptance of the fact that Cross and Resurrection are always objects of faith, never objects of verification. The empty tomb as a miracle is as little able to verify the resurrection as Jesus' throwing himself down from the pinnacle of the Temple would have verified his Messiahship.

While this statement of Bultmann's position has, of necessity, been brief, it can already be seen what grave problems the future discussion had to face. There were, for one thing, the apparent inconsistencies within the demythologization procedure itself, above all the question as to whether God's act in Christ, even in Bultmann's version of it, was not, after all, a mythological remnant. There was the truly alarming correlation of Christian formulations with those of modern existentialism, putting in grave doubt the necessity of adhering to the *kerygma* in any form at all. Finally, there was the question whether, in fact, Bultmann had not reduced Christ to a datum of consciousness. Had not the *Christus pro me* very subtly become a *Christus in me?* If so, was Christianity not reduced to an immanent process in human consciousness in a way different only in terminology from that of Schleiermacher or William James? And, if one thinks of Schleiermacher, one also thinks of Husserl. Is Christianity here not treated as a phenomenon in the sense of *epoche,* and, when Bultmann dismisses all questions of the cosmic significance of Christ as mythological, is he not actually putting phenomenological brackets around something taking place in the human consciousness?

Developments of the Position

As the controversy proceeded in the years following the publication of the original essay, both Bultmann himself and his followers produced a large number of explanatory statements, using arguments ranging from epistemology to exegetical analyses of certain New Testament passages. However, the essential concern of these statements had to be the solution of the grave problems indicated above. Needless to say, the fierce attacks on the Bultmann program, both from the "right" and the "left" of his position, brought these problems into even sharper focus.

Friedrich Gogarten defended the program at length from the viewpoint of a philosophy of history.[12] He defends Bultmann against the accusation that he filled the New Testament with contents derived from existentialist philosophy by denying that existentialism has any such contents in the first place. Existentialism is not a *Weltanschauung* because it does not tell man how he is to exist; it only points out to him what existence means.[13] He also defends Bultmann against the accusation that, by saying that Christ can only be encountered in the *kerygma,* the historicity (*Geschichtlichkeit*) of the Christian message is denied.[14] Gogarten maintains that both sides of the controversy maintain that Christ antecedes the human encounter with him—the question is only, how? Bultmann, it is argued, does not deny that Christ exists over and against the human experience of him; he only denies that this preexistence is a matter of objectively verifiable historicity (*Historizitaet*). He attacks the theologians of the "right" for allowing themselves to remain in a "Babylonian captivity" brought about by introducing into theology an alien concept of "scientific objectivity," of the search for

[12] Friedrich Gogarten, *Entmythologisierung und Kirche* (Stuttgart, 1953).
[13] *Ibid.,* pp. 51 ff.
[14] *Ibid.,* pp. 56 ff.

"objective facts." [15] This attitude is attacked as a subjection of Christian theology to thought patterns alien to the New Testament. The irony of this statement, in defense of a theological position designed to make Christianity understandable to modern man, does not seem to be apparent to Gogarten.

An early and very forceful defense of the Bultmann position is that of Goetz Harbsmeier. [16] He takes up the defense at precisely the point at which Bultmann had been most sharply attacked: one Lutheran critic had ironically paraphrased the Apostolic Creed according to Bultmann— Christ, not conceived by the Holy Ghost, not born of the Virgin Mary, really suffered under Pontius Pilate, crucified and buried, but not descended into hell, not risen from the dead on the third day, not ascended into heaven, not sitting at the right hand of God, from whence he will not come to judge the quick and the dead. Precisely, says Harbsmeier, here our faith is narrowed down to the naked human being hanging on the cross. Everything else is "finished," and even that human being is "finished," because he is the crucified one. And then, just then, faith finds its object in the crucified Christ, who becomes Lord and Redeemer. It is this Christ, no longer protected by dogma or myth, with whom the Bultmann program wishes to confront man. In defending themselves against Bultmann, the theologians of the "right" are defending themselves, in reality, against the scandal of the cross. [17]

Harbsmeier, who himself was wounded in the war, stresses the problem of communication, or, as he calls it, translation. The message of the New Testament must be translated into the language of modern man. But we must realize that God always, in the Bible as elsewhere, speaks through human beings in human language. The task of translation is, therefore, not the purification of the divine Word from its human

[15] *Ibid.,* pp. 98 ff.
[16] Bartsch, I, 54 ff.
[17] *Ibid.,* pp. 68 ff.

elements and presentation of it in this purified form. This cannot be done. It is rather the proclamation of the Christian message in our language, just as in the New Testament it is proclaimed in the language of mythological man. The attempt to hold onto the mythology is romanticism, the yearning for a world that is dead for us and cannot be resurrected.[18]

Bultmann himself developed his position in a final rebuttal to his critics.[19] He reiterates his analysis of mythology as illegitimate objectivization of the transcendent and the need to speak of existence in other terms. He points out that much of the fear of demythologization may be due to a tacit assumption that one's propositions have to be either mythological or scientific, thus failing to understand the existential language in which the *kerygma* is to be presented; for instance, the sentences "I love you," or "please forgive me," are neither mythological nor scientific, but speak directly and simply of existential realities. The same sort of language is to be used in presenting the realities of the Christian life. He stresses the point, also made by Harbsmeier, that existentialism does not furnish the content of his program, but only its formal presuppositions.

He then returns to the crucial question about the possibility of speaking of "God's act" within the demythologization program.[20] God does, indeed, act "objectively," that is, outside of and over against human consciousness. However, I can only become aware of God's acting within my existence, which takes place in space and time. Within this existence, it is only faith which can recognize God's act. To all eyes but those of faith, only natural, causally explainable acts take place. Within these, however, are God's acts hidden. Nowhere does God "break into" the world of natural phenomena. He always remains the *Deus absconditus*. For

[18] *Ibid.,* pp. 78 ff.
[19] Bultmann, "Zum Problem der Entmythologisierung," in Bartsch, II, 179 ff.
[20] *Ibid.,* pp. 191 ff.

this reason, faith must always retain its paradoxical character, perceiving the hidden act of God in spite of that which is visible to the eyes of all. It is clear, though, that, by saying that God is visible to faith only, we are not saying that God exists only within the consciousness of that faith. It follows that God's act in Christ also can be perceived only in the encounter of my existence with the *kerygma* hidden within the Bible. It cannot be objectively discovered, verified, made visible as a historical fact. This realization does not diminish the "once and for all" (*ephapax*) quality of Christ. As I accept Christ through faith, I recognize him also as having redeemed me once and for all, in the sense of the New Testament.

Bultmann presents demythologization as the final consequence in the area of understanding of the Pauline conception of justification by faith without the works of the law. Reformation thought emphasized that there are no sacred places in the world, that the world as such and as a whole is profane. Well, says Bultmann, it must be recognized that nature and history in their entirety are profane also, that we cannot locate the sacred places within them by factual observation. Only faith sees the hidden hand of God acting within the world.

We thus see Bultmann's position as an extreme and radical consequence of the Protestant alienation between God and man. The Catholic *analogia entis,* the hierarchical universe connecting man with God through the angels, is denied as never before. God is totally hidden and man is totally alone within his profaneness. Faith, therefore, is totally paradoxical. Is this perhaps, finally, a reduction to total absurdity of this approach to religion?

Attack from the "Right"

The bulk of the attack on Bultmann's position naturally came from the "right," from the side of orthodoxy, both "neo" and otherwise, Lutheran and Reformed. By 1950 the official organs of German Protestantism, particularly the Evangelical Church in Germany (EKID) and the United Evangelical-Lutheran Church in Germany (VELKD), felt called upon to debate the matter officially. These official statements are marked throughout by considerable restraint, a willingness to listen to what Bultmann has to say (despite the repeated accusation by his followers that his position is always "misunderstood"), but a generally firm rejection of the entire procedure.

The first official statement came out in 1950. It was issued by the Church of Hesse-Nassau, the United Church of which Martin Niemoeller became president after the war.[21] It discussed various aspects of the controversy without taking a definite position, but is generally negative in tone. This attitude was characteristic of the circles of the Confessing Church, from which, after all, Bultmann himself had emerged.

The most violent controversy broke out, not surprisingly, in pietist Wuerttemberg. Early in 1951 Bishop Haug of the Wuerttemberg Church (Bishop Wurm's successor in that mildly Lutheran territory) issued a pastoral letter on Bultmann which, for the first time, officially warned against the consequences of the position and, without trying to coerce the conscience of the pastors in that Church urged them to seriously question the implications for their ministry.[22] The attacks on the part of Wuerttemberg's "Bible-believing" circles were less restrained. A pamphlet published in the same year boldly proclaimed "The Bible is at stake!" and passionately condemned Bultmann as a heretic undermining the very foundations of the Protestant faith.[23]

While the EKID hesitated to take a public position on the matter (it was discussed at several conferences), the Lutherans of the VELKD came out with a clear warning and re-

---

[21] *Kirchliches Jahrbuch fuer die Evangelische Kirche in Deutschland,* 1951 (Guetersloh, 1952), pp. 185 ff.

[22] *Ibid.,* pp. 199 ff.

[23] *Ibid.,* pp. 210 ff.

jection. In 1953 the Conference of Bishops of the VELKD issued a statement on the Bultmann controversy urging pastors and congregations not to be confused and not to deviate from the traditional proclamation of the Gospel.[24] This warning was reiterated in subsequent synods of the VELKD and by a theological commission appointed by that body.

The discussion by the theological world proper was intense in circles ranging from the orthodox Lutherans to the Barthians. Its range of approach was equally wide. An example of a rather naïve approach is an article by Ethelbert Stauffer, in which the author confronts Bultmann with what he terms "realistic theology." [25] Stauffer attempts to show, by the results of archeology and other scientific investigations, that the Bible is much more credible today than it was when Bultmann began his critical work in the 1920's. This approach hardly touches the meaning of the demythologization program.

An early very serious discussion of Bultmann from the "right" was that by Julius Schniewind.[26] Schniewind questions Bultmann's premises as well as his deductions. Mythology is defined as any attempt to represent the invisible by the visible, the unspeakable by that which can be named. It may be asked, then, whether man's thought can ever escape mythology, unless it is to fall into complete nihilism. The very mention of God, even philosophically, involves us in mythological thought. If one is to remain completely unmythological, God can only be spoken of negatively, in the manner of the mystics' *via negativa*. Indeed, Bultmann might be understood from that philosophical tradition. Christianity, however, makes positive assertions about God and God's actions. The paradox (*skandalon*) of Christianity lies, at least partially, in this "mythology," not, as Bultmann maintains, only in the naked Man on the cross. Moreover, Christianity

[24] *Informationsdienst der Vereinigten Evangelisch-Lutherischen Kirche Deutschlands,* November 1953, pp. 107 f.
[25] Ethelbert Stauffer, "Entmythologisierung oder Realtheologie?" in Bartsch, II, 13 ff.
[26] Julius Schniewind, "Antwort an Rudolf Bultmann," in Bartsch, I, 85 ff.

is such a paradox, not only to modern man but to man as such. By escaping from historicity into the "here and now" of existential decision the full weight of the Christian paradox is avoided. The *skandalon* lies precisely in Christ's presence "in, with and under" the events of history, one certain history. It is then, again, asked urgently whether this procedure does not destroy the heart of the Christian message.

A sharp attack from the Lutheran side came from Helmut Thielicke.[27] He starts the attack by discussing Bultmann's concept of faith. This faith, though couched in the aura of the Reformation's *sola fide,* is really a perversion of it. The Reformation understood faith as objectively bound to and dependent on Jesus Christ, not as a pale, abstract maneuver of man's consciousness. Faith, according to Bultmann, becomes a process within man's consciousness. The history reported in the New Testament becomes nothing but a prolegomenon to what goes on in my consciousness; the question of its extraconscious reality is pushed aside. Christ, at best, stands only in the background of the Christian existence. Like the chained men in Plato's cave, we can only see the reflections on the wall. Perhaps, indeed, our consciousness of Christ presupposes the extra-conscious reality, but the former is understood as being "deistically started" (*"deistisch angekurbelt"*) by the latter—there is no actual encounter with the living Christ. Bultmann sets up the idol of a secular world view within theology, says Thielicke. The result of this is a "philosophical palace revolution," against which Bultmann can only defend himself feebly. Demythologization becomes the reduction of theology to philosophy. This entails the destruction of the Christian message, not its communication to modern man.

Scandinavian theology entered the controversy in an interesting contribution by the Danish Lutheran Regin Prenter.[28] Prenter reduces the controversy to two basic

[27] Helmut Thielicke, "Die Frage der Entmythologisierung des Neuen Testamentes," in Bartsch, I, 177 ff.

[28] Regin Prenter, "Mythos und Evangelium," in Bartsch, II, 70 ff.

questions: Has Bultmann succeeded in the demythologization program itself? Does his program reach the understanding of God and man in the New Testament? Both questions
are answered negatively. Bultmann does not, in fact, remove
mythology. He merely interprets it existentially instead of
cosmologically. A better name for his program would be
"decosmologization." This entails a contradiction: either
one eliminates mythology, but then one cannot interpret it;
or one gives an interpretation of mythology, but then one
cannot speak of demythologization. Bultmann seeks to
maintain the Christian existence as the acceptance of God's
gift, living towards transcendance, open to the future. Measured by the standards of secular existentialism or Bultmann's modern world view, these concepts are as mythological as the breathing-in of the *pneuma* in the New
Testament, which Bultmann finds unacceptable.

Again, as in the characterization of Bultmann's procedure
as an expression of the *via negativa,* he is presented by Prenter
with a mystic label. If Christ loses his past significance, in
any historical sense, then his "presence" can only be understood mystically, that is, ultimately in the sense of a psy-
chologism. Christ becomes only the example, and the Christian life becomes an *imitatio Christi.* What is the end result
of Bultmann's program? The Christian picture of God, rejected as mythological, is replaced by a concept and a feeling
of God. When mythology disappears, metaphysics takes its
place. Also, when mythology disappears, emotionalism takes
its place. In this way Bultmann is again placed in a heretical
tradition within Protestantism, that of the crucial alliance
between rationalism and pietism which once before spelled
the end of Protestant orthodoxy.

Karl Barth entered the controversy with some remarks
in the third volume of his monumental *Dogmatics.*[29] His
main broadside, however, was fired in a pamphlet published in 1952, ironically entitled *Rudolf Bultmann—An At-*

[29] Reprinted in Bartsch, II, 102 ff.

tempt to Understand Him.[30] The pushing back of Christ into a vague causality of the Christian consciousness is represented by Barth as an absorption of christology into soteriology, the entire loss of any christological concern in the preoccupation with my own salvation and its processes. It is a complete reversal of the Christ-centered theology of the Reformation, which cannot be hidden by a facile quotation of Melanchthon's saying that to know Christ is to know his benefits—a saying which, before Bultmann, had been as piously quoted by the old liberals. And Barth asks whether Bultmann does not, indeed, reduce the Gospel to a new law, the law of my own consciousness, in which, when all is said and done, it is man's act rather than God's act which accomplishes my salvation. It is as if Christ goes forward toward his resurrection—in us. He then sharply attacks Bultmann's conception of mythology, his "canonization" of the modern world view and particularly its expression in existentialism.

Barth concludes with some interesting questions regarding Bultmann's historical antecedents. He feels that Bultmann cannot be understood only within the Marburg tradition of mercilessly grim "intellectual honesty," in spite of the absolute readiness to sacrifice the belief in demons before the universal use of the telephone. Also, Bultmann cannot be simply understood as an apologist or a historian. Barth, with considerable *Schadenfreude,* would like to address Bultmann above all as a Lutheran, and warns those who would strike at Bultmann to look out, as they might accidentally hit Luther. It is already in Luther that one finds, according to Barth, this absorption of christology into soteriology. Luther's *theologia crucis* carried within itself much of what later became experiential interpretations of Christianity. Moreover, Luther's conception of the world, its profaneness and autonomy, finds its echo in Bultmann's slavish acceptance of nature and history as "closed." It may be asked,

[30] Karl Barth, *Rudolf Bultmann—Ein Versuch, ihn zu verstehen* (Zollikon-Zuerich, 1952).

therefore, whether Bultmann's position could have developed anywhere but on Lutheran ground. And was not, after all, the Lutheran Kierkegaard the father of modern existentialism, including Heidegger's?

After this Calvinist smirk Barth returns to the matter at hand and sums up his attack on Bultmann. One cannot approach the New Testament with a preconceived idea as to how much one can and how much one cannot understand. One cannot argue with God in this way. The New Testament must be approached humbly, in faith, with a willingness to listen rather than argue. The deepest difficulty Barth feels with regard to Bultmann is not his many negations and pronouncements of biblical statements as "finished," but his basic anthropocentric approach—something which Barth aptly describes as "pre-Copernican."

Attack from the "Left"

Bultmann's position has been under attack not only by the orthodox, who felt that he had gone too far, but by those on the "left," who felt that he had not gone far enough. In the objective analysis of his concepts these two sides often agreed, as is not surprising.

Fritz Buri, a Swiss follower of Karl Jaspers, submitted the thesis that Bultmann's demythologization must be followed by a "dekerygmatization," adding, as Barth points out, another unfortunate term to the poor German language.[31] The *kerygma*, which Bultmann tries to save, is nothing but the last intolerable remnant of New Testament mythology. The Christ-myth is nothing but a symbol of an existential process within man's consciousness, of his transcending his closed-in selfhood (what the existentialists have called *Eigentlichkeit*) and receiving the gift of freedom, a process which may be described by the word grace. The paradox of our existence lies in our acting decisively despite our

---

[31] Fritz Buri, "Entmythologisierung oder Entkerygmatisierung der Theologie," in Bartsch, II, 85 ff.

knowledge that all we know is historically bound. We must not let this genuine existential paradox be obscured by an unreal mythological paradox. The task of such a "de-kerygmatized" theology is to work together with philosophy in clarifying and appealing to man's understanding of himself. There is nothing any more to be proclaimed.

Jaspers himself entered the controversy through a series of exchanges with Bultmann published in 1954.[32] He sharply attacks the premises of Bultmann's program and denies their right to present themselves as philosophy. Jaspers attacks, first of all, Bultmann's conception of science and the scientific view of the world.[33] Bultmann exaggerates the differences between the various world views, such as those between our own and that of the New Testament. What all ages have in common is, on the one hand, crass realism and materialism resisting all thought; on the other, the willingness of people to believe the absurd. What Bultmann calls the scientific world view is not really scientific. Science, properly understood, has no world view, can never have one. What Bultmann has in mind is rather the scientific superstition, the "scientism," of our age, for long an object of Jaspers' wrath. So much for Bultmann's understanding of science. As to his understanding of philosophy, it seems to be limited exclusively to the one major work of Heidegger, and even that, says Jaspers, largely misunderstood. Bultmann's conception of philosophy is doctrinaire, narrow, full of an objectivizing spirit, as if existential decision could be combined with scientific objectivity. Bultmann is as much a stranger to philosophy as to science.

Also, Bultmann's conception of mythology is inadequate.[34] The function of the myth is to tell a story, to think in terms of representations instead of general concepts. As such, mythology is a vital part of our thinking processess.

[32] Karl Jaspers & Rudolf Bultmann, *Die Frage der Entmythologisierung* (Munich, 1954).
[33] *Ibid.,* pp. 9 ff.
[34] *Ibid.,* pp. 18 ff.

Demythologization would involve a radical impoverishment of all human thought. We must, it is true, understand and grasp the message of mythology, but this is not really demythologization. The philosopher is aware of God's total transcendence, over and above all mythological imagery. He knows that one cannot possess God in these images. He also knows that magic, demons, angels, and all the beings and events of mythology have no empirical reality. Yet he will struggle with the contents of mythology to clarify his own existence. The Bible is for western man the preferred place for this struggle. This, however, is not to eliminate the Greek epics and tragedies, or the sacred books of Asia. Bultmann not only restricts himself to the Bible, as, indeed, he must as a Protestant theologian, but very narrowly to certain parts of the Bible. He has no use at all for the Old Testament, very little for the Synoptic Gospels. Bultmann's *kerygma* is restricted, in fact, to the Johannine and Pauline literature.

If Bultmann is full of the spirit of a false enlightenment, he is ultimately to be counted also among the orthodox. For orthodoxy is the coming-to-rest of reason in the illusion of knowledge as a firm possession. Philosophy, as the free exercise of reason, never reaches this stage. It is in continued movement, always open, always ready for communication.

One voice is markedly absent on the "left" of the controversy. Heidegger did not raise his voice. It was left to others to discuss Bultmann's relationship to his philosophy.

Conclusion

Once more, it is important to see the Bultmann controversy in its sociological context. It reflects the situation of Protestantism in a state of acute alienation within European civilization, at any rate on the continent. In the immediate post-war years in Germany, it seemed for a while that this alienation had been broken through. A great religious renascence seemed in the offing. The development of the new Germany, particularly (and embarrassingly) the economic

"German miracle" following the currency reform, showed that these expectations were unfounded. It is understandable, therefore, that the demythologization question, involving, as it does, the relationship between church and "world," should stand in the center of German theological interest. It is an agonizing self-questioning on the part of a church no longer at home in this "world," an attempt to grasp and solve intellectually this problem of alienation.

As Barth points out in his discussion of demythologization, there is something peculiarly Lutheran in Bultmann's program, despite its clash with the neo-Lutheran orthodoxy in Germany. It is an extreme development of Luther's doctrine of the "two kingdoms," as it were, a final acceptance of the autonomy of the "world" on the latter's own terms. Also, here the denial of the Catholic *Analogia entis* (which Barth has claimed to be the sharpest dividing line between Catholicism and Protestantism, both Lutheran and Calvinist) is carried to its final conclusion. Man is totally alone, enclosed by a nature and history which at no point are or can be "broken into" by God, except in the paradox of faith, whose object may never be seen or experienced. Demythologization becomes an extreme expression of the *sola fide*—faith *alone* in the most terrible sense of the word.

Two other trends in German Protestant theology may be mentioned which, despite their differences from the demythologization program, may be understood as arising out of the same sociological situation. The one is that broad movement of thought, having many aspects outside the theological area proper, which seeks to bring back to modern man an understanding of what is regarded as the reality of mythological perspectives. Within theology in Germany, the liturgical-sacramental movement associated with the name of Bishop Staehlin comes closest to expressing this trend. It is generally associated with "high church" Lutheranism, breathing an atmosphere of much Anglican and Scandinavian inspiration. However, beyond theology, we find this trend in the broad neo-mythologism rampant in post-war Europe, within

which we may classify such divergent movements as the re-
newed appeal of Anthroposophy and the *mode* of Jungian
psychology. Here, as it were, the problem of alienation is
attacked from the opposite pole: instead of seeking to demythologize religion itself, as Bultmann does, the attempt is
made to bring modern man back to mythological thought
patterns now re-interpreted as objective facts (even if only
psychological facts) whose significance has been lost in the
historical process of western civilization.

Another trend, perhaps not very influential but highly
interesting in conception, is Dietrich Bonhoeffer's theory of
the "world come of age," and of "non-religious Christianity."
It is an even more radical formulation of the problem than
Bultmann's, but it is free from the debatable epistemological
position of the latter. Here the radical statement is made
that, with Christianity and its doctrine of the Incarnation,
the dichotomy between the sacred and the profane is destroyed. Since this dichotomy is the foundation of all religion,
we may speak of "non-religious Christianity." The Christian
life, therefore, is not lived in an area separated from the
"world," but right within it. Christianity is not a religion of
"marginal situations," but takes place in the center of life.
It is altogether worldly. Therefore, the Christian must cease
to deplore the "secularization" of western civilization, which
only means that modern man has come of age. Instead of
trying to lure him back into religious dependency by playing
on his weaknesses and failures, Christianity should accept
him in his freedom and maturity. Unfortunately, Bonhoeffer
only knew of the demythologization program in its very beginnings and could only make a few critical remarks about it
before his death at the hands of the Nazis in 1945. Bonhoeffer
states that Bultmann does not go far enough: not only the
mythology, but the religion of Christianity must be abandoned. What is interesting in his attempt is that here, as
contrasted with Bultmann, the Lutheran conception of the
"two kingdoms" is discarded completely and the Christian

life is understood as, by its very nature, "worldly," yet also attacking the "world's" autonomy.

All these attempts to rehabilitate Christianity in the modern world express the same underlying alienation. They are products of a Protestantism with its back to the wall. The importance of this situation becomes evident when we reflect on what faces this Protestantism today—that "new faith" from the East, to which the West is as much of a mission territory today as it was to Christianity when the latter first emerged from its Oriental background.

Sources and Acknowledgments

John C. Greene, "Darwin and Religion," *Proceedings of the American Philosophical Society,* CIII (October 1959), 716–25, reprinted by permission of the American Philosophical Society and the author. Mr. Greene is Professor of History at the University of Kansas. His principal works are *The Death of Adam: Evolution and Its Impact on Western Thought* (1959) and *Darwin and the Modern World View* (1961).

Robert V. Daniels, "Fate and Will in the Marxian Philosophy of History," *Journal of the History of Ideas,* XXI (October–December 1960), 538–52, reprinted by permission of the *Journal of the History of Ideas* and the author. Mr. Daniels is Professor of History at the University of Vermont. His principal works are *The Conscience of the Revolution: Communist Opposition in Soviet Russia* (1960), *A Documentary History of Communism* (1960), *The Nature of Communism* (1962), and *Russia* (1964).

Hajo Holborn, "Wilhelm Dilthey and the Critique of Historical Reason," *Journal of the History of Ideas,* XI (January 1950), 93–118, reprinted by permission of the *Journal of the History of Ideas* and the author. Mr. Holborn is Sterling Professor of History, Yale University. His principal works are *Ulrich von Hutten and the German Reformation* (1937), *The Political Collapse of Europe* (1951), and *A History of Modern Germany* (1959–63-—).

Philip Rieff, "The Origins of Freud's Political Psychology," *Journal of the History of Ideas,* XVII (April 1956), 235–50, reprinted by permission of the *Journal of the History of Ideas* and the author. Mr. Rieff is University Professor of Sociology, University of Pennsylvania. His principal works are *Freud: The Mind of the Moralist* (1959), *The Analytic Attitude: Uses of Faith after Freud* (1965), and *The Triumph of the Therapeutic* (1966).

Franklin L. Baumer, "Twentieth-Century Version of the Apocalypse," prepared for the International Commission for a History of the Scientific and Cultural Development of Mankind, and published in the *Journal of World History,* I (January 1954), 623–40, issued by the Editions de la Baconnière, Boudry, Neuchâtel, Switzerland. Reprinted by permission of the Secretary-General of the International Commission. Page 640 (a chronological bibliography) is omitted. Mr. Baumer is Randolph W. Townsend Professor of History, Yale University. His principal works are *The Early Tudor Theory of Kingship* (1940), *Main Currents of Western Thought* (1952, Second Edition, 1964), and *Religion and the Rise of Scepticism* (1960).

Gustav Krüger, "The 'Theology of Crisis'," *Harvard Theological Review,* XIX (July 1926), 227–58, reprinted by permission of the *Harvard Theological Review.* Pages 249–58 are omitted. Mr. Krüger was Professor of Church History at the University of Giessen. He died in 1940. His principal works include *Geschichte der altchristlichen Literatur in den ersten drei Jahrhunderten* (1895, English edition, 1897) and *Das Papstthum* (1907, English edition, 1909).

Herbert Dingle, "The Scientific Outlook in 1851 and in 1951," *British Journal for the Philosophy of Science,* II (August 1951), 85–104, reprinted by permission of the *British Journal for the Philosophy of Science.* Mr. Dingle is Professor Emeritus of History and Philosophy of Science at University College, University of London. His principal works include *Modern Astrophysics* (1924), *Through Science to Philosophy* (1937), *Science and Literary Criticism* (1949), and *The Scientific Adventure* (1952).

Alfred Cobban, "The Decline of Political Theory," *Political Science Quarterly,* LXVII (September 1953), 321–37, reprinted by permission of the Academy of Political Science, Columbia University, and the author. Mr. Cobban is Professor of French History at University College, University of London. His principal works include *Edmund Burke and the Revolt against the Eighteenth Century* (1929), *Rousseau and the Modern State* (1934), *Dictatorship* (1939), *The Crisis of Civilization* (1941), *The Debate on the French Revolution* (1950), *History of Modern France* (1957–61), *In Search of Humanity: The Role of the Enlightenment in Modern History* (1960), and *The Social Interpretation of the French Revolution* (1964).

Helmut Kuhn, "Existentialism—Christian and Anti-Christian," *Theology Today,* VI (October 1949), 311–23, reprinted by permission of *Theology Today.* Mr. Kuhn is Professor of Philosophy at the University of Munich. His principal works include *Die Kulturfunktion der Kunst* (1931), *Sokrates: Versuch über den Ursprung der Metaphysik* (1934, Second Edition, 1959), *A History of Esthetics* (with Katherine Everett Gilbert) (1939, Second Edition, 1953), *Freedom Forgotten and Remembered* (1943), *Encounter with Nothingness: An Essay on Existentialism* (1949), *Begegnung mit dem Sein: Meditationen zur Metaphysik des Gewissens* (1954), and *Das Sein und das Gute* (1962).

Mikel Dufrenne, "Existentialism and Existentialisms," *Philosophy and Phenomenological Research,* XXVI (September 1965), 51–62, reprinted by permission of *Philosophy and Phenomenological Research* and the author. Mr. Dufrenne is a member of the Philosophy Department of the University of Paris. His principal works include *Karl Jaspers et la philosophie de l'existence* (with Paul Ricoeur) (1947), *Phénoménologie de l'expérience esthétique* (1953), *La Personalité de base* (1953), *La Notion d' "a priori"* (1959), *Language and Philosophy* (1963), and *Le Poétique* (1963).

Peter L. Berger, "Demythologization—Crisis in Continental Theology," *Review of Religion,* XX (November 1955), 5–24, reprinted by permission of Columbia University

Press. Mr. Berger is Professor of Sociology at the Graduate Center of the City University of New York and editor of the journal *Social Research.* His principal works are *The Noise of Solemn Assemblies: Christian Commitment and the Religious Establishment in America* (1961), *The Precarious Vision: A Sociologist Looks at Social Fictions and Christian Faith* (1961), *Invitation to Sociology* (1963), and *The Human Shape of Work: Studies in the Sociology of Occupations* (1964).